Transce

Bloomsbury Studies in Philosophy

Series Editor: James Fieser, University of Tennessee at Martin, USA

Bloomsbury Studies in Philosophy is a major monograph series from Bloomsbury. The series features first-class scholarly research monographs across the whole field of philosophy. Each work makes a major contribution to the field of philosophical research.

Transcendental Ontology
Essays in German Idealism

Markus Gabriel

B L O O M S B U R Y
LONDON • NEW DELHI • NEW YORK • SYDNEY

Bloomsbury Academic
An imprint of Bloomsbury Publishing Plc

50 Bedford Square	175 Fifth Avenue
London	New York
WC1B 3DP	NY 10010
UK	USA

www.bloomsbury.com

First published by Continuum International Publishing Group 2011
Paperback edition first published 2013

British Library Cataloguing-in-Publication Data
A catalogue record for this book is available from the British Library.

ISBN: HB: 978-1-4411-1629-1
PB: 978-0-5670-5780-8

Library of Congress Cataloging-in-Publication Data
Gabriel, Markus, 1980-
Transcendental ontology : essays in German idealism / Markus Gabriel.
p. cm.
Includes bibliographical references and index.
ISBN-978-1-4411-1629-1
1. Ontology—History. 2. Idealism, German. 3. Schelling, Friedrich Wilhelm Joseph von,
1775–1854. 4. Hegel, Georg Wilhelm Friedrich, 1770–1831. 5. Fichte, Johann Gottlieb,
1762–1814. I. Title.
B2745.G34 2011
141.0943—dc22

Typeset by Newgen Imaging Systems Pvt Ltd, Chennai, India

Contents

Acknowledgments

This book contains a variety of essays on German or post-Kantian idealism. Earlier versions of some of these essays have been published in German. I would like to thank Tom Krell for his help with the translation of large parts of these original essays into English, and Julian Ernst, Jens Rometsch, and Francey Russell for their critical comments on the translated essays, which led me to significantly change and unify them into a book. I would also like to thank Matt Congdon for his help with editing the manuscript and his critical comments. In addition to this, I thank all participants in the *First Annual International Summer School in German Philosophy* that was held on the topic of "Transcendental Ontology" in Bonn in June 2010. Particular thanks go to G. Anthony Bruno, Jon Burmeister, Karen Ng, Andreja Novakovic, Sebastian Ostritsch, Daniel Smyth, Clayton Shoppa, and Sebastian Stein for discussions during their stay in Germany. As always, I am deeply indebted to Wolfram Hogrebe, discussions with whom have consistently inspired me over the last ten years.

Introduction: Transcendental Ontology in Context

According to a widespread standard picture, modern philosophy is defined by an alienation of thought from being. While ancient metaphysics set out to grasp being as such, modern philosophy instead humbly investigates our access to being. In modernity, being turns into the external world, made up of objects suitable for an investigation *more geometrico*. Mind (thought) and world (being) come to be opposed as a result of a general (methodical) skepticism. Given that from this skeptical vantage point our access to the world appears such that it potentially distances us from what there is (being), it is at least prudent to secure the access to what there is prior to the somewhat naïve attempt to grasp being.[1] Modern philosophy thus seems to be defined as epistemology, which replaces ontology as *prima philosophia*.

To a certain extent, this picture corresponds to the current state of the art in analytic philosophy. Analytic philosophy still talks about mind and world as if there were an epistemic realm of minds on the one hand, and on the other, an ontological realm of things/facts, defined primarily through its opposition to mind as mind-independent reality. Despite various attempts to overcome this Cartesian dualism, analytic philosophy (in its narrow academic sense) has never dared to question its notion of the world. Of course, in particular the Harvard school (Quine, Goodman, and Putnam)—and to some degree also Davidson—have undermined the methodological Cartesianism of analytic philosophy in such a way that one has referred to them as post-analytic philosophers. However, as Rorty correctly pointed out, they nevertheless remain within the framework of modern philosophy as epistemology, investigating the nature of the conceptual structure of our access to what there is.[2] What there is becomes conceptually tied to our access to what there is: "to be is to be the value of a variable."[3]

Continental philosophy, on the other hand (a label even fuzzier than that of analytic philosophy), and in particular some of the most prominent developments in twentieth and twenty-first century French and German philosophy, can be seen as a rediscovery of being. This is obvious if we look at phenomenology's attempt to overcome the implicit Cartesianism of modern epistemology. In this sense, Heidegger has argued against Husserl's methodological solipsism in favor of a notion of Being as the temporality of Dasein's constitutive relationship with its own finitude. This led him to a new attempt to rethink the concept of the world both in *Being and Time* and in other writings.[4] Most recently, Alain Badiou has developed his own ontology on the basis of a reconsideration of the relation between Being and the necessarily nonexistent whole, to name but one example.

Be that as it may, both the so-called analytic and the so-called continental movement are generally reunited in their opposition to post-Kantian idealism. Analytic philosophy with Russell and Moore grew out of an epistemological skepticism, which bred well-founded suspicions against an exaggerated Hegelianism, while phenomenology suspected the whole movement of post-Kantian idealism of an illicit wish to transcend (Kantian) finitude and immanence. Against this alleged act of transcendence, Heidegger in particular argued that finitude is constitutive of Being, because Being is nothing but the domain of sense available to finite agents defined by their being-towards-death. And despite the overarching influence of Hegel on twentieth-century French thought, much of French philosophy in the wake of Lévinas and Derrida remains critical of his claim to totality and, just like Heidegger, suspects Hegel of a negation of finitude, which cannot be justified in the face of the modern gesture of a self-limitation of reason's claim to being.

Despite all of this, there is a recent Hegel renaissance in contemporary philosophy. Robert Pippin, John McDowell, and Robert Brandom (to name but some protagonists of this movement) argue that Hegel can be reconciled with epistemology such that his philosophy turns out to be a reflection on the normative constitution of the modern subject, rather than as a Neoplatonically inspired hyperonto-theology.[5] They all agree that Hegel does not break with transcendental philosophy, but rather remains within a fundamentally Kantian framework, which they see him trying to improve upon. In this manner, recourse to Hegel's conceptual holism and inferentialism seems to support their more courageous moves within the narrow framework of analytic philosophy without committing them to what might be perceived as a relapse into precritical ontology. Their reference to Hegel serves the goal of moderating the ontology of bald naturalism, according to which everything that exists is an object of our best scientific theories, by saving the normative dimension of conceptually structured subjectivity (mind) from its reduction to a nonconceptual order.

Yet they avoid approaching Hegel's own ontology—let alone defending it. And while Hegel is thus deflated and returns in the disguise of a somewhat deviant American pragmatist, Fichte or Schelling are hardly even mentioned in the contemporary renaissance of "German Idealism" within Anglo-American analytic philosophy.[6]

In this book, I will show that post-Kantian idealism (in particular the philosophies of Fichte, Schelling, and Hegel) can be seen as occupying a middle ground between one-sided (and despite itself scientist) contemporary Anglo-American transcendental epistemology and the return of ontology in recent French philosophy (Badiou, Meillassoux). This middle ground involves precisely articulating what I call a *transcendental ontology*. On my account, the project of post-Kantian idealism will turn out to be both closer to ontology than "normativity Hegelians" would have us believe and more reflected and complex than speculative realism would like it to be. I will also argue that neither Fichte, Schelling, nor Hegel transcend finitude and that Heidegger's classification of German Idealism within his history of Being misses some of this movement's essential points.

Transcendental ontology investigates the ontological conditions of our conditions of access to what there is. It sets out with the simple insight that the subject (in whichever way conceived) *exists*, that the analysis of the concept of existence is, hence, methodologically prior to the analysis of the subject's access to existence. The subject with its conceptual capacities actually exists; it is part of the world. Therefore, the question arises: what conditions have to be fulfilled by being (the world) in order for it to appear to finite thinkers who in turn change the structure of what there is by referring to it? To use a term introduced by Slavoj Žižek in his reading of Schelling, transcendental ontology investigates into the "phenomenalization"[7] of being. Thereby, it overcomes the dualism of being and appearance (objectivity and subjectivity, world and mind) and rather asserts that being is in one way or another dependent on its appearing.

For example, this is exactly what happens in the *Logic of Essence* in Hegel's *Science of Logic*, where Hegel discovers that "*Being is illusory Being* [*das Sein ist Schein*]."[8] "Being" in Hegel turns out to be the same thing as an expressive dimension he calls "actuality" or "manifestation," and his overall project can be read as the very attempt to reconstruct Being's transition into its manifestation to finite thinkers. This is also obvious for any reader of the late Fichte, in particular of his 1804 *Science of Knowing*, in which Fichte explicitly calls his theory of phenomenalization a "phenomenology,"[9] a term introduced by Lambert and famously picked up by Hegel.

Nevertheless, I will not deny that there is a tendency towards onto-theology in German idealism: Fichte, Schelling, and Hegel are no doubt in the bad habit of sometimes transcending the limits of transcendental ontology and relapsing into onto-theology. After all, philosophy trivially is a product of its own time, and in their time these thinkers still had to defend themselves against the charge of atheism, even though I will try to offer "translations" of some of the onto-theological terms frequently used by post-Kantian idealists. However, the original contribution of this book consists in reconstructing some important moves of post-Kantian idealism in terms of a transcendental ontology and in defending the outlines of such a project of a transcendental ontology under contemporary conditions. I pick up some essential motives of transcendental ontology in post-Kantian idealism and I try to disembed them from their onto-theological context.

This book is meant to be a historical introduction to a larger systematic project in which I will lay out in full detail a new transcendental ontology, the outlines of which will be sketched propaedeutically in what follows. I hope to be able to steer a course between the Scylla of a merely epistemological approach and the Charybdis of a one-sided ontology à la Badiou, which lays claim to a universal first-order ontology.

I What Is Transcendental Ontology and Why Do We Need It?

Kant famously believed that his transcendental method disposed of the classical project of ontology.[10] He argued that ontology was premised on a naïve epistemological assumption according to which being (the thing in itself) would immediately be available to thought. Against ontology in this sense, Kant was eager to prove that everything that exists has to be constituted by thought, given that thought can only grasp what is compatible with the logical form of referring to something, which differs from the fact of being referred to. Instead of laying out the structure of being as such, he assigned philosophy the task of reflecting on the constitution of objects qua objects of thought.

One of the fundamental rationales for this transcendental turn can be made out in its antiskeptical import. If thought constitutes its objects by imposing its forms (categories) onto the given, then the given must itself have a form that is at least minimally compatible with being grasped by thought. Hence, there could be no absolute ontological gap between the order of things and the order of thought (of judging). If in truth-apt discourse we assert that *p* is the case, and if *p* is the case, then there cannot be any in principle unbridgeable gap between the content of thought and the objective order.

Thus, in order to eradicate the possibility of Cartesian-style skepticism, Kant believed that thought had to constitute its object. For this reason, the unifying activity that makes judgments about anything possible, yet which is not itself a judgment, had to be located within the subject. The subject came to be understood as a theory-building process without which objectivity is impossible. If judgment is the locus of truth, then it opens the very open region within which something can truthfully take place, and there can be no more truth without the subject (the subject being the name for the synthesizing activity that puts the elements of a judgment together in the first place).

However, Kant did not sufficiently take account of the seemingly trivial fact that the subject *exists*. The subject is itself part of the world. By excluding the subject from the world qua totality of objectively available states of affairs, Kant in effect turned the subject into a nullity. This is the kernel of truth in Jacobi's observation that transcendental idealism amounts to nihilism.[11] Transcendental idealism indeed destroys the subject by reducing it to an empty logical form, which can never become the content of a thought on pain of giving up its proper position as the subject. Hence, the subject ultimately vanishes, it dissolves into its judgments and cannot judge itself. Of course, Kant believed that this was the only way to preserve the possibility of freedom, given his belief that the network of appearances was so conceptually taut that it could not be otherwise. Kant rightly understood that freedom presupposes contingency, in the sense of the subject's possibility to be otherwise than its appearance as an empirical entity.

Yet in response to Kant, Fichte, Schelling, and Hegel—each in his own way—have convincingly made the case that Kant's reasons for replacing ontology with transcendental reflection are not sufficient, for Kant's overall argumentation turns out to be dialectically unstable. Hegel, for example, has argued that Kantian autonomy proves to be heteronomous on a higher order of reflection, for autonomy is defined with recourse to spontaneity, and spontaneity is only defined in opposition to receptivity. Hence, autonomy is contingent on heteronomy, the possibility of freedom presupposes the actuality of necessity, and so forth. In order to secure freedom, post-Kantian idealism investigates into the ontological constitution of the Kantian edifice, because the higher-order heteronomy of autonomy is ultimately resultant of Kant's (despite himself) ontological distinction between the thing in itself and the world of appearances. Post-Kantian idealism, then, can be seen as the creation of a new ontology in which freedom turns out to be the very meaning of being.

Nevertheless, the post-Kantian creation of a new ontology does not amount to a naïve relapse into traditional metaphysics. Quite to the contrary: Fichte, Schelling, and Hegel all accept the crucial lesson to be learned from Kant, namely that the proper method of philosophy is higher-order reflection, thought on the constitution of thought's relation to objects that are not necessarily thoughts. Mutatis mutandis the question to be answered remains Kantian: how is it possible to refer to anything that is not a judgment by a judgment? How is it possible that we have thoughts about the way the world is, even though our thoughts are not identical with the way the world is? The thought that transcendental ontology adds to this question is *that our thoughts about the way the world is are themselves a way the world is.* My occurent thought that the skyscraper over there exists is not itself a skyscraper. However, though my thought is not itself a skyscraper, my thought itself exists.

Therefore, in order to answer Kant's fundamental epistemological question, it is necessary to refer to the constitution of transcendental constitution, or more precisely, to the ontological conditions of the conditions of possibility of truth-apt reference. Given that the subject exists and that it refers to the world and intramundane states of affairs from within the world, how is it possible that the world refers to itself through our reference to it? How does the world manage to become self-referential in reflection? If we no longer exclude the subject from the world (as Cartesian-style dualism does, which till today lies at the basis of epistemology), the world finally has to be credited with the capacity to become intelligible to itself in our conceptual capacities.

In this context, it is remarkable that John McDowell, who defends a sophisticated version of a Kantian theory of intentionality, hardly ever mentions the world in his book on *Mind and World.* The notion of the world remains completely obscure. McDowell even combines elements of a theory of intentionality from Wittgenstein's *Philosophical Investigations* with the *Tractatus* definition of the world as "everything that is the case."[12] Thus, in McDowell's picture, the world turns out to be a totalizable domain of facts immediately available to truth-apt thought. In the case of a true thought, "thinking does not stop short of the facts,"[13] as McDowell points out. An obvious—but ultimately too simple—objection to McDowell's claim that there is an "unmediated openness of the experiencing subject to 'external' reality,"[14] involved in thought's interaction with the world might assert that McDowell underestimates fallibility. However, this objection falls short of the truly problematic aspect of the project defined in *Mind and World* and its successor papers. As I will elaborate in Section 3 of this introduction, McDowell indeed succeeds in making a transition from a Cartesian to a Kantian metaphysics of intentionality. Yet, there is another more severe problem in McDowell's account of reference, which partly motivates the transition made in the present book from mere transcendental reflection to transcendental ontology. The problem lies in the off-base, ultimately premodern notion of a thoroughly determined, totalizable world. In McDowell, it looks as if there were a homogeneous field of facts (the world) such that one only needs to guarantee the possibility of an unproblematic access to this always already established unitary field of facts.[15] However, let us just take a look at the following example: I raise my left hand and claim truthfully that there is a hand in front of me. If there is a hand in front of me, then my thought that there is a hand in front of me does indeed not stop short of the fact that there is a hand in front of me. In true thought, objects and states of affairs seem to become part of my thought in an unproblematic manner. There is no picture-like Cartesian representation involved that potentially separates my thought from my hand. However, at the same time, there is not only a hand in front of me, but also a swarm of particles. I might truthfully judge that there is a swarm of particles in front of me. The same is thus at the same time a hand, a swarm of particles, and many other things (depending on how many possibilities of truthfully accessing It might be granted at a given time).

Things become even more complicated once we recognize that even *this* very description of the metaphysical situation—that is, some "thing" or state of affairs on the one hand, and a plurality of ways of truthfully accessing *It* on the other—is partial. It still tries to identify It, thereby accessing the apparently unproblematically singular It under one description among others. This simple reflection should make it plain that the notion of a homogeneous, extant field of always already individuated ready-mades is not an acceptable notion of the world.

Even Frege was very well aware of this problem, though he tries to conceal it to a certain degree in order to make room for scientific certainty. He notoriously points out that we have no way to access reference (and hence to assert existence) without sense. His famous example of morning star and evening star thus has an obvious shortcoming. According to Frege, the proper names "evening star" and "morning star" refer to the same thing, that is, Venus. However, "Venus" is also a proper name, and proper names have a sense even if we use them to denote the referent of a plurality of senses.

The sense of a proper name is grasped by everybody who is sufficiently familiar with the language or totality of designations to which it belongs; but this serves to illuminate only a single aspect of the reference, supposing it to have one. Comprehensive knowledge of the reference would require us to be able to say immediately whether any given sense belongs to it. To such knowledge we never attain.[16]

In other words, there is no immediate access to reference. Even though sense should indeed not be conceived as a barrier or misleading veil between an objective state of affairs and our attempts to grasp it, there is an inherent plurality in the notion of sense. *Sense is a medium of difference, whereas reference is meant to limit the sheer proliferation of senses without a referent.* Nonetheless, there can be no grasp of It independent of the possibility of grasping It otherwise. If this also holds for the attempt to give an account of our epistemic finitude in terms of an ontology according to which there is a thoroughly individuated domain of referents on the one hand, and a plurality of senses on the other hand, which serves to make the determinacy of things available to truth-apt discourse, then the very ontology we use in this case to make finitude available to higher-order thought about thought itself turns out to be finite. By the same reasoning that led to the insight into the contingency of sense, the very thought that tries to grasp this finitude and contingency becomes finite and contingent. Hence, transcendental thought loses its classical a priori status, which McDowell still tries to vindicate.

For this and other pertaining reasons, we need a more reflected ontology, an ontology that takes account of the existence of a plurality of fields of sense and the constitutive contingency of everything that might be the content of truth-apt discourse. Such an ontology needs to preserve both the methodological insights of transcendental philosophy and the insight that transcendental philosophy leads to the formulation of a new ontology of reflection. As the essays collected in this volume are meant to show, this is exactly what the whole movement of German idealism is about. It was intended to establish a middle ground between the methodological Cartesianism of Kantian transcendental reflection and an uncritical relapse into traditional ontology.

The basic ontological claim that I will defend based on Fichte, Schelling, and Hegel is that Being itself is the source of contingency. Being is nothing other than a side effect of the transfinite, nontotalizable plurality of fields of sense. Being, thus, is not conceived in terms of something given in advance, it is not some metaphysical entity behind or beyond appearance.

There is no underlying hidden reality, because there is only a plurality of fields of sense. Yet this plurality of fields of sense remains hidden to those who endorse either a metaphysics of common sense or that of scientism.

Being is manifold. However, this plurality is not quantifiable, but is rather a plurality of fields of sense, each of which simulates an origin, hints at something that cannot be given to any particular field of sense. In the course of these essays I will refer to this as a constitutive withdrawal, a withdrawal that opens up the domain of that which exists.

II From Kantian to Post-Kantian Metaphysics of Intentionality

Recently, McDowell has argued that the transition from Kant to Hegel should be understood in terms of a development within the metaphysics of intentionality. According to McDowell, Hegelian idealism's central tenet has it that "the very idea of objectivity is to be understood in terms of the freely self-determining operations of a self-conscious intelligence."[17] Of course, this formulation has an obvious Kantian ring to it, and I believe that it misses the truly Hegelian, ontological move.

For Hegel (as for Fichte and Schelling), Kant is not capable of applying the results of transcendental philosophy to transcendental reflection itself. Kant remains stuck in a subjectivist (Cartesian) notion of synthesis because his very starting point is a form-content dualism. Subjectivity is the activity of judging—an activity that in Kant primarily serves the function of determining spatiotemporal states of affairs. Synthesis, for Kant, establishes relations within a given material, which is given through sensibility. Givenness, for Kant, is sensory givenness. Hegel's real problem with givenness is not simply that Kant seems to subscribe to a variety of the empiricist "myth of the given," and thereby to a semantic atomism that Hegel will go on to replace with a form of radical conceptual holism. For even on a model of conceptual holism about empirical concepts, cognition would still be based on albeit conceptually structured sensory givenness. However, the very thought that what is given in sensory experience is conceptually structured transcends sensory experience by investigating into the relation between how something is given and the position to which it is given. The very object of this thought—the structure of experience—cannot itself be experienced among other objects. Therefore, philosophical thought cannot conceive itself in terms of sensory givenness. For this reason, already in the "Sense-Certainty" chapter of the *Phenomenology*, Hegel's primary target is Kant's empiricist restriction of thought to a processing of sensory material. Hegel's overcoming of Kant can therefore not consist in an enhancement of the notion of the given as always already conceptually structured. Such an account would again be subject to a Hegelian criticism, because it still conceives of thought's proper content as empirical in the empiricist sense of experiential input.

Hegel believes that Kant is roughly right in understanding subjectivity as constituting logical forms of reference (categories) outside of which nothing determinate can be apprehended. However, Kant does not apply this thought to itself. It is not only within the apprehension of *empirical* material that synthesis comes into play, but synthesis is a property of intentionality as such and, therefore, also applies to higher-order intentionality, that is, to theorizing about intentionality. The (Kantian) categories turn out to be constituted by thought's own activity; they are just as little brute facts about ourselves as spatiotemporal objects are raw givens for Kant himself. The categories are themselves the result of a synthesis, a synthesis Hegel famously calls "the Concept." The Hegelian concept is, thus, nothing more than his name for the attempt at a coherent higher-order metaphysics of intentionality, which allows for a dialectically stable metatheory.

It is crucial here to distinguish between *analytic* and *dialectical contradiction*, a distinction that corresponds to Hegel's famous distinction between *Verstand* and *Vernunft*. Analytic contradiction is the standard form of contradiction on the level of the propositional content of a theory. A theory might explicitly contradict itself or be implicitly committed to a contradiction if it contains both the theorem T and the theorem ¬T. Even if there might be true contradictions, as paraconsistent logicians hold, analytic contradictions always only concern propositional content.

Dialectical contradiction, on the other hand, arises as the contradiction between the motivational structure and the execution of a theory.[18] Object-directed theories generally tend to mask the role of theory-decisions, which open up the object domain of the theory. This even happens to Kant. Kant refers to intentionality and its constitutive structures (categories, ideas, schemes, space, time, etc.) as if these were metaphysically stable items that make up the framework of any rational, finite subjectivity (= intentionality). The conceptual nucleus of Kant's discovery, however, is not that rational, finite subjectivity necessarily has a particular content—its constitutive structures—but rather that intentionality as such has an *as if* character: in order for us to have anything *in view*, which is even potentially distinct from our *having* it in view, we need to refer to it at least *as if* it was independent of this act of reference. Objectivity is the very domain that is

supposed to correspond to this "fact" about intentionality. If Kant's fundamental discovery is as general as this, then it also applies to the framework
itself. Hence, the question as to the objectivity of the framework of objectivity arises as soon as we try to refer to transcendental reflection as to
another object. And transcendental reflection is indeed just another object
given that it can be referred to in a particular theory-language (say that of
the first *Critique*).

Seen in this light, the general motivation of transcendental reflection,
its scope qua metaphysics of intentionality, contradicts its actual outcome,
namely that synthesis only takes place between a domain of judging and an
empirical domain of content to be synthesized. Kant notoriously does not
address the question of the truth-conditions of the propositions of transcendental reflection. Are the very statements of the first *Critique* analytic
or synthetic? If they are not analytic (which seems obvious), then they have
to satisfy the conditions of possibility with respect to content for synthetic
judgment. Now, according to the explicit theory, synthetic judgments
mediate between sensory content and logical form. Yet what could the sensory content be, which corresponds to this very statement? In what sense
does Kant's most general judgment about judgments have an empirical
grounding? *In other words, the Kantian metaphysics of intentionality is dialectically contradictory under self-application precisely because it does not reflect on its
own position, on its own constitution.* Kant misidentifies the origin of synthesis because he believes synthesis to be a structure mediating between the
sensory given and our awareness of it. However, synthesis is an activity of
thought, which is also exerted in thought's reference to itself.

All of the so-called German idealists are looking for a transcendental
method which is thoroughly dialectically stable under self-application.
They all practice various forms of higher-order reflection thereby distinguishing between the levels of reflection. A very clear example as to how
this leads to transcendental ontology is the late Fichte, in particular his
1804 *Science of Knowing*, in which Fichte analyzes the notion of "absolute
knowing."[19] Absolute knowing is neither more nor less than higher-order
intentionality. The term refers to our insight into the structure of reference. Fichte uses this notion as a starting point for his dialectics, which
leads him to "knowing's absolute being."[20] "Being" here is the name for
the facticity of absolute knowing, for the fact that we make the concept of
knowledge explicit after having already claimed some knowledge or other
about something or other. Being, in other words, is thought's belatedness
with respect to itself. At the same time, this discovery itself retroactively
generates being, the facticity of knowledge, by claiming higher-order or

absolute knowledge about knowledge. This insight turns being (which means the being of knowing) into an object of itself, thereby transforming it into a result of an objectifying activity. This leads Fichte to the insight that the objectifying performance, which takes absolute knowing and thereby being as its object, is being's self-reference. According to Fichte, this is the highest possible insight, which is nothing but a movement of self-application. This is the master thought of his transcendental ontology, by which he tries to solve the key question of philosophy: "Philosophy should reveal and discover *being in and of itself*."[21] The crucial move is to identify Being with its self-reference in philosophical thought such that Being is not conceived as a relatum in the relation of grasping it, but as the very relation in which It necessarily withdraws insofar as I mistake it for its mere *Doppelgänger*, for Being as an object of thought.

> If being cannot ever get outside of itself and nothing can be apart from it, then it must be being itself which thus constructs itself, to the extent that this construction is to occur. Or, as is completely synonymous: We certainly are the agents who carry out this construction, but we do it insofar as we are being itself, as has been seen, and we coincide with it.[22]

Schelling makes a similar point in various ways across the different phases of his thinking. A particularly clear statement can be found in *The Grounding of Positive Philosophy*.[23] There, Schelling reminds us that the *Critique of Pure Reason* draws on a twofold notion of "reason," a distinction that Kant himself does not avow. The two forms of reason would be **reason in its application to the sensible realm** and **reason in its self-application**. Kant mainly considers reason in this first sense, that is, in its capacity to structure sensible experience with the help of regulative ideas. In this way, Kant neglects "absolute reason,"[24] that is, reason insofar as it explicates itself. The very use of reason in transcendental reflection has to be distinguishable from the use of reason in experience: this is a distinction that Kant does not clearly draw, even though he makes philosophy its own proper object in the *Transcendental Doctrine of Method*.[25]

Schelling takes Kant as the starting point for his own transcendental ontology by emphasizing a point made both by Hegel and McDowell (among many others): the apparently merely given is already conceptually structured. Otherwise, it could not even be given to any rational position. The minimal presupposition about the given has to be that it exists, as some notion of "being" is even implicit in that of the "unknown something,"[26] which can be made available to thought.

However, the remark cannot be repressed that it is quite impossible for the *object* to be given to us through only receptivity. For no matter how general and undetermined we may think the concept "object," there are already determinations of the understanding to be encountered in it; indeed, there is at least the *determination* that it is something that is a being, something that is real.[27]

Given that the given is given *to* a position, it is already determined, and be it *as* the given. Givenness is evidently not itself given, it is already a position within higher-order thought.[28] This very reflective insight can be called a claim to "absolute reason" in that it takes reason in its application to sensible experience as an object. Taking reason itself as an object of reason is an act of reason; of a reason, however, whose conditions of contentfulness cannot be empirical in the usual sense.

This move can also be illustrated by reference to a notorious blind spot of simple-minded verificationism. If the criterion of contentfulness of a thought or a proposition is the possibility to verify it by way of sensible experience, then the proposition that states this alleged fact about the nature of content would have to be subjected to the same criterion as all other propositions. Yet, there is no way to verify the verificationist principle with reference to any particular sensible experience or other. Hence, the verificationist thought about thoughts belongs to a different order of reason. Verificationism is not capable of referring to the theory decisions that constitute it without engendering paradoxes. As Anton Friedrich Koch has shown in his *Essay on Truth and Time*, these paradoxes are manifestations of subjectivity, of absolute reason.[29] "Subjectivity" is his name for the combination of negativity and self-reference, that is, negativity applied to itself. Such negativity drives thought to higher-order intentionality. The nature of higher-order intentionality cannot be investigated in terms of higher-order logics in a narrow sense of "formal logics," because negativity is an *ontological* structure. Given that ontology can neither be based on logics nor reduced to it (it is rather the other way around), logics in this narrow sense has no proper grasp on negativity.

While Fichte, Schelling, and Hegel each take Kant in very different directions, their common project is transcendental ontology in the form of an ontology of the transcendental subject. This project combines both the methodology of higher-order reflection initiated by Kant and the traditional attempt to grasp being as being. The crucial post-Kantian innovation consists in the reflection that the "as" in ontology's classical definition is reflection itself. Thought intervenes in being in such a way that a distance between thought and what there is is established. This distance, which is constitutive of objectivity—of the capacity to get it right *or* wrong—is the proper object of transcendental ontology.

At this point it is important to emphasize the difference between *objects* and *objectivity*. Post-Kantian idealism is not a first-order theory according to which there would be no objects if there were not any subjects in the universe. In other words, it is not committed to ontic nonsense, as Meillassoux's criticism of "correlationism"[30] suggests. Of course, the project of transcendental ontology would be guilty of straightforward nonsense if it denied the truth-value of "ancestral statements," that is, statements concerning the past before the existence of judging creatures. Post-Kantian idealism is rather a higher-order theory, the content of which is objectivity, that is, the very possibility of objective states of affairs being manifest to finite thought.

In this respect, Brandom's distinction between *sense-* and *reference-dependence* is very fruitful for distinguishing two forms of idealism.[31] Roughly speaking, *reference-idealism* claims that there is only a particular kind of object (say a spatiotemporal object) if there is a corresponding act of judging. *Sense-idealism*, however, claims that being given in a particular kind of way constitutes a particular kind of domain of objectivity. The ways in which objects are given determine the possibility of getting something right *or* wrong about them such that modes of presentation in part determine what there is (by determining *what* there is).

Sense, the medium of different modes of presentation, also exists within the world. It belongs to the totality or to the "whole" in a sophisticated idealist sense of the "whole." (The notion of the "whole" is frequently confused with the notion of the "all," a confusion that lies at the very heart of Badiou's repudiation of Hegelianism despite his Hegelianism.[32]) Brandom's reconstruction of the basic movements of the idealist "sonata," as he calls it, unfortunately also misses the properly Hegelian, higher-order point about totality due to the remnants of Cartesian epistemology in his semantics. It is not the case that there is a stable, completely determined "world" on the one side of a dividing line and a precarious, potentially contradictory domain of sense and reference on the other, as Brandom's deontological difference between things and discursive commitments presupposes.

> The *process* on the *subjective* side of *certainty* that corresponds to the *relation* of incompatibility of facts or properties on the *objective* side of *truth* is *resolving* incompatible *commitments* by revising or relinquishing one of them. [. . .] *objectively* incompatible properties *cannot* characterize the same object (objectively incompatible facts cannot characterize the same

world), while *subjectively* incompatible commitments merely *ought not* to characterize the same subject.[33]

In this quote, world and subject are opposed such that the subject is excluded from the domain of the world. Yet, how does this square with Brandom's correct remark that Hegel's notion of "infinity" is the "holistic successor conception to a world of *facts*"?[34] It is, therefore, obvious that the semantic differential characterization between the objective world and the subject in terms of two forms of incompatibility cannot suffice as an interpretation of the Hegelian whole. In other words, Brandom's own conception of the world seems to fall back to a cosmological, pre-Kantian conception. For even Kant has pointed out that the world does not exist, that there is no such thing as an all-encompassing entity, an "all," even though the idea of an all regulates our epistemological enterprises. The all is nothing but a (necessary) illusion, and as such it is the content of transcendental dialectics, which Kant designs in order to reveal this illusion. As Žižek aptly remarks,

> . . . the mistake of the identification of (self-)consciousness with misrecognition, with an epistemological obstacle, is that it stealthily (re)introduces the standard, premodern, "cosmological" notion of reality as a positive order of being: in such a fully constituted positive "chain of being" there is, of course, no place for the subject, so the dimension of subjectivity can be conceived of only as something strictly codependent with the epistemological misrecognition of the true positivity of being.[35]

Subjectivity exists, sense qua object of reference has to be included in the world. This higher-order insight makes up the whole, which is the message of Hegel's dictum that "the true is the Whole."[36] Hegel consequently does not claim that there is some mega-entity, the whole, which encompasses everything else, from spatiotemporal objects to art, religion, and philosophy; the *whole* is not the *all* or some kind of other set. Again, Hegel's monism is not ontic nonsense, as some recent interpreters would like it to be.[37] That the true is the whole means rather that the very possibility of truth, of getting things right *or* wrong, can only be made sense of in higher-order reflection, for it refers to the constitutive conditions of truth-apt thought. In higher-order reflection we discover that the subject belongs to the world, that there is no objective world from which thought can be excluded. This does not entail that there is only thought. It just means that we have to explain the fact that thoughts *exist* too.

The move from Kant to Hegel cannot be made without taking into account the overall atmosphere of post-Kantian idealism and its thoroughgoing anti-Cartesianism. Analytic philosophy, in general, remains within the confines of Cartesian epistemology as long as it refers to the structure of reference without taking account of intentionality's existence as an object within the world. To tear down the barrier between mind and world is neither to fall into the trap of a subjective idealism nor to simply make the world immediately available to thought, but rather to include "mind" in the world. There is no such "thing" as the world, the unitary set of referents accessed by us by way of our sense-mongering activities (such as thinking), precisely because sense belongs as much to the world as the referents made available by sense.

The Kantian metaphysics of intentionality is designed to overcome the empiricist variety of a myth of the given and thereby to domesticate (or "exorcize," as McDowell has it) certain varieties of skepticism with regard to our access to the external world. Its central claim is that the structure of sensible experience can be analyzed into transcendental constituents, thereby enabling the substitution of always already structured givenness for the idea of a nonconceptual given. However, its focus remains on **sensible** experience: *having the world in view, it does not reflect on thereby also having experience of the world in view.* Kantian metaphysics of intentionality therefore also implicitly draws on "having the world in view" in view. Post-Kantian metaphysics of intentionality begins by making this level of reflection explicit: it is here that it does its whole work. On this level, there is no object that does not include its being an object in view. For this reason, it is legitimate to say that on this ontological level being and thought are one and the same, an identity one might simply call the whole.

III Logics and Ontology—Against Badiou

In particular in his "Dialogue with Pünjer About Existence," Frege has convincingly pointed out that "existence" cannot be a proper property of objects. He claims that it is rather the property of concepts to have an extension that is larger than 0.[38] To assert that there are horses is to assert that the concept *X is a horse* is not empty, that is, that something falls under it. Existence is, therefore, according to Frege, *a higher-order predicate.* Modifying Frege, one could defend his claim as follows. A long-standing rationalist tradition has thought of concepts in terms of sets of "marks" in order to understand objects in terms of sets of properties.[39] According to this tradition, any object has a finite set of properties by reference to which it is distinguishable from other objects. Horses are animals, they are supposed to have legs, a particular genetic code, and so forth. The very function of the idea of properties of objects in our epistemic economy is to make objects available to judgments in order for us to be able to refer to a world made up of different objects. Properties that do not serve this function of distinguishing an object within the world from others are, hence, not proper properties.[40] Given that there are no objects in the world that do not exist (although there might be nonexisting objects in the logical space of possibilities that is therefore distinguished from the world), existence cannot be a proper property of objects in the world. However, it remains that existence is a property, but just not of objects. For this reason, one could agree with Frege mutatis mutandis and say that existence is a higher-order predicate. It distinguishes concepts from each other by dividing a logical space of concepts into empty and nonempty concepts. Hence, the property of existence fulfills a discriminatory function, but only on the level of concepts, not on that of objects.

Frege ties the notion of existence as a higher-order predicate to his notion of reference. The extension of a concept constitutes the in principle quantifiable range of objects which fall under it. In this way, his notion of existence perfectly squares with his attempt to build mathematics on formal semantics, because number theory can be based on set theory, and set theory is tied to formal semantics (*Begriffsschrift*). Existence thus turns from mysterious metaphysical Being into the existential quantifier.

Prima facie there seems to be nothing wrong with this move. However, it ultimately neglects the dimension of sense, which is constitutive for the distinction between sense and reference. As Frege himself points out, we have no way to access reference (and hence to assert existence) without sense. As we saw, the proper names "evening star" and "morning star" refer to the same thing, that is, Venus, but this same thing in turn is nothing but another sense. Frege's disregard of sense in his theory of existence leads him to identify existence with quantifiability.

This identification is echoed by Badiou's identification of ontology and set theory. Set theory only appears as the best ontology as long as we think of existence in terms of quantifiability, as Badiou does.[41] However, as long as existence is only thought of in terms of the existential quantifier, we miss the fact that there is not one single homogeneous domain of objects that consists of in principle countable objects that fall under concepts. On the contrary, there are various domains of objects, and this plurality of domains of objects simply cannot be made sense of in terms of set theory.

To be sure, Badiou himself understands "existence" as the transcendental degree of self-identity of an entity's appearing-in-a-world. For him, to
exist is to appear in a world with a degree of phenomenal intensity, which
is larger than 0.[42] In this way, he spells out the details of a new transcendental logic, which is based on an "objective phenomenology." However,
if the existential quantifier belongs to transcendental logic, how can it be
applied to ontology in Badiou's sense? How can we claim that there are sets
by ascribing properties to them without thereby creating or entering the
world of set theory? This contradicts the ontological status of set theory in
Being and Event. Once more, Badiou struggles with his metaphysical division between ontology and logics, between the realm of pure multiplicity
and the realm of appearance, precisely because he disavows the fact that
ontology appears (to him) to be such and so. Otherwise, there could not be
any claimable true existential propositions in his ontology.[43]

Even though Badiou draws a distinction between the universe (the all
that does not exist) and his worlds, he himself ultimately claims that there
is a universe, the universe of set theory, of atomic elements, which abide
independently of any conceptual activity of synthesizing or organizing
them. Yet, how can he access this Platonic realm of pure multiplicity without making sense of it? And by making sense of it, it immediately loses its
alleged ontological status of consisting of pure sense-less referents. The
very split between *Being and Event* and *Logics of the Worlds* either destroys the
insights of the former or of the latter. For these and other pertaining reasons, it is necessary to develop a notion of existence that does not conflate
existence with the existential qualifier and its associated one-sided focus
on reference. In order to get there, it is necessary to replace the idea of sets
as the elements of ontology with the notion of fields of sense.

According to Cantor, the formation of sets presupposes a twofold abstraction. In order to build a set, say the set of all objects on a table, we have to
abstract both from the "quality" of the objects in question and from "the
order in which they are given."[44] If we count the objects on a table, it does not
matter which way they are arranged. Yet, this evidently does not hold for all
domains of objects. If the art historian talks about abstract expressionism or
Renaissance art, she has to take into account both the quality and the order
of presentation of objects. There are many domains of objects, which are constituted as fields of sense and not only as fields of reference. Some domains
of objects are fields of sense, which trivially entails that not all domains of
objects are sets. Therefore, set theory cannot account for the existence of a
plurality of domains of objects, and it has to dominate this field of differences
in terms of one specific domain of objects among others, namely set theory.

For this reason, I suggest we replace Frege's one-sided focus on reference with a notion of existence as a higher-order predicate, which allows for sense to become integral to our theory of existence. The *modified Frege-thesis*, therefore, claims that predicates are functions, which constitute domains. Existence would then be a property of domains of objects (of fields of sense), namely the property that something appears within them. To assert that Goya's *Saturne dévorant son fils* exists is to assert that it appears within a particular domain of objects, for example the domain of nineteenth-century Spanish painting, which is a field of sense.

The theory of domains of objects, which I identify with ontology, promises a new logics of sense by integrating sense into existence. Everything that exists exists under some mode of presentation or other. There might be a universe of purely quantifiable objects, but this universe is smaller than the world, because the world encompasses a plurality of domains, the universe of physics or mathematics being just some domains of objects among others. The formation of a set of sense-less, uninterpreted (mathematical) objects cannot furnish us with the ontology of all domains, because there is no such thing as an underlying pure multiplicity in a work of art (to name but one example). Works of art do not have a unified structure of sense; they do not form a single world in Badiou's sense, but open up different worlds.

Hence, despite some structural similarities between my domain-ontology and Badiou's *Logics of the Worlds*, there are various crucial differences. Badiou draws a distinction between ontology, the subject matter of which is pure multiplicity, governed by the laws of set theory, and the transcendental logic of worlds, which is a theory of appearing. Badiou, thereby, opposes the theory of being qua being, ontology, to the theory of appearing, which he understands as a theory of being-there. In this sense, his notion of ontology remains thoroughly Platonic and, just like traditional Platonism, he is not capable of explaining the transition from pure ontology to the realm of appearing, from being to being-there.

However, there is an even more fundamental problem. I fully agree with Badiou's claim that the All does not exist. In his language, the *universe* does not exist, whereas there are many *worlds*.[45] Yet his argument for the nonexistence of the All or the universe draws on set-theoretical paradoxes, particularly Russell's antinomy. Badiou argues as follows: If the All existed, it would have to exist as a member of itself. Otherwise, there would be an all outside of which something else, namely the All, existed. Hence, the All has to be a member of itself. Thus, there is at least one set, which is a member of itself. Nevertheless, there are obviously sets that are not members

of themselves. The set of all bananas is not itself a banana. This entails
that the All consists both of sets which are members of themselves and sets
which are not members of themselves. Given that the set of all sets that are
not members of themselves famously leads into Russell's paradox, the All
cannot exist, because its existence would entail an antinomy.

From this train of thought, Badiou infers that there can be no all-
encompassing situation in which all beings take place, thus there has to be a
plurality of worlds with no grounding unity as their background. However,
worlds in his sense are not sets according to the strict definition of the term.
For this reason, Badiou conflates his set-theoretical argument for the nonexistence of the All, the order of ontology, with a theory of worlds, which
belongs to a logics of appearing. He does not prove that the laws of ontology
also hold for the "worlding [*mondanisation*]"[46] of beings. Even though the
notion of intensity, which plays an important role in Badiou's transcendental logic, is not fully quantifiable, he does not seem to be aware of the crucial difference between an ontology of quantity and a logics of sense.

The advantage of a domain-ontology is that it starts with the notion of
sense right away and thereby does not even allow for the split between the
project of *Being and Event* and *Logics of Worlds*. Whatever exists only exists
within a field of sense. This also holds for fields of sense. *Fields of sense only
exist within the field of sense of fields of sense.* So, the multiplicity domain-ontology
deals with is never a quantifiable multiplicity. Many fields of sense are fuzzy
and their limits are, at the most, vaguely defined. Consider, for example,
the field of contemporary art. Objects are made up, which would not
have been part of the field of art of yesterday. The very field is constantly
changed by the objects, which appear within it. Other fields of sense, say,
set theory, are obviously not in the same way flexible, fragile, and open to
historical change by the objects that appear within them.

Concepts and predicates are functions that constitute fields of sense.
There is no transcendental universal logic for all fields of sense, as Badiou
believes. Appearing, and not only being, is also manifold. There is no single
set of laws of appearing, but rather a multiplicity of fields of sense, which
is as manifold and dynamic as our use of concepts. This insight is a post-
Kantian radicalization of Aristotle's anti-Platonic reminder that the sense
of being is manifold.[47] Of course, Aristotle believes that there is a focal
meaning of being, of existence, whereas I, in a modification of Aristotle,
take this focal meaning to be the property of a domain having something
appear within it. Being, therefore, is inextricably linked with appearing.

However, even though the nonexistence of the all in set theory that
results from Russell's paradox is restricted to one domain of objects among

others, and can therefore not be a universal truth about all domains, the whole also does not exist. The next step in the argument for this insight consists in a crossbreeding of modified Frege with Hegel. Hegel notoriously claims that "determination is negation posited as affirmative."[48] This can be reconstructed in terms of a domain-ontology as follows. It is impossible that there be just one object domain. If there were only one object domain, this object domain could not appear within a higher-order object domain, since it would have to be the only domain. Hence, the domain would have to appear within itself. Yet, the appearing domain could not be identical with the domain within which it appears for the trivial reason that it would have at least one different property, namely that of appearing within a domain. The domain within which something appears is trivially not identical with anything that appears within it. Hence, if there were only one domain, there would be none. Therefore, if anything exists at all, there are ipso facto many domains.

Now we can raise the question of whether the domain of all domains, the DD, in fact exists. If it existed, there would have to be a higher-order domain DD* that contained both the DD and all other domains. In this case, DD* would be what we were looking for, when we tried to grasp the idea of a domain of all domains. Therefore, DD* would be the "true" instance of a DD. If we ask the question whether DD* exists, we will have to form the notion of a DD** and so on ad infinitum. Therefore, there is no ultimate, all-encompassing object domain, no field of sense that would be capable of encompassing all fields of sense.

Even though the domain of all domains does not exist, the universe exists qua object domain of physics. There is no problem with the existence of the universe as long as we understand that the universe is just one object domain among others. If it were the only object domain, as physicalism tries to make us believe, then it could not exist, because it is impossible that there be just one object domain. As soon as an object domain exists, many object domains exist, and this goes for anything and everything determinate. And as soon as many object domains exist, the domain of all domains does not exist anymore. Of course, it never existed. As Heidegger thus correctly pointed out, Being is Nothing, for it does not exist.[49]

Already the early Heidegger uses the notion of object domains in his reading of Scotus.[50] And it is quite naturally derived from a particular reading of Aristotle's definition of what has later been labeled "ontology":

There is a science, which investigates being as being and the attributes, which belong to this in virtue of its own nature. Now this is not the same as any of the so-called special sciences; for none of these others treats universally of being as being. They cut off a part of being and investigate the attribute of this part; this is what the mathematical sciences for instance do.[51]

The science that investigates being as being, ontology, is here distinguished from any special science. While the special sciences deal with a particular object domain, ontology spells out the very concept of a domain as such. This already presupposes a plurality of domains, an assumption without which ontology could not get off the ground, as we can now see.

Aristotelian ontology is, as is well known, directed against Platonism. Platonism divides totality into pure being and being there, just as Badiou does. However, this raises the question of a transition from being to being there. Badiou wants to explain this transition in terms of his logics of appearing, which would be a new transcendental philosophy in his sense. Yet, this operation only results from the questionable assumption that ontology is set theory. If you replace the notion of sets by the notion of domains, it is both possible to maintain the transfinite nontotalizable existence of a plurality of worlds, that is to say of domains of objects, and to reduce set theory to one domain among others. This also allows for the elaboration of a logics of sense not committed to the quantifiability of existence.[52]

Of course, there have been attempts at an intensional logic after Frege.[53] However, the logics of sense cannot be modeled after mathematical logic at all, because it sets off with an account of a plurality of fields of sense, each one constituted by different rules, which define what can appear within a field of sense in order to then assess what actually appears within it.

IV Contingency and General Incompleteness

Logic—if we grant that there is a homogeneous field of formalizable logic— has turned out to be just one field of sense among others, one way for objects to be given to a position defined by rules. Logic is, thus, just a region of being in the traditional sense, such that we have to credit ontology with a primacy over logic. Of course, there might be a mere doing that we call "logic," a mere manipulation of signs according to rules, a certain reflectively undemanding practice. However, as soon as we interpret this doing in terms of an ontology, we wind up with a flawed metaphysics, which credits itself with the capacity to grasp the essence of what there is. This is already Plato's mistake, namely, to believe that the realm of pure forms could be more real in the sense of constituting a transcendental matrix for everything that exists. Contrary to this tradition, it is crucial to emphasize the overall discovery of post-Kantian idealism, a discovery most succinctly pointed out by Hegel when he reminds us that even his *Science of Logic* is a "realm of shadows."[54] Uninterpreted structure cannot be the essence of what there is.

Modern philosophy after Kant has inverted the Platonic order of explanation: the individual in "its infinite value"[55] constitutes the universal retroactively. Only by being there, it generates the domain within which it appears. The universal is strictly speaking nothing without the individuals it comprises, just as a concept has no meaning (in the Fregean sense, i.e. no reference) if nothing falls under it. If the whole (the ultimate universal dimension within which everything takes place) does not exist, its appearance is only generated retroactively by the contingent being there of a plurality of fields of sense. We can summarize the overall crucial ontological shift of modernity with the slogan that *Being becomes its own belated retrojection*: Being, the domain where everything, and therefore a plurality of fields of sense, takes place, only takes place as the imaginary whole generated from within a particular field of sense. Elsewhere, I have referred to this as the inevitability of "mythology."[56]

The primacy of ontology over logics entails that we cannot read our ontology off some established practice of manipulating signs. This is particularly obvious in the case of the metaphysics of the modalities. The metaphysics of contemporary modal logic, that is the metaphysics of "possible worlds" is only a ridiculous science fiction variety of Leibniz's *Theodicy*, but it even involves various conceptual shortcomings, some of which are pointed out in the final chapter of this book. The very role the notion of a "possible world" plays in the metaphysics of modal logic in fact involves a devastating circularity: it explains possibility, actuality, contingency, and necessity by reference to *possible* and *actual* worlds! The modals are already presupposed in the notion that is supposed to explain or even to define them.

I believe that reflection on the modalities leads to an insight into the contingency of necessity, a thought I have also already sketched elsewhere.[57] One of Aristotle's most profound philosophical insights is his discovery of the relation between truth and contingency. Contingency (τὸ ἐνδεχόμενον) in Aristotle refers to "that, which could be otherwise [ὃ ἐνδέχεται ἄλλως ἔχειν]."[58] If we assert that *p*, we claim that *p* is true. However, to claim that *p* is true, to take *p* for true, is evidently not identical with *p*'s necessarily being true. What can be asserted, could be otherwise.[59] In order to refer to a state of affairs, which is not identical with the act of being referred to, we need to be able to distinguish truth and taking-for-true. For this reason, judgment constitutes a realm of contingency. Even if we assert that p is necessary, this necessity is itself contingent. Truth is tied to assertion because it presupposes the possibility of error.[60]

If we import this observation into a domain-ontology, we get a result more radical than Aristotle could have envisioned from the perspective of his own ontology. Contingency and necessity can only be asserted within a particular domain. Given that nothing exists independent of some domain or other (because existence is a property of domains), contingency and necessity can only take place under the condition that there be domains. The rules that constitute the modalities of objects within a particular domain, such that it is distinguishable from other domains, do not necessarily apply to the domain itself. By virtue of the validity of a set of axioms and rules, it is necessary that $5 + 7 = 12$. However, this necessity presupposes the establishment of rules, which is not by itself necessary. Not only are there alternative arithmetical systems, but not even the laws of arithmetic apply to objects outside of the domain of arithmetic.[61] If you add 2 drops of water to 2 drops of water, you do not wind up with 4 drops of water.

Of course, the arithmetical notion of "addition" defines quantification in such a way that the water case does not fall under the concept of "addition." Yet, this difference is not reflected within the necessities of arithmetic. It is not a theorem of arithmetic that arithmetic is not identical with Spanish or with a subway ride in Hong Kong, even though we could not assert the truths of arithmetic without the capacity to locate it within a particular domain. Given that the difference between domains is ontologically constitutive of anything's existence whatsoever, nothing can exist that could not be otherwise.

Moreover, assertion *exists*, and because of this contingency has an impact on ontology. The ontological fact of contingency—expressed in the fact that everything turns out to be contingent on some level of reflection or another—generates the incompleteness of everything that exists. Some things are straightforwardly contingent, but, more radically, some a priori truths turn out to be higher-order contingent. There can be no complete theory of anything, because every (rule bound) theory is constituted by a blind spot: it cannot both refer to the objects of its domains and the rules that constitute it, because the constituting rules can only ever be the object of a higher-order theory. This higher-order theory is in turn constituted by rules, which are not objects of the theory, and so forth.

Therefore, no domain is complete in the sense that it can never both consist of truths about its objects or contents and of the rules which constitute it or open it up. The very assertion of all truths about its objects or contents and its rules would generate its contingency. Every theory is distinguished from other theories. However, this very defining feature can never be completely mapped within the theory. The theory could therefore always be otherwise than it appears to us, even though its objects or contents appeared to us in just the same way as they will continue to appear once we discover the limitations of the theory.

Despite the general incompleteness of everything determinate (which is a consequence of everything determinate being assertible) that also applies to ontology itself, philosophical thought is the paradoxical attempt to grasp the DD. This attempt fails if one thinks of the DD as if it were some entity or other. Domain-ontology is in itself an incomplete theory of incompleteness, because there might be other ways of formulating the thought it spells out that cannot be envisioned from the standpoint of domain-ontology. For example, one could argue in a Heideggerian vein that domain-ontology presupposes a unified, too general notion of objecthood, which might have to be replaced by a more fine-grained notion of the "thing." If late Heidegger is right, then the ultimate origin of the meandering of the philosophy of subjectivity is not the subject, but a problematic notion of the thing, which he aims to overcome.

Domain-ontology is one contingent field of sense among others, even though it tries to become universal. Be that as it may, no theory is capable of ruling out alternative modes of presentation. Just like any other theory, domain-ontology is defined by certain historically contingent rules and it generates its own blind spot. It will never be possible for any theory (nor for any ontology for that matter) to make its contents and its form explicit in such a way that it surpasses its being conditioned. There is no unconditional insight.

One might want to object that the mode of presentation of incompleteness adopted in this book still remains within the confines of the metaphysical wish to transcend the very finitude that is constantly pointed out. However, as I will argue in the course of the essays, finitude and infinity belong together. After Fichte, Schelling, and Hegel, it has become possible to think the dialectics of finitude and infinity in an anti-Platonic manner such that the infinite (Being) is not some predetermined, ready-made hyper-object, but the very result of our transcendence: *belated retrojection*.

Of course, the insight into the finitude and incompleteness of Being itself has hermeneutical consequences for any enterprise of interpreting the philosophical tradition.[62] If it is conceptually naïve to believe that objects might be fully determinate entities that exist independently of their capacity to be registered in a plurality of fields of sense, this also applies to the ontology of texts. We experience the meaning of a text only within the horizon of our own creative capacity to invest it with meaning. At the same time, the object, the text, responds; it conditions our conditions of referring to it. In other words, the overall structure of Being, the constitution of constitution laid out by transcendental ontology, also applies to our being towards texts.

This does not entail that there are no constraints in constituting objectivity. On the contrary, as I argue here and elsewhere, objectivity is sense-dependent on a plurality of fields of sense. The object, It, is only retroactively constituted as soon as conditions for identity—an identitary system—are established. Given that the texts of Fichte, Schelling, and Hegel respond to a reading in terms of a transcendental ontology, and given that this project can be philosophically defended (as I hope to show here and in the future), the web of interpretations laid out in this book at least opens up another field of sense between a normative reading of "idealism" and the contemporary French fallback to Platonic metaphysics.

Chapter 1

The Ontology of Knowledge

Modern philosophy seems to be characterizable in terms of a clear-cut distinction between epistemology and ontology. In the still dominant Quinean frame, ontology is modeled after epistemology insofar as it only describes the ontological commitments of a theory without thereby committing itself to a particular ontology.[1] Quine accepts the modern primacy of epistemology over ontology and, therewith, the distinction between *our access to what there is* and *what there is*. However our access to what there is is as much something that exists as anything else. Insofar as we are able to relate to conditions of truth or knowledge, those conditions have to exist. Only if we haphazardly identify existence with a realm of existing things in space-time, can we either deny that our access to what there is exists or feel the pressure to include it into the natural realm. Yet this forced choice is completely groundless and implicitly based on an unreflected ontology. Hence, the primacy of epistemology over ontology is already an ontology of knowledge with an obvious Cartesian outlook.

Against this background, it is evident that post-Kantian idealism (and actually already Kant) breaks with a certain ontology rather than just modifies epistemology. This is Hegel's point against the primacy of epistemology in the "Introduction" to the *Phenomenology of Spirit*. We cannot circumvent ontology by "modestly" sticking with epistemology, because this presupposes an ontology of knowledge. Therefore, post-Kantian idealism does not simply elaborate on Kant's epistemology, but reconstructs thought's ontological conditions. Those conditions are available to thought, because being turns out to be related to our conceptual capacities.

In this chapter, I investigate some consequences of this shift from transcendental epistemology to transcendental ontology. The first task is to reconstruct the role skepticism plays in the motivation of a post-Kantian ontology. As I read them, both Schelling and Hegel spell out a metaphysical truth of skepticism. The metaphysical truth of skepticism consists both in a realization of our finitude and in the adjacent insight into the nonexistence of the world. According to Kant and post-Kantian philosophy, the world is a "regulative idea" or a "horizon."[2] As we shall see, this neither entails "correlationism" nor "finitude" in Meillassoux's sense. On the contrary, the reflection on the ontological constitution of finite objective knowledge turns out to be the absolute itself. The absolute is not opposed to knowledge as an unattainable beyond, but identified as the very process of a subjectivization of being in the form of finite objective knowledge.

Next, I will turn to Hegel's Jena conception of "absolute identity" in order to argue that this is the crucial point of deviation from Kant. The transition from Kant to Hegel is the latter's move to a reflected ontology of the subject. Hegel accepts Kant's analysis of subjectivity, adding that the subject is but one instance of the very scheme of existence.

The last essay in this chapter reconstructs the further development of Hegel's ontology of the subject in the anthropology section of the *Philosophy of Subjective Spirit*. There, Hegel gives a genealogical account of intentionality (or "consciousness," as he calls it) in terms of a pathological splitting of a feeling monad. Hegel asserts the primacy of feeling and the disciplinary organization of an undifferentiated "feeling totality" into an arrangement of emotions. This forges the subject that, therefore, is always grounded in feelings. Those are connected to its surroundings in such a manner that we can never even assert the position of a Cartesian, potentially solipsistic subject. Hegel's move away from empiricism and the "myth of the given," thus, anticipates some of the philosophically valuable insights of psychoanalysis.

I Schelling, Hegel, and the Metaphysical Truth of Skepticism

One can distinguish at least two forms of naturalism. On the one hand there is *reductive naturalism*, which represents the metaphysical thesis that in truth only those objects that square with the necessary ontological assumptions of our best scientific theories can be properly said to exist.[3] To wit, then, there is no supernatural realm, nothing extranatural whatsoever, and what counts as "natural" is defined by our best scientific theories. Reductive naturalism claims that all ontological assumptions that we might make in our everyday lives, that is, in or regarding the human community, or in any context other than a natural scientific theoretical one, must be reducible to natural scientific assumptions: The manifest image must ultimately be reducible to the scientific image of man.[4]

On the other hand, there is *liberal naturalism*, which also begins from the thought that there is nothing super- or extranatural, yet admits that there is a human or second nature. While the latter cannot simply be reduced to first nature, it is nevertheless continuous with nature as conceived by our best scientific theories. Liberal naturalism thereby expands the concept of the natural by including a particular *human* nature therein. For example, McDowell has famously defended a variety of liberal naturalism in the form of a "naturalized Platonism,"[5] which is to say, Aristotelianism. In general, contemporary liberal naturalists tend to be Aristotelian precisely because Aristotle is trying to concede a space for mind in nature. In Aristotle, the philosophy of mind is part of the philosophy of nature.[6] Yet the presence of second nature in first nature does not change the ontological structure of first nature. The classical German idealist question—which properties do we have to ascribe to first nature in order to explain its capacity to become second nature, at least in the form of a creature gifted with second nature—is not within the scope of contemporary liberal naturalism. One reason for this is probably that it tries to avoid a revisionary form of metaphysics. Instead of facing science with the challenge of second nature, it rather acquiesces in science. The driving force of both forms of naturalism is the common enemy of religion, in particular religion in the form of creationism or other forms of creepy ontic, antiscientific claims. Just as its reductive sibling does, liberal naturalism wants to take account of the position of man in the cosmos without positing any supernatural dimension, without falling back into metaphysics in the pejorative sense of a weirdly premodern onto-theology.

However, reductive naturalism makes explicit metaphysical claims to the knowledge of reality as a whole, asserting that there is nothing that actually takes place (and no possible state of affairs) that our best scientific theories cannot take up as their object. Now, one can understand *metaphysics* as the project of thinking the world *as* world, that is, of developing a theory of totality that makes claims over the world as world rather than over some particular, determinate content in the world. Metaphysics is therefore characterized by a *reaching out to the whole* in which it should become determinate what the whole is. In this sense, reductive naturalism is unquestionably a *meta*physics, in that it claims that everything that actually exists, all content of the world, is describable in natural scientific terms. With this claim, an idea of the whole is anticipated and projected that cannot simply be inductively read off of a finite set of empirical data. Rather, a concept of the world corresponding to the scientific logic of discovery is assumed, which determines all available information as possible contents to be recorded in a to-be-achieved unified theory; even if it is not at present clear how a reduction of ostensibly nonnatural phenomena to the order of nature could take place, reductive naturalism assumes precisely that such a reduction is possible.

Reductive naturalism is therefore notoriously liable to skeptical challenges that bring into question how it is that it justifies its propositions about the nature of the world as world. Reductive naturalism presupposes that our empirical data processing is reliable and that the anticipation of the whole underlying the process of data collection is in turn justified by the successful collection of data. Skepticism famously disputes that this circular epistemological structure can or ever could be grounded in anything external to it, precisely because the circle itself constitutes the very possibility of reference to a natural order. According to the skeptic, any logical form of reference presupposes an anticipation of the domain over which it quantifies, an anticipation that can never be justified by determining what takes place within the domain. The very establishment of a sphere of intelligibility for understanding seems thus to be undermined by its fundamental transcendental structure. Thus, employing a set of classical arguments and paradoxes, the skeptic sets out to provoke reductive naturalism, to make manifest both the metaphysical tenor of its claims and the ultimate indefensibility of any and all reductive claims.

Liberal naturalism, however, has from the outset been thought of as an *antiskeptical* strategy and as a kind of therapy for the metaphysical tenor and tendency of reductive naturalism. It defuses the skeptical threats associated with reductive naturalism—or so it claims—by supplementarily equipping its naturalist ontology with a robust concept of human, second nature: ultimately, this move is meant to free the human community from total reduction so as to preserve the space wherein we negotiate and manage our beliefs. This move is a crucial step in liberal naturalism's effort to show that skeptical doubts are mere pseudoproblems that arise only for a theoretically alienated subjectivity, that is, subjectivity that has reflected itself out of the world.

In contemporary epistemology, it is only infrequently noted that liberal naturalism repeats a crucial moment of ancient (Pyrrhonian) skepticism to help ward off the charge that its withholding of judgment would lead to a complete practical paralysis.[7] While reductive naturalism flagrantly makes metaphysical claims and cannot defuse the skeptic's charge, liberal naturalism is a more subtle theoretical position, usually occurring as an antimetaphysical quietism that conceives of skepticism as a result of a tempting, but ultimately false, metaphysical transcendence. This transcendence is to be remedied by a therapeutic diagnosis that enlightens us as to why the transition from our finite discursive practices to a comprehensive view from nowhere presents itself as a temptation in the first place.

On even a superficial reading of German idealism, it should be obvious that Schelling and Hegel aim at a refutation of both forms of naturalism. As good students of the Antinomies chapter of the *Critique of Pure Reason*, they both criticize reductive naturalism as a reification of totality: with the help of a "skeptical method,"[8] such reification can be pointed up and destroyed. In a rather easy move, Schelling and Hegel break down metaphysical, reductive naturalism in light of Kant's famous diagnosis that metaphysics has for too long stayed a "battlefield of endless controversies"[9] because it has not made its own theoretical conditions the subject of a theory: it is thus imperative to bring the theory-conditions of metaphysics under reflective scrutiny. In this effort, reductive naturalism reveals itself as being, at best, a kind of half-baked metaphysical theory and, at worst, shameless ideology.

The quietism of liberal naturalists, on the other hand, will face the charge from Schelling and Hegel of being a dialectically inconsistent figure of thought. They attack it by demonstrating that quietism despite itself is based on a skeptical ground, which is incompatible with the position of reflected naïvety that quietism ultimately claims for itself. The supposed liberation from metaphysical claims, that is, the therapy of our natural tendency to metaphysics, itself leads to the adoption of a specific conception of human freedom, which quietism has to employ to distance itself from reductive naturalism. However, the liberal naturalist is, *according to his own theory*, in no position to lay claim to such a concept of freedom, and so maneuvers himself into a quietist trap; this is why his position ends up in dialectical contradiction.

Following Hegel, we can draw a distinction between an *analytic* and a *dialectical contradiction*. A theory is said to suffer an *analytic contradiction* if it can be shown either that there are obvious and direct logical incompatibilities between some explicit theorems of the theory (which is rare), or if it is shown through an analysis of the inferential role of some theorems of the theory in question that there are logical incompatibilities, that is, that when spelled out, a theory comes to oppose two of its own theorems such that it is impossible that both could be true. On the other hand, a *dialectical contradiction* arises when the motivational structure of a theory is incompatible with its manifest propositions (both on the level of axioms or theorems), without a direct, logical contradiction arising *within* the already established structure of the theory.

Now, every philosophical theory must be, explicitly or implicitly, motivated prior to its articulation. Hegel even reckons, just like all other post-Kantian systematic philosophers, that the motivation of a philosophical position must be spelled out within the theory itself, that is, that it is crucial that the conditions of a theory be justified and reflected within that very theory. Hegel creates his own theory *a limine* under the conditions of a maximally methodological self-consciousness, in an effort to prevent the possibility of dialectical contradictions in his own theory. This is precisely what skepticism could not achieve: "the thoughtlessness of skepticism about itself"[10] must therefore be remedied. As we shall see, liberal naturalism suffers from a dialectical inconsistency; it is not capable of being motivated without cancelling the motives that lead to its formulation in the first place.

Schelling and Hegel both seek to build skepticism into their methodology in order to motivate their move from first-order to higher-order metaphysical theorizing. Metaphysics after Kant no longer has an object without itself becoming its own object to begin with. Their strategy is thus both antiskeptical and skeptical, inasmuch as they both seek to make use of the skepticism initially leveled against reductive naturalism: they both employ the destructive energy of skepticism, which explodes the taken-for-granted character of our common explanations and experience, in order to motivate a metatheoretical standpoint from which the theoretical conditions of metaphysics in general will be discussed and scrutinized. From this vantage point, it turns out that liberal naturalism violates human freedom, which as Hegel and Schelling see it, consists in the fact that we are above and beyond all that is given at any given time and that things *überhaupt* can only be grasped within the horizon of an unconditioned, infinite, or absolute. In its attempt to purify the human condition of its tendency toward transcendence, since this potentially leads to a skeptical loss of the world, liberal naturalism deprives us of the specifically human dimension of an unconditional freedom, that to which Schelling and Hegel in their utterly antireductionist attitude consistently lay claim.

The question of the tenability of this strategy—that is, whether it is possible to integrate skepticism into the construction of metaphysical theories, while at the same time rendering quietism impossible—is essentially the question of whether or not metaphysics in a post-Kantian idealist sense is feasible. Hegel had first pursued this strategy when he leveled the antinomies discovered by ancient skepticism against common sense and its implicit claim to sense-certainty. Consider, for instance, Hegel's early essay "The Relationship of Skepticism to Philosophy,"[11] as well as his confrontation with skepticism in the *Phenomenology* and in his *Lectures on the*

History of Philosophy.[12] The proof of the implicit philosophical assumptions of common sense and the ensuing dialectic that displaces and destroys such assumptions has a definitively skeptical moment, as Hegel emphatically states. However, Hegel's dialectic ultimately domesticates skepticism by way of reflectively installing it in his own theoretical construction. At the same time, it shows the quietism (of Pyrrhonian skepticism) to be an instance of the figure of theoretically mediated immediacy, which under genuine skeptical conditions would lead to dialectical inconsistency and contradiction.

In his lecture course *Initia Philosophiae Universae* (held in Erlangen, 1820–1), Schelling also lays out a strategy of skeptical metaphysics, which can be explained using the example he develops in his Erlangen text *On the Nature of Philosophy as Science*.[13] Schelling understands skepticism as delivering a crucial lesson about the structure of human knowledge, whose constitutive finitude he insists constitutes the infinite. While Hegel uses skepticism to motivate the thought that the education of consciousness leads, through genealogical, retrospective understanding, to absolute knowledge, Schelling reconstructs the path of metaphysical knowledge as the discovery of nonknowledge by and through the breakdown of all dogmatic determinations of the whole. It is crucial to note that with their respective conceptions of metaphysical knowledge, both Hegel and Schelling distance themselves from *any* determinate concept of the whole, always keeping in mind Kant's thesis that the whole cannot possibly be a content of propositional knowledge.

In what follows, in Section 1, I will begin by reconstructing Schelling's account of a metaphysical "knowledge of non-knowledge"[14] and its relation to and departure from Kant's conception of totality. In this context it will be shown exactly how Schelling understands skepticism as a crucial lesson about the structure of human knowledge.[15] In contradistinction to liberal naturalism, Schelling reinterprets the result of skepticism, viz. that no knowledge can be had of the whole or of our position in it, in a metaphysical manner, elucidating what one might call the metaphysical "truth of skepticism."[16] After this, I will turn, in Section 2, to outline what results from Hegel's skeptical heuristic, that is, his concept of *true* or *veritable infinity* and its relation to his claim that the ten tropes of ancient skepticism make the naïve realism of common sense and sense-certainty impossible. Finally, in Section 3, it will be demonstrated that Hegel points up a dialectical instability in the liberal naturalist's position that results from the fact that its motivation, the "freedom of self-consciousness,"[17] is incompatible with its conclusion, viz. that the skeptic should simply content himself with what is given, so long as one does not seek to establish the given through philosophical claims.

1. The Knowledge of Nonknowledge (Schelling)

According to Kant, it is the nature of reason to reach out beyond itself to the whole, because, as the very organ of the pursuit of knowledge, it is oriented towards the "idea of absolute totality."[18] Without the anticipation of a whole, that is, without a concept of the world, it could not be expected that our representations relate to a representable world, which always provides more information than we can grasp in any single moment or mode of knowledge. Any determinate concept of the world is a stand-in for the (nonexistent) unity of actuality as a whole. With regard to this unity of actuality as a whole, we must reckon, however, that if indeed everything that exists is in some manner or other determined, then it will be differentiated through its properties from all other existent things and consequently that it will stand in potentially predicable relations of inclusion and exclusion to all other things. Everything that exists stands in such exclusive or inclusive relations with everything else and therefore has, by definition, certain limits, in virtue of which it is differentiated from everything else. This ensures, according to Kant, that everything that exists is part of a comprehensive unity and therefore can be interpreted as a limitation of this unity. The idea of an "*omnitudo realitatis,*" "the unlimited," or "the All"[19] leads us never to abandon the search for the proper predicate for a given thing: our progressive attitude is motivated by the idea that our determinations will eventually find their proper place in the totality of predicates.

The unlimited itself, however, cannot be limited and, consequently, one cannot determine it *as* something. It is a motivating idea in the economy of the human intellect, not an object of knowledge: it is not a knowable, but rather that which spurs the desire that subtends the whole project of knowledge. The unlimited itself is nothing definite, nothing that is the case, as Wittgenstein would have it. Therefore, clearly, the unlimited cannot be identified with nature as conceived by the natural sciences. Nevertheless, it belongs to the logic of natural scientific research to anticipate and project the whole, whose laws the theory-building process aims to reveal and render transparent. The presumption of a whole cannot be inductively proven, but it is a heuristic presupposition without which cognitive projects could not even be set in motion.

It is impossible that empirical evidence could speak for or against any particular concept of the world without a concept of the world being anteriorly at play according to whose criteriology empirical data would be arranged such that they might speak for or against this or that concept of the world. The world itself cannot be represented as the ultimate context of all that exists without (and this is trivial) itself being brought into the world. Therefore, the world cannot be a determinate object among others.

According to Kant, totality does not exist independently of the human project of knowledge, neither as a *summum ens* nor as a mere natural mechanism. The concept of the world itself thus has no objective reality, since the utter and total ontological context cannot be given in any intuition. Again, the world as a whole is no real entity, though it persists for the understanding as the impetus of a striving: it motivates the effort to formulate an optimal system of statements about actuality, wherein all of these statements would be progressively rendered epistemically transparent. The idea of the world is that which motivates the progressivism of the project of knowledge, and this project cannot exist apart from this progressivism. The search for knowledge cannot terminate in any totality, that is, it could never discover an object that corresponds to the concept of the whole, because totality as such cannot, in principle, exist as an object. Stephen Mulhall also succinctly renders the same point with reference to Wittgenstein and Heidegger:

> The world is not a possible object of knowledge, because it is not an object at all—not an entity or set of entities. It is that within which entities appear, a field or horizon of assignment-relations; it is the condition for the possibility of any intra-worldly relation, and so is not analyzable in terms of any such relation. In short, the Cartesian conception of subject and world opens the door to skepticism because it interprets both subject and world as entities (or sets of entities)—as if the world were a great big object, a totality of possible objects of knowledge, rather than that wherein all possible objects of knowledge are encountered.[20]

Schelling interprets this insight as asserting that the human qua rational being or concept-mongering creature can only be comprehended within the horizon of an absolute. This horizon can itself be no thing: therefore the world as a whole must not be thought of as an object to which certain properties belong, through which it can be differentiated from other things. In this sense, Schelling already saw in his early essay *Of the I as the Principle of Philosophy or on the Unconditional in Human Knowledge* that the task of philosophy consists in "finding something which absolutely cannot be thought of as a thing."[21] If there were no unconditioned, there would be for us, to wit, no things within the horizon of a whole: it is through the absolute alone that the promise of thoroughgoing determinacy can be made and a priori secured.

Schelling insists that if it is the nature of reason itself to reach out to the whole, then the reification of totality cannot simply be an artificial and ultimately contingent result of philosophy having gotten on the wrong track at some point in its history. In this insight Schelling is in perfect agreement with Kant, for this tendency to reify totality attests to and is an inalienable feature of our "common reason" (which should not be confused with common sense), and the effort to grasp the whole is a "quite natural illusion"[22] (which should not be understood as natural in the natural scientific sense).

We have, indeed, a tendency to reify our own activity: we are constantly compelled to make that which is the ultimate condition of possibility of the search for knowledge (*totum*) into a specific content of knowledge to be revered (*totem*). To become enlightened about the reason behind our compulsion to reification, Kant insists that we must adopt a "skeptical method."[23] Specifically, this method will work by reflecting on thought and revealing those moments of *isostheneia* or equipollence that make manifest the activity of reason in its attempt to reify totality. This method is skeptical because it shows that there is no world independently of the functioning of the concept of a world in the epistemic economy of finite cognitive beings.[24] Yet this method itself elicits no skeptical charge because it makes no claim on the substantive nature of the All. It is not skeptical in the sense that it deprives us of our knowledge of the (external) world, it rather denies the existence of such a *thing* without denying that there are other things. The only thing, the existence of which it questions, is the all of reality. It merely seeks to bring to light the specific function of the concept of the world in our epistemic economy: an objectified concept of the world, as that about which judgment should be suspended, functions in our ordinary cognitive projects as the background in accordance with which questions are determined as meaningful.[25]

In his Erlangen lecture *On the Nature of Philosophy as Science*, Schelling highlights, with Kant, a discovery of ancient skepticism, which he reinterprets as a metaphysical lesson about the true status of the absolute in the epistemic economy of finite knowers. The methodology of the Antinomies chapter of the *Critique of Pure Reason* plays a pivotal role, for there skepticism has already been integrated in the reflection of reason. Skepticism is for Schelling a moment that must be installed in metaphysical reflection itself if metaphysical reflection is to be valid: that is, skepticism represents a crucial moment in any mode of metaphysical knowledge that seeks to avoid the reproach of reifying totality. In order to avoid reifying the unconditioned, one must, with Kant, undertake a reflection on the structure of human knowledge. Thus Schelling inherits from Kant the effort of localizing totality within the *search* for knowledge, that is, to conceive the whole as a crucial part of the dynamics of reflection, rather than as an extant entity. In order for the project of knowledge to go on, an unconditional horizon of expectation must at all times be set in place, which decides in advance what can appear as a *thing* in question, what can come into question in our investigation. But if things only exist for us in the horizon of an unconditioned upon which our world is grounded yet from which we are indeed cut off—for it cannot be determined as a content of the world or grasped in any propositional manner—one can say that things exist for us only insofar as we are always already beyond everything that is or could be given. Things exist for us, therefore, only on the basis of an inexorable transcendence that is the very motor of reason itself. This is why we are compelled and obliged to conceptually anticipate the whole in order to guarantee the *systematic unity* of our empirical data processing: without an image of the whole in mind, no authority could be derived on the basis of which we could make true statements about the whole (let alone identify false ones). Hence, totality is a projection of reason, a "*focus imaginarius*,"[26] but is not a possible object of propositional knowledge.

The systematic unity of knowledge which Schelling himself refers to as "coherence"[27] can therefore never be fully realized. As Schelling puts it at the outset of his lecture, this fact is expressed in the plurality of metaphysical systems. The diagnosis of the plurality of metaphysical systems has since antiquity motivated a skepticism *in metaphysics*. Thus Pyrrhonian skepticism, in response to the supposedly undecidable disputes of various philosophies, asserted that philosophy's problems are constitutively unsolvable. Skepticism misconstrues the "inner disputes"[28] of metaphysicians as the impossibility of metaphysical knowledge as such: this is what must be avoided if the post-Kantian skeptical method is to fight shy of the typical conclusions of skepticism.

The skeptical method can be seen particularly clearly in the structure of the so-called five tropes of Agrippa's Trilemma, which has become a popular reference point for contemporary epistemology.[29] The five tropes present a skeptical *argumentum ex dissensu*, the structure of which can be recapitulated as follows. The initial step of skeptical arguments in all instances is the "trope of difference of opinion" (ὁ ἀπὸ τῆς διαφωνίας). The theoretical work of the skeptic consists first and foremost in bringing together the plurality of dogmatic assertions, such that an irresolvable conflict can be staged and Agrippa's Trilemma can be initiated. The trilemma effectively arises when a fundamental disagreement between at least two parties leads, in any attempt to decide between the parties, to (1) an infinite regress of reasons, where the arguing opponents will each time require a further reason for their opponent's fundamental assumptions (ὁ εἰς ἄπειρον ἐκβάλλων). (2) The infinite regress can be avoided if at least one of the parties asserts that their position is groundless (ὁ ὑποθετικός) or (3) is guilty of begging the question (ὁ διάλληλος). Yet, (1)–(3) are altogether highly questionable "options".

The trilemma of Pyrrhonian skepticism serves to shatter absolutist prejudices in all doxastic systems (and a fortiori in all metaphysical systems). It does so by revealing not only the background assumptions harbored by such positions—which can neither be blindly accepted nor justified by reference to their logical implications—but also by demonstrating the background assumptions of any position which would allow us to adjudicate between positions. For this reason, "the trope of relativity" (ὁ τοῦπρόςτι) represents the bottom line of the canon of the five tropes. Sextus argues for a form of global relativism, which states that we will never be justified in deciding between different doxastic systems. We can say with Strawson that the five tropes are Sextus's "relativizing move."[30] In this sense, Sextus can be called a diligent historian of philosophy, for he recognizes the history of philosophy as a testimony of the undecidability of its own problems.

Schelling concedes to the skeptic that, in principle, the plurality of metaphysical systems must precede the one true system of totality. Without some original "*asystasia*"[31] or inconsistency, no system is possible, because a system is only intelligible for us as the arrangement of something that before was not arranged. The very space of ignorance, which is replaced by a system, is an inconsistency relative to the system. Analyzing what it is to acquire, accumulate, and systematize knowledge presupposes an a-systasy, a position of nonknowledge within our epistemic economy.

This general claim is, of course, nothing more than a reflected form of the skeptical insight of the *Antinomy of Pure Reason*: the plurality of metaphysical systems is a necessary feature of metaphysics, not a sign of its impossibility. It is crucial to note, however, that without this reflective insight into the antinomy of pure reason, the precise metaphysical reason of the antinomy itself could not be discovered.

Skepticism for Schelling invites the construction of a *system theory*, that is, a theory whose proper content consists in the very theory conditions of metaphysics. According to Schelling, metaphysics as a theory of totality must therefore be constructed as a metatheory. One cannot *intentione recta* design a system, for it would immediately be confronted with its negation: what the insight of the skeptical principle of *isostheneia* teaches us is that every assertion can be countered by an equipollent, opposite one. When metaphysics is confronted with skepticism, it must develop a different model of theory construction, one wherein the content of metaphysical theory is not totality tout court, but is rather the totality of metaphysical systems, the totality of the history of concepts of totality. For Schelling, metaphysical knowledge is thus possible only in the context of a theory that has the conditions of possibility of the plurality of metaphysical systems as its object, such that metaphysics with Schelling becomes a metatheory.

Skepticism teaches the metaphysician that a theory of totality can provide no simple answer to the question of what the whole is. As historical examples of such simple answers Schelling mentions ancient naturalism (e.g. some pre-Socratic natural philosophers) and the dualism of spirit and nature (which he attributes to Anaxagoras), as well as abstract spiritual monism (which he attributes to the Eleatics).[32] All these positions fail in Schelling's eyes by virtue of the fact that they do not install their negation, the ineradicable equipollent claim that opposes their own theory, into their own theory construction. Thus, when the skeptic challenges these positions, the skeptical *isostheneia* principle devastates their theories. The *dogmatism of skepticism*, as it were, consists in the unswerving commitment to the thought that the whole cannot straightforwardly be determined without generating a metaphysical *isostheneia* situation. According to Schelling, the theory of metaphysical systems in general, and thus the very system he himself seeks to achieve, must therefore take the form of a "unity of unity and opposition,"[33] such that skepticism can be reinterpreted as the real agent of metaphysics.

The clash of metaphysical systems is not an accidental controversy of various thinkers, but is rather the expression of an "inner irresolvable conflict in human knowledge."[34] Schelling develops this skeptical diagnosis in response to a basic and fundamental antinomy in human knowledge, which consists in its necessary oscillation between the finite and the infinite. This antinomy is not an accidental determination of our thinking about reality as a whole, but is rather constitutive of *human* knowledge as such. Human knowledge as such is antinomical because, on the one hand, the human is beyond all that is given and therefore grasps things only in the horizon of an unlimited absolute and, on the other hand, something is only known inasmuch as it is conceptualized and ipso facto determined or limited. Knowledge presupposes a process of something "becoming an object for someone,"[35] an effective *taking to be true*, which is a necessary component of the concept of knowledge. *One cannot know what one cannot at the very least take to be true.* What one takes to be true must be conceptually determinate and therefore epistemically distinguishable from other objects. Taking to be true implies, therefore, a discriminatory capacity and an ability to recognize inferential relationships. If knowing implies taking to be true, and taking to be true would not be possible without inferential capacities or the ability to recognize relations of inclusion and exclusion, then every and all determinate content of human knowledge is a moment in a whole, which of course could not be a content of human knowledge properly speaking. Hence Schelling asserts that this insight into holism provides a "peculiar knowledge," viz. that the whole is "one and always already another."[36] He writes,

> Knowledge is neither in that which always remains one, which does not transcend itself, nor in that which is totally dispersed and diverse, in that which is without unity and context; knowledge is coherence, one and yet many, always another and yet always one.[37]

Human knowledge, in undertaking the construction of metaphysical systems, thereby seeks to dissolve its ownmost antinomy: in engaging in metaphysics, the human ultimately fixes its essential transcendence in an object through which it seeks to get hold of the infinite, to "include it within determinate limits."[38] That is, human knowledge seeks to *de-fine* the infinite, in the proper sense of definition, that is, limitation (ὁρισμός). What can be defined, however, must itself be definite: "that which lets itself be defined can be nothing but what by nature is enclosed within determinate limits."[39] The project of human knowledge to determine the whole as something and to make its unconditional horizon into an object constitutes the dialectic of human knowledge: it can only ever grasp its infinity by way of the finite knowledge of *something*, which is to say that it cannot, in principle, *know* this infinity.

One can also explain this antinomy as follows: the infinite as condition of the *search for knowledge* is necessarily lost as soon as one sets out to *secure knowledge* of it.[40] Every effort to secure knowledge consists in the de-finition (in the literal sense) of an object, that is, in the search for the right concept: the one object to be known must be sufficiently delimited from and over against some others in order for it to be known.[41] Every effort to secure knowledge by determining the unconditioned or the infinite as the condition for the possibility of the search for knowledge necessarily displaces the infinite by virtue of this determination.

> Here we have the contradiction that the human destroys that which it wants through its wanting it. From this contradiction arises this internal

drivenness, such that he who is looking for something moves that which he is looking for ahead of itself in a constant flight from himself.[42]

According to Schelling, all finite knowledge of the determinate is resultant of the effort to define the infinite. Thus, every successful predication misses its goal, as it were, but in a constitutive manner. Every predication aims at a definition of what was indefinite for knowledge before its attempt to grasp it in concepts. Therefore, knowledge claims delimit the infinite and always already miss it. While the skeptic argues that this condition for possibility of knowledge makes it finite in such a way that it might turn out to be impossible, the apparent shortcoming of knowledge for Schelling is constitutive of its very possibility. Knowledge need not be conceived as defective in its confrontation with the infinite, as long as we keep in mind that it is both finite and defined by its reaching out for the whole. The desire of the infinite does not destroy knowledge, but makes it possible.

As the infinite is always only grasped in a certain "shape,"[43] that is, as something determinate, the infinite ipso facto "drives itself in front" of these shapes; by virtue of this excess of the infinite over its determination, the judging subject's predicative practice must itself carry on ad infinitum. Skepticism teaches us that a constitutive ignorance lies at the heart of human knowledge; it also teaches us, however, that as a consequence of this ignorance, the attempt to bring knowledge to an unsurpassable closure is itself impossible.

Sextus famously draws a distinction between *Pyrrhonian* and *academic* skepticism. While academic skepticism *claims* that we cannot know anything and thus seeks to demolish the search for knowledge as such, Pyrrhonian skepticism insists that the search for knowledge cannot be brought to rest by way of some specific claim regarding the impossibility of knowledge. The Pyrrhonian search for knowledge does not come to tranquility, that is, to *ataraxia*, by holding onto some determinate knowledge claim, not even the claim that we cannot know anything. Instead, *ataraxia* arises only when the Pyrrhonist gives himself over to the ultimate groundlessness of knowledge.[44] Only in reason's last desperate act, as it fully experiences its antinomy, does the Pyrrhonist come to see the world "for what it truly is." Sextus expresses this with the famous metaphor according to which the giving up of knowledge is like kicking away the very ladder one has climbed;[45] Wittgenstein seems to be echoing precisely this.[46]

In this thought one can see with Stanley Cavell the "truth of skepticism," which asserts that "our relation to the world as such is not one of knowing."[47] Cavell recognizes this insight (just as Schelling had) in Kant's doctrine of the *transcendental ideal*: he points directly to Kant's doctrine in his interpretation of the thesis that our relation to the world as a whole is not theoretical. It is for exactly this reason that the Kantian idea of God has its proper place in practical philosophy, for as Kant showed, we do not relate to the world *as* world by virtue of *knowing* something about it. Cavell sees Kant's critical intention of limiting human knowledge as a consistent effort

> to show that knowledge is limited not in the sense that there are *things* beyond its reach [. . .] this is something his idea of God is meant to show: that I have, and must have if I am a rational creature, a relation to reality which is not one of knowing.[48]

The lesson that skepticism teaches us, following Cavell, is that our relation to the world as a whole is not primarily theoretical and therefore cannot be an object of knowledge. The world as a whole is not an object that either exists or does not exist such that one would have to secure oneself against skeptical doubts about the existence of this immeasurable, excessive object. According to Cavell, it is rather the case that the project of epistemology as such distances us from the world, convincing us that we are correct in "looking at the world as if it were another *object*."[49] This does not entail that metaphysics is altogether a senseless undertaking, but rather just that the standard epistemological view of objective knowledge is not suited to understanding the world. Thus, epistemological accounts of the world will, without fail, provoke skepticism.

It is crucial not to lose sight of the metaphysical potential that Cavell's diagnosis unleashes: thus, we should recall the metaphysical consequences and the consequences for metaphysics that Schelling had extrapolated from his similar diagnosis. Schelling accepts the truth of skepticism with the important addition, what he conceives as a metaphysical (in his qualified sense) lesson about the absolute, namely that the absolute cannot, in fact and in principle, be known with any epistemic security. The system-theoretical reflection on the possibility of a theory of totality shows that absolutely all metaphysical systems set out to **determine** the absolute or infinite, and all fail to do so because this very attempt finitizes the infinite. Schelling shares this lesson with Sextus.

This lesson, however, does not necessarily entail that we should simply resign to a liberal naturalism or quietism, according to which human knowledge has nothing left but to retreat to the practices of the community and refrain from its reaching out to the whole.[50] The truth of skepticism rather draws our attention to the fact that we cannot get hold of what we originally sought in our metaphysical efforts, that is, a definite answer to the question of what the whole is, for it reveals that the whole is nothing determinate.

Schelling thus replaces the classical ontology of completeness, which opposes the world as the completely determinate domain of things to mind as the fallible excess over what is the case, with an ontology of incompleteness: the domain of all domains is not a thing, but a withdrawal constitutive of the possibility of something being given to knowledge. In this way, he avoids Cartesian-style skepticism by changing the background ontology, which motivates skepticism about the (external) world. The very concept of an (external) world, which is still prominent in epistemology today, is completely obscure. It seems to designate a huge kind of object or, at best, a homogeneous, singular domain of objects, which can be quantified over. However, this very conception of the world, and not its assumptions about knowledge, is the flaw of modern epistemology. Instead of refining our concept of knowledge so as to make it suitable to our ontological assumption of the world as an object or homogeneous, singular domain of objects, as most of contemporary epistemology does, we need to change the underlying ontology of knowledge. This leads to a *docta ignorantia*, to nonknowledge about the world, which differs from the skeptical ignorance about intraworldly state of affairs/facts. We cannot know the world as an extant entity, which does not entail that we cannot know anything.

The *docta ignorantia* concerning the world or the absolute is itself a reflexive knowledge through which the constitutive ignorance of human knowledge is known. Yet, have we not thus merely made "the undefinable the definition"[51] of the absolute? Have we not overturned our claim that the absolute is not an entity or object of knowledge? If so, the unconditioned would be determined as infinite in contradistinction to the finite, as "the negation of finitude."[52] That means, however, that it would faute de mieux be determined through its opposition to the finite. Yet Schelling counters this "threat of negation"[53] by seeking to solve the problem of "how unity can consist in coexistence with opposition and opposition with unity, or better, how for their own good, each necessitates the other."[54] This complex dynamic is only possible if the unconditioned is understood as the very process of its reification in finite consciousness. The struggle with the inconsistencies of reification, thereby, ultimately serves the goal of forcing consciousness from the level of first-order knowledge to higher-order theorizing.

The attempt to think the whole, according to Schelling, leads us to discover the metaphysical truth of skepticism, which says: we cannot know the whole, because it is essentially nonobjective. The higher-order reflection on the plurality of metaphysical systems gives rise to this insight. The plurality of definitions of the whole that have been offered over the history of philosophy indicates, in Schelling's metatheory, not that no sufficient definition of the whole has yet been given, but rather that no adequate definition is possible. All metaphysical systems strive to determine the whole, so that it might be "the absolute subject"[55] of all metaphysical judgments. Nonetheless, it cannot be successfully determined in any judgment without becoming an object. In seeking to capture the whole in a system-theoretical reflection, one cannot but think the absolute as the subject of a theory of the whole.

This claim must not be thought of as an epistemological problem, but rather as identifying something about the absolute: the infinite must be structured such that it always and only appears as the finite. In order to avoid setting infinity and finitude in mere opposition, Schelling identifies the infinite with the "self-destruction"[56] of human knowledge, the essential reflexive act of the knowledge of nonknowledge. This reflexive metatheoretical insight into the antinomy of human knowledge *is* the infinite. We come to recognize this insight through the antinomy without the absolute thereby becoming an object of knowledge. It remains in the position of the subject of knowledge, it knows its own nonobjectivity by knowing about the impossibility of becoming an object in any particular domain. The inconsistent determinations of metaphysical knowledge that lead to the plurality of metaphysical systems exist only so that the infinite can ultimately manifest itself, for without this improper manifestation it would simply be determined in opposition to the determinate. Only "by assuming a shape, yet at the same time victoriously transcending any shape, does it show itself to be the ungraspable, the infinite."[57] Thus, *human knowledge itself is the infinite,* since on the one hand it seeks to determine the infinite, to grasp it as a specific object, while on the other hand it is always already beyond all that is given. The infinite is not set against human knowledge—neither as an ungraspable beyond nor an object too big to be grasped—for it would thus be determined through this opposition.

The specific freedom of the human consists in the fact that human knowledge is, in its first-order usage implicitly and in philosophical reflection explicitly, beyond all that is given. Therefore, however, this specific freedom is at the same time dependent on the given, for *freedom consists in a relation to the given that is gone beyond.* In human freedom the "eternal freedom"[58] of being beyond all that is given is exhibited. Yet, when human knowledge seeks to catch its eternal freedom as an object, it of course only generates this object as a thing in the horizon of the absolute. Thus eternal freedom necessarily and at all times appears to consciousness qua finite knowledge as non-freedom, that is, as reified totality. If the unconditioned were "only freedom in such a way that it could not be not-freedom, that it had to remain freedom, then freedom would become its limit, would become its necessity: it would not really be absolute freedom."[59]

Only knowledge of the unconditioned in the mode of nonknowledge leads to the true determination of human freedom in knowledge as eternal freedom.[60] The "concept of eternal freedom" cannot therefore be something "remote from our knowledge,"[61] that is, eternal freedom is not some inaccessible object. In showing that the infinite is nothing other than the finitude of human knowledge which reflects upon itself, Schelling demonstrates that our search for knowledge in system-theoretical reflection is the infinite's own search for itself.

All of these dialectical speculations might sound like grandiose metaphysical claims, but they are rather simple, if not almost trivial. For, if we set out to know what knowledge is, we try to determine the right concept of knowledge. However, this presupposes that knowledge was indeterminate for us before. Given that knowledge only exists as knowledge for us (it is not like a stone or any other typical mind-independent object), knowledge only becomes determinate and thereby finite in our attempt to know it, to make it an object of knowledge. Knowledge therefore only exists as such in its own objectification. Yet this objectification does not usually grasp knowledge in its transition from indeterminacy to determinacy. Forgetting this transition, our standard conception of knowledge indeed reifies knowledge and generates the bad background ontology of completeness as a correlate of objective knowledge. This motivates Cartesian-style skepticism, which in turn makes us aware of the structure of knowledge in its transition from indeterminacy to determinacy. Thus, without the flawed view of knowledge of the world as a relation between two objects or two kinds of objects, we could not get to the correct view, which integrates the very indeterminacy of the transitory moments of knowledge into our conception of knowledge. All of this can be called an attempt of the infinite (aka the absolute, the world, the domain of all domains, eternal freedom, the unconditioned, etc.) to finitize itself in order to become aware of its true infinity, its being nothing but a belated withdrawal.

In this movement of generating knowledge of nonknowledge, eternal freedom is shown in its essence to consist in "a search for itself,"[62] which terminates in the insight that metaphysical knowledge is only actual in its "self-destruction."[63] Eternal freedom can, hence, only be recognized *after* the attempt to reify it and only *after* a certain metaphysical theory of totality is advanced and defended. The metaphysical error of dogmatism is thus an anterior theoretical condition of the knowledge of nonknowledge. In order for eternal freedom to reveal itself as the truth, a long history of the false is needed: eternal freedom is recognized only at the end of a process. This process is the history of philosophy as the historical sequence of dogmatic systems.

The antinomy of human knowledge leads to a "state of lacerating doubt and eternal unrest,"[64] from which antimetaphysical quietism seeks to liberate itself in its promise of *ataraxia*. Yet, in metaphysics, specifically human freedom—being nothing other than being beyond everything that is given—is at play and at stake. This freedom leads to eternal unrest only so long as philosophy fails to understand that freedom as such cannot be limited, cannot be bound to a particular content through which it would lose its specificity as freedom. The metaphysical insight into constitutive finitude and thus the nonknowledge of human knowledge is the only possible *ataraxia* that can be attained while preserving the specificity of human freedom.

Schelling therefore objects to the quietist that the latter's theory has a constitutive blind spot. At the outset of his theory, the quietist must make use of the specifically human freedom that Schelling discovers in the antinomy of human knowledge; in order to arrive at the concept of, say, second nature, human freedom must be exercised over against the modern concept of the space of natural laws. Yet, at a later stage in his theory construction, the quietist denies the role said freedom plays: he attempts to silence the role of human freedom in his theory by affirming the finite, discursive practices of the community as absolutely primary over our reaching out to the whole.

The motivation of quietism indeed depends on the freedom of transcendence, which is an unassailable feature of human knowledge: yet quietism goes on to make a claim on the absolutely primary, reifying the specifically human freedom to be beyond everything that is given that it initially presupposes. Quietism thus seeks a kind of epistemic security in the search for knowledge that, if it were truly achieved, would, *ad absurdum*, bar the possibility of the construction of its own theory. Otherwise put: quietism only succeeds as a theory by failing to reflect on the consistency of the conditions of itself as a theory.[65]

Returning to the distinction with which we began, we can now see how Schelling's philosophy can be mobilized against both forms of naturalism. *Reductive* naturalism is guilty of reifying the whole and of making a claim on totality that for human knowledge is utterly untenable. *Liberal* naturalism is indeed the lesser of two evils, inasmuch as it renounces and seeks to displace reductive naturalism's baldly metaphysical, subreptive claims on the whole. While it succeeds in displacing reductive naturalism, its quietism fails to account for the specifically human freedom that Schelling, following Kant, insists upon: quietism fails to appreciate the fact that man, as a knowing being, has an inexorable, "natural" tendency to metaphysics and, further, that by and through this tendency, what man makes manifest is a manifestation of eternal freedom.

2. Skepticism and the True Infinite (Hegel)

It is well known that Hegel also spotlights the Antinomy chapter of the *Critique of Pure Reason*, subjecting it, of course, to a metacritical revision. Though Kant can be credited with discovering the fact that reason itself is antinomical, the deep significance of this discovery was lost on Kant: because of his fixation on epistemological finitude, he remained blind to the possibility that antinomies could be made the engine of a positive dialectic, rather than merely leading to the opposition between the finite and the infinite. Hegel and Schelling indeed take this next step, articulating a metatheory on the ground of the insight of the antinomies. Hegel accepts Kant's thought that the absolute (the unconditioned) cannot be any *thing*, yet modifies the Kantian conclusion, as Schelling had, by insisting that the sublation [*Aufhebung*] of finite knowledge is itself the activity of the infinite; the infinite comes to itself in the sublation of the finite. Like Schelling, Hegel is therefore eager to grasp finitude as such as a manifestation of the truly infinite; this structure is completely central to Hegel's system-theoretical reflections.

Hegel asserts that metaphysical knowledge, properly speaking, can itself be nothing other than the presentation of a series of "definitions of the absolute"[66] in a speculative metatheory (the *Science of Logic*); this thought directly parallels Schelling's conception of metaphysical knowledge that we have already explicated. All definitions of the absolute save one (i.e. the Hegelian *Absolute Idea*) thus fail, for in order for the infinite to be finite (to be *de-fined*), the infinite must be set over against the finite, thus in principle barring its capture in a definition. The Idea serves as the conclusion of Hegel's dialectical circle because it has the reflection on the process of the finite itself as its own content. It stands to reason, then, that the infinite only truly arises in the metatheoretical reflection on the structure of finitude.

Now, in order to bring thinking onto the speculative path of the definitions of the absolute, Hegel must provide an introduction. This introduction is necessary because natural consciousness is least of all inclined to busy itself with accounting for the structure of its own reflection. The problem of an introduction arises because we are not always already in the position from which we would be motivated to secure our everyday knowledge through philosophical knowledge. Therefore, natural consciousness must have an experience of "rupture" in order to make its transition into philosophical knowledge, that is, an experience of skeptical "confusion": "Philosophy must, generally speaking, begin with confusion in order to bring about reflection; everything must be doubted, all presuppositions given up, to reach the truth as created through the Concept."[67] According to Hegel, therefore, without the engine of skeptical disorientation, absolutely no impulse to philosophize would arise in natural consciousness.

The transition into philosophy is constructed such that its own necessity is thematized within philosophical knowledge, wherein philosophy's specific genealogy is made explicit. This genealogical account is intended to bridge the gap that has been torn by skepticism between empirical and transcendental consciousness. Healing this wound does not happen simply by virtue of philosophical knowledge modestly submitting itself to some common sense, but rather by a retrospective justification of philosophy's own standpoint. Hegel's conflict with the phenomenon of skepticism is thus twofold. *On the one hand*, a dose of skepticism is needed in order to alienate natural consciousness from itself: this is the starting condition of philosophical reflection *überhaupt*. *On the other hand*, skepticism must not be allowed to resolve itself by way of a reflexive restoration of natural consciousness, for by Hegel's lights this is a dialectical contradiction. The dual role of skepticism, then, is that, on the one hand, it is the condition of philosophy and, on the other hand, if it is allowed to resolve itself in quietism, it turns into a threat to philosophy. Hegel dissolves this paradoxical structure by distinguishing between two forms of skepticism; he already discussed this distinction in the early "The Relationship of Skepticism to Philosophy" and repeats this move in the skepticism chapter of the *Lectures on the History of Philosophy*.[68]

(1) An original ancient skepticism is to be employed against "healthy" common sense and is used to teach it a basic lesson about human finitude. This skepticism leads to a positive dialectic and can be credited as that which initiates philosophy, as the promise of philosophy. Hegel identifies this original ancient skepticism with Sextus's catalogue of the ten tropes, which are on his interpretation older than the five tropes that the Pyrrhonian skeptics had used to bar all metaphysical knowledge.

(2) The later five-trope Pyrrhonian skepticism is understood as that variety of skepticism that turns against or threatens philosophy. This form of skepticism culminates in skeptical quietism.[69] In insisting on the skeptical motivation of his positive dialectic, Hegel must convincingly show that it can entertain the first form of skepticism without falling into skeptical quietism: otherwise, the skeptical moment with which Hegel begins would in effect diffuse from the outset his metaphysics and his notoriously far-reaching knowledge claims. Hegel must show, therefore, that the turn from the truth of skepticism to quietism, from (1) to (2), is dialectically inconsistent and unstable. In a word, Hegel needs the explosive power of skepticism, but must avoid blowing up his whole enterprise.

Ad (1): In his "The Relationship of Skepticism to Philosophy," Hegel explains *expressis verbis* that the skeptical rejection of the sense-certainty of common sense is the "noblest side of skepticism."[70] He discovers the constitutively antinomial character of the purported immediacy of sense-certainty or common sense: this, Hegel says, is its "untruth."[71] The sensuous is constitutively finite because any claim on sensory input relates to a determinate position in time and space and thus differs from all others, without thereby indicating as such the relationship this input maintains with everything else. Hegel justifies his criticism of sensuous finitude with reference to the ten skeptical tropes. These tropes destroy sense-certainty "because they make evident against the finitude of dogmatism that from which it abstracts, viz. dogmatism's opposite at any given position, thereby generating the antinomy."[72] One is indeed justified in situating Hegel's critique in the context of the ten tropes insofar as these tropes are leveled against the dogmatism of a naïve realism which states that the material world is given and, further, that its unobstructed reception in thought is the criterion of truth. Already the academic skeptics had themselves argued against the Stoic concept of a simple "kataleptic representation" (καταληπτικὴ φαντασία), which would have the special property of its *certainty* being at the same time its *truth*, that is, a representation in which both the certainty of the relation between sense perception and objective reality and the relation between sense perception and mental representation are unquestionably secure.

The ten tropes themselves use classical skeptical arguments against the reliability of sense perception, employing just the same tactics as the pre-Socratic critique of the perceived world. The reasoning that lies behind the ten tropes and that has always played an important role in epistemology can be summarized *modo grosso* as follows: if we had direct, immediate access to the world by way of sensible representations such that we were always able to process the information that is given to us from the outside (through causal influence on the organs of sense perception), then one could not explain how failures of perceptions (hallucinations, illusions, etc.) occur. To explain how failures of perception are even possible it must be assumed that our representations potentially differ in content from the various external things taken to cause those representations. In order for deception to be possible, and thus for a genuine disagreement about the things that are sensibly presented to us to take place, it must also be assumed that there can be two subjects that can present the same object differently. This holds for all sensible representations, such that the mere presence of a representation alone is not sufficient to guarantee epistemic success, even if it motivates a certain conviction and compels us to assume that its intentional content is indeed what is the case. After all, one crucial feature of the phenomenological experience of sensory deceptions is that we do not necessarily see through them: we can be compelled to assume that our hallucinations are what is the case.[73] Due to this operative intransparency of our belief systems, films like Scorsese's *Shutter Island* are capable of shattering our self-understanding.

Consequently, a so-called criterion of truth must be found, which holds true in all veridical perceptions and which allows us to distinguish with complete clarity those representations that are empty from those that are properly contentful. The very fact that no such agreed upon truth criterion exists should indicate that we need to refrain from assuming that we have immediate access to the world (that which a direct realism assumes) and indicates that we should, instead, assume the contrary: our cognitive access to the world is in some manner inexorably mediated. Given that our access to the world is essentially mediated, it cannot be a priori ruled out that we have absolutely no contentful representations, which would mediate between our thought and the things themselves. In the extreme case, the illusion argument leads therefore to a skeptical solipsism that deprives us of any justification that our ideas are actually based on, that is causally related to an object in the sense of a robust, extramental correlate.

Sextus spells this thought out not only in the explicit case of sensory mistakes, but also by reference to the patent plurality of sensual and conceptual configurations by which cognitive beings are related to the world. Suppose we came in contact with another cognitive being, whose reference to the world were intentional and who referred to what we would call a "table" in some prima facie unintelligible manner. Already in our everyday contact with animals it can be seen that the manifold different configurations of sensory and conceptual equipment among creatures leads to a plurality of ways in which the world gets divided and ordered. From this thought it seems to follow that the world in itself, behind the plurality of its appearances, disappears in the plurality of differently predisposed cognitive beings.

Sextus's tropes are clearly directed against the dogmatism of the Epicureans and the Stoics, whose commitment to mental representationalism falls in direct conflict with the tropes. According to Sextus, mental representationalism follows from the assumption that our sensory representations come to us through causal influence, such that the effect (representation) and the causative, original thing can be distinguished. Given that the same effect can be resultant of a variety of causes, nothing stands in the way of the thought that our representations stand in a generally misleading connection with things. If this assumption cannot be cleared out of thought's way, dogmatism must give way to skepticism.

Hegel sees in Sextus's supposedly destructive result, that is, "that everything is relative,"[74] a novel notion of reason, which opposes a form of reason, which assumes fixed rules of understanding. According to Hegel's Kant-inspired view, reason is "the faculty of the *unconditioned*"[75] and therefore the "principle of totality."[76] Therefore the rational is nothing more than "the relation to self,"[77] because it is directed towards the web of relations, that is, the whole. The real motor of skepticism is reason, which seeks to grasp the whole and therefore refuses to content itself with the finite, instead seeing that the finite always takes place within a broader horizon, the infinite. Skepticism serves, therefore, as the insight into this connection of the finite and the infinite, in that it motivates an "*immanent* transcendence [*Hinausgehen*]"[78] over the finite fixity of the understanding. According to Hegel, it is at the moment of this transcendence that the properly speculative work of philosophy begins. The demonstration of this connection leads to the thought that no claim can be laid to a thing in itself, because in order for something to be what it is, to be either logically or ontologically determinate, it must stand in differential relation to everything else, that is, to that which it is not. Determination is therefore "negation posited as affirmative,"[79] as Hegel interprets Spinoza's *omnis determinatio est negatio*. The idea of a thing in itself fails not for epistemological, but for ontological reasons: relationality determines difference and thereby existence in Hegel's sense, that is, in the sense of a network of relations first between things and their properties and then between things.[80]

In "The Relationship of Skepticism to Philosophy," Hegel first of all limits the heuristic function of Pyrrhonian skepticism to showing that direct realism is challenged by the ten tropes, that such realism would require some better account of how it acquires the immediate cognitive access to the world it assumes. However, Hegel's firm conviction is that such an account of immediacy cannot be given; for, if such immediacy existed, why would the transition from sense-certainty to any other form of consciousness ever have taken place?

Hegel thus does not decide between direct realism and mental representationalism, but rather must undo the fixation on the finite essential to the (Kantian) epistemological standpoint: Hegel insists that we must move beyond the presumption that knowledge consists foremost in the presentation of a sensible intuition. It is his stated intention to motivate a position capable of "truly" entering the realm of the infinite, beginning its thought from an "affirmative infinity" and therefore capable of bringing the absolute into view. This standpoint is, of course, incompatible with the assumptions of natural consciousness, and so a transition from natural consciousness to the position of philosophical knowledge must be staged, which does not already presuppose that philosophical knowledge be the judge of natural consciousness, that is, which does not presuppose the position of the philosopher from the outset. That is, natural consciousness turns out to be driven by an immanent motor to seek a philosophical understanding of its own structure. Otherwise one could not explain why there are any philosophical knowledge claims at all. This motor is skepticism, which can only be interpreted as a metaphysical lesson about the truly infinite if its destructive tendency can be curbed shy of disabling the natural transcendence of the human.

Hegel conceives of the truly infinite as the relation of the infinite and the finite, which is only possible in reflection on the fact that the infinite and the finite cannot be determined as set against each other without ipso facto setting them in relation: any attempt to fix the infinite as the other of the finite irrevocably leads one to render it finite. This reflective insight is the only possible way to avoid reifying the absolute and getting stuck at the standpoint of finitude. Thus, for Hegel the absolute is obtained in a metatheoretical reflection. This means, then, that the absolute is not some exceptional object of propositional knowledge to be determined as *supremum ens*, but rather is that which escapes all definitions of the absolute and drives the search for knowledge to incessantly move forward. This ultimately leads to the reflective insight that the absolute is not an object and, further, that it cannot be determined in opposition to the finite. If one wishes to avoid conceiving the absolute as the opposite of the relative (determinate, finite, etc.), one must employ a figure of thought that allows the absolute to come to thought despite its being presented as the nonabsolute. In seeking this proper figure of thought, Hegel counters the classical substance-metaphysics, which had set substance (οὐσία) and relation (πρός τι) in opposition, therefore fixing the infinite always only in some exceptional in-itself, to which the finite is accidentally opposed: the key difficulty of such substance-metaphysics is, after all, understanding why the finite exists at all.

Therefore, Hegel is committed to defending skepticism's principle that everything is relative as a supremely rational notion. For the rational itself consists in the fact that, as the skeptic pointed out, there is no immediate being that is not yet mediated: the taking place of the actual, that is, all extant things (matter included, that which is taken to be primary by unreflective realism), is therefore primarily a matter of relation. With his model of true infinity, Hegel thus turns against purely negative dialectics, the paradigm of which would be Plato's *Parmenides*: on this view, though all finitude is destroyed, in the last act the finite is opposed to the infinite in such a way that it is clear how the infinite can proceed to the finite. Thus Hegel identifies the negative dialectic of Plato's *Parmenides* with the specific intention of ancient skepticism.[81] The concept of a positive, processual dialectic, that is, the anti-skeptical concept of a "*determinate* negation,"[82] had not yet been reached. The principle of determinate negation ultimately states that the negation of a metaphysical determination leads to a further determination, in which the first determination has been sublated in a three-fold sense. All position is therefore a negation of a negation and is resultant of a relation (negation). The first step of determinate negation, the so-called "negative-reasonable [*negativ-Vernünftige*],"[83] lies in the critique of reification of the given categories (positions). The second step, the corresponding "positive-reasonable [*positiv-Vernünftige*]" or the "speculative,"[84] leads to another determination. This process can only come to a close when it sees through itself and no longer sets out to make some determinate thing into the absolute content, that is, when it ceases to determine finite things in opposition to the infinite. The truly infinite cannot therefore be anything in particular, which is to be distinguished from the finite. Rather, the finite must be described as the process of self-overcoming [*Selbstaufhebung*] and the infinite as the process of its own finitization, these processes culminating in the methodological self-consciousness of dialectical knowledge.[85] This is the crucial result of ancient skepticism, directed against common sense: human finitude is not merely negative, but leads to a positive dialectic. Dialectics in Hegel's sense is therefore not only the pointing out of dialectical contradictions in given philosophical positions, but the ultimately hierarchical organization of philosophical theories according to the way in which they aim at solving the dialectical problems of their respective predecessor theories. Philosophy is therefore nothing but a series of attempts at a positive theory of the absolute that all fail. Yet every failure motivates a new account such that all philosophical theories co-respond to another.

This relation between philosophical theories is what Hegel calls "determinate negation." Determinate negation is therefore not an operation performed on a homogeneous singular set of entities or a domain of objects. For Hegel, there is no single conceptual whole structured by rules of inference. For this reason, Brandom's interpretation of "determinate negation" misses Hegel's point (which does not speak against the specific semantic points Brandom himself is defending).[86] For Brandom's inferential holism operates on the assumption of a homogeneous singular domain of referents, the world, and adds the principle that determination implies negation to the determinacy conditions of the elements belonging to that domain. Hegel, however, conceives of the whole as of a series of attempts to determine such a domain, which all ultimately fail because they think of the whole (the absolute) as of an object. Nonetheless, there is a logic of failure involved in the classical metaphysical attempts to define the absolute, and Hegel's program is to discover the laws that drive the process of metaphysical failures.

3. Skepticism and Metaphysics Reunited (Schelling and Hegel)

Ad (2): Hegel thus accepts, similar to Schelling, the (metaphysical) lesson of Pyrrhonian skepticism, viz. that true metaphysical knowledge can have no content other than the finite as such, that metaphysical knowledge is the presentation of its own coming to be in the history of failed attempts to grasp the infinite in a particular form. Thus true metaphysical knowledge only has a processual content, that is, the history of metaphysics as the finitization of the infinite and, through this, the production of antinomies and their successive dissolution. Therefore, true metaphysical knowledge carries no further substantive determinations of the whole. Both reductive naturalism (with its reduction of subjectivity to nature) and its extreme counterpart, subjective idealism (which reduces nature to subjectivity), are determined to commit the mistake of determining the infinite, such that both can be seen to be a "merely jejune assurance": in this we can hear Hegel's dictum that with all such assurances, one "counts for just as much as another."[87] The effort to conceive the absolute as immediacy (Being, Nature, the Not-I) or as the reverse, as conceptual mediation alone (the I, Thinking), must fail because any such one-sided claim can be met with and contradicted by an equipollent opposite claim.[88] Skepticism shows, therefore, that the absolute cannot be determined: it is no accident that it defines itself with the slogan "to determine/define nothing at all (οὐδὲν ὁρίζειν)."[89]

However, the fact that neither the naturalist nor the idealist could convince or persuade their opponents should not be taken to entail that metaphysical knowledge in a demanding sense is impossible. Rather, the question should be: how can we *relate* to the whole in any manner without *ipso actu* reifying it? This important methodological question lies at the heart of Hegel's own program of a processual critique of all categories in the *Science of Logic*, which itself uses a skeptical method to sublate [*aufheben*] all definitions of the absolute that had been offered up to Hegel's day. Hegel's conclusion is, of course, that after his massive deconstruction of the history of all attempts to determine the absolute, only a methodological consciousness of philosophy's own procedure stands a chance of being an appropriate concept of the absolute: this is the meaning of Hegel's *Absolute Idea*. Thus, Hegel instrumentalizes the merely "negative dialectic" of Pyrrhonian skepticism as a weapon against the standpoint of finitude.[90]

Hegel is, however, not himself a skeptic, since the dynamics of Pyrrhonian skepticism end up in an antinomy, which turns the skeptic against himself. Hegel is not assured by the jejune metaphysics of skeptical quietism, for this position is revealed under the pressure of Hegel's dialectical procedure to be unstable and one-sided. After all, Sextus's thought ultimately returns to and resolves itself in a paradoxical liberal naturalism. It is paradoxical because under the skeptical conditions he has already established, Sextus cannot claim this position as a *theory*. However, the skeptical procedure shows something the pronouncement of which it necessarily blocks, viz., that it is the nature of the human to take measure such that our lives are generally set up in such a way that we do not require a philosophical foundation for or account of our forms of life. In this way, practice replaces the discovery of *pragmata* (things). The Pyrrhonian relies, therefore, on a concept of theoretically mediated immediacy, which, in Hegel's eyes, leads to dialectical opposition just as soon as it is substantiated.

Nevertheless, in Hegel's theory skepticism has a crucial dialectical advantage over dogmatism, which is rooted in his discovery of the "freedom of self-consciousness."[91] Skeptical self-consciousness is ultimately tied to no determinate content because it realizes the meaning of withholding judgment in the active search for knowledge: all possible content is entangled in antinomies and contradictions, and therefore any given content's claim to absolute validity is nullified. Hegel sees skeptical *ataraxia* as an expression of the freedom from finitude won by the skeptical consciousness through placing any and all content under skeptical suspicion. "Thought becomes the thinking that annihilates the being of the *manifoldly determinate* world, and the negativity of free self-consciousness in the heart of these multifarious shapes of life becomes in its eyes real negativity."[92]

The motivation of skepticism is, on Hegel's interpretation, the very freedom of self-consciousness, which effects a return of consciousness to itself (reflection), dissolving the opposition of consciousness and the Not-I in the ultimate negativity of self-consciousness. It effects this transformation by demonstrating that all being stands essentially in relation to the circumstances of its conceptually mediated registration, which means that it is simply impossible to capture being as it is in itself. Being is relationality, the openness of what there is to thought. Yet, there is no single transcendental matrix of all thoughts, no absolute logical form of thought, but only a (for Hegel dialectically ordered) multiplicity of logical forms. To determine reality is to take it up as something or other, not as it is in its immediate state. What skeptical argumentation has always sought to do is dissolve claims to knowledge of the in-itself: thus, Hegel's description of the skeptical approach is no doubt an accurate one, even though his own conclusion is far from being skeptical.

What skepticism takes up as its contents and sets in opposition are, on the one hand, everyday life, and on the other hand, its philosophical thematization: it shows that a dispute arises between these two modes of being and, by *argumentum ex dissensu*, it initiates the argumentative strategy of the five tropes in response to this dispute. Skeptical consciousness takes up its content, therefore, from what is accidentally or conventionally known and destroys the assumptions harbored by such conventions with its negative dialectic. Through this effort the skeptic proves her freedom and arrives at *ataraxia*.[93]

Skeptically motivated quietism achieves the freedom of self-consciousness only through the extradition of all theoretical claims to a knowledge of the in-itself and a blind surrender to appearances, which the skeptic must necessarily hold onto, without in turn making a claim about the true being of said appearances.[94] Thus Pyrrhonian skepticism leads straightaway to a conservatism, which states that it cannot but assent to the forms of life, that is, the customs and practices (νόμοι καὶ ἔθη) of its community, for it cannot take up the position of an external observer or anyone who would be situated in a critical position relative to her community.[95] The Pyrrhonian therefore has no choice but to receive her life and to follow her nature as if they were utterly necessary: she follows the laws of her community and insists that each ought to follow what *appears* to her at each instance to be good, without thereby making any claim to a substantial knowledge of what *is*, in fact, good.[96]

This means, however, that as she arrives at the very summit of her freedom, the skeptic loses the basis of her freedom, instead surrendering to being blindly guided by the given, against which she has nothing to oppose, for she can mobilize no substantial, community-transcending claim for or against anything whatsoever: this deadlock is resultant of the fact that any attempt to hold onto her freedom would employ destructible claims to knowledge. The skeptic acknowledges, therefore, that her consciousness is

> a wholly contingent, single, and separate consciousness—a consciousness, which is *empirical*, which takes its guidance from what has no reality for it, which obeys what for it is not an essential being, which does those things and brings to realization what it knows has no truth for it.[97]

Through this, however, she forfeits the freedom that was the actual moving impulse of her position. The skeptical freedom of self-consciousness thus nullifies itself in a blind acquiescence to everything that is given and sacrifices the critical power of philosophy that was, after all, its original agency. Skeptical quietism is thus dialectically incompatible with its motivation, viz. the desire to achieve a certain critical distance from the given: Hegel takes up this discrepancy and utilizes it against the conservative quietism resultant of skepticism.

Skepticism is shown therefore to be "a self-contradictory consciousness."[98] It is motivated and maintained by virtue of skeptical consciousness freeing and distancing itself from all content. This theoretical detachment is, however, rendered impossible as soon as it is taken to lead to the insight that metaphysical knowledge is as such impossible. Thus the original immediacy results in a second immediacy relative to which the claim to the original immediacy is inconsistent, for the original motivating immediacy which would have to have been carried out in an already *philosophical* knowledge, that is, precisely what the second immediacy claims to defuse.

The mediated immediacy of skeptical quietism is hence dialectically inconsistent: Hegel has shown that Pyrrhonian skepticism simply cannot lead to *ataraxia* without the help of reflection, which it, itself, claims to have rendered impotent and meaningless. *Ataraxia* ultimately does not represent the immediate life of the community. Skepticism instead discovers that philosophy is rooted in the immediacy of the community: otherwise it could not explain where the impulse to philosophy, that is, that which expels us out of immediacy and motivates skepticism, comes from. Skepticism therefore discovers against its own will that the tendency toward philosophical thinking must already exist within the community: skepticism itself must be therapeutically treated before reflected immediacy could possibly take place.[99] *Ataraxia* as consciousness purged of all metaphysics and theoretically uncluttered is itself a theoretical result or an ideal that the skeptic cannot continue to defend by way of skeptical argumentation.

Hegel accepts as a truth of skepticism that our orientation towards the whole cannot be exclusively a matter of objective knowledge. This truth does not, however, lead him to quietism, but rather to the starting point of his own metaphysics, that is, to the fact that truth is not (only) substance, that is, is not the in-itself, but is (also) subject. Hegel thus conceives truth as a process of making hidden relations explicit, which actually constitutes the elements of a given domain of objects, without this constitution being reflected within the domain. In order to show how the metaphysical interpretation of skepticism is to avoid being yet another jejune assurance, Hegel points up the way in which skeptical quietism falls into dialectical contradiction.

Hegel opposes reductive naturalism, just as Kant and Schelling had, insofar as it reifies totality; he insists that such reification must be remedied by way of a critique of the categories employed in reductive naturalism's claims on totality. Liberal skepticism is, however, charged with harboring the paradox of a mediated immediacy, the theoretical mediatedness of which is incompatible with the immediacy it seeks to achieve. The specifically human freedom that Pyrrhonian skepticism discovers is thus lost in the process of its own implementation. The transcendence of the human spirit, the fact that everything that is given could only be so given in the horizon of an unconditioned, in what I call the *spielraum* of contingency, is indeed recognized by quietism to be a feature of the *conditio humana*: however, this condition is betrayed by the effort to integrate this condition into a given nature, which the human is constitutively always already beyond. The constitution of human freedom, to be beyond what is given thanks to its reaching out to the whole, is not natural in the sense of something necessary and reliable. This self-conception of the human is rather a fragile historical achievement, nothing we can simply rely upon. Rather, specifically human freedom constantly has to be defended against reductive ideologies.

We can see, then, that Schelling and Hegel are hand in hand in the effort to make skepticism a basic feature of metaphysical thinking. However, the end to which each philosopher sees this effort is very different: for

Schelling, this effort should lead to a knowledge of nonknowledge, while Hegel, on the contrary, seems to want to follow this effort out such that he can be in the position to lay claim to absolute knowledge. Nonetheless, both Hegel's absolute knowledge and his absolute idea have the same system-theoretical structure as Schelling's *docta ignorantia*: both, after all, are based on the insight that the infinite cannot be known in a propositional manner, for a certain, unassailable oscillation between the finite and the infinite is constitutive of human knowledge as such.

Nevertheless, Schelling defends a plurality of modes of presentation of this insight in order to illustrate eternal freedom as the constant transcendence over any given position. This does not commit him to a classical Platonic conception of static or vertical transcendence. Transcendence depends on immanence; it is nothing but the failure of absolute theoretical closure. Transcendence is the very contingency of all ways in which the infinite withdraws in our efforts of grasping it. The infinite therefore depends on the finite. In Hegel, on the contrary, there is a clear tendency toward an absolute mode of presentation of the infinite, even though the true infinite is also not an object or any other kind of hyperphysical entity to be discovered by philosophical thought. Also for Hegel, the infinite is tied to finite knowledge. Yet the insight into the structures of finite knowledge yields an unconditional mode of presentation, dialectics, which cannot be superseded by any other mode of presentation. For this reason, Hegel clearly argues for the superiority of philosophy over art and religion, in which he sees an inferior mode of presentation of the contents of philosophical thought, while Schelling admits a plurality of modes of presentations through which content is retroactively generated as that which eludes any particular mode of presentation (including the mode of presenting it in terms of a plurality of modes of presentation).

Be that as it may, both elaborate on the meaning of Kant's defense against the reification of totality, which they mobilize against reductive naturalism. By seeing how they share this position with skepticism, one can gain insight into what motivated their respective theories, as long as one understands, further, that both thinkers insist that skepticism misses one crucial thought (hence its resolution into conservative quietism), which must be defended: specifically, that human freedom consists in being beyond all that is given. Liberal naturalism loses sight of this freedom in its dialectic, even though it plays an indispensable role in the beginning of its own theory and is precisely what it itself mobilizes against reductive naturalism. Skeptical quietism must be replaced, then, by a "consummate skepticism,"[100] without which metaphysics, that "intellectual twin of skepticism,"[101] would not be possible.

Mutatis mutandis this also holds for the theory-conditions of contemporary liberal naturalism. Without its confrontation with skepticism and therefore with the human freedom of transcending any given position, it could not try to return to a *second naïveté*. In confronting the world as world in its relation to mind, it transcends everything that is given without reflecting on this act of transcendence as constitutive of its position. I suspect that it is for this reason that McDowell does not elaborate on the notion of the world as a totality and avoids spelling out what Hegel's obvious return to ontology (which is really the creation of a new form of ontology) means.

As Hegel famously remarks, "it would be just as remarkable for a nation to lose its metaphysics as it would for a nation's constitution, national sentiments, ethical customs and virtues to become useless."[102] Metaphysics is associated with a particular practice of freedom, in that in attempting to render the infinite finite, it thereby achieves the twofold insight into the fact that (1) the infinite cannot be accessed from any particular position, and that (2) this very negativity is the infinite. If we give up metaphysics, we give up human freedom. Of course, we need to understand metaphysics as a system-theoretically motivated metatheory, a practice of higher-order thought, and not some wild speculation about the supernatural. But, then, no metaphysician of the tradition has ever been as naïve about metaphysics as contemporary naturalists and many philosophers who call themselves analytic metaphysicians. Unfortunately, a huge number of academic departments worldwide and the associated organs of publication seem to be willing to forbid metaphysics because they are suspicious of free philosophical thought. Today, at the beginning of twenty-first-century philosophy, the prohibition of metaphysics and free thought is no longer the result of the well-motivated post-metaphysical gestures of twentieth-century philosophy. It seems to be nothing other than a manifestation of the aggressive suspicion that free thought cannot be refuted by weak spirits, but only suppressed by committees, philosophical societies, and journal editors. Yet, as long as people continue to philosophize, there will be people who remember the original motivation for doing philosophy, namely the strange feeling that things might be otherwise.

II Absolute Identity and Reflection: Kant, Hegel, and McDowell

The normative theory of intentionality originating from the work of Wilfrid Sellars has played a crucial motivational role in the Hegel renaissance that is currently taking place in Anglophone philosophy, something the continental-European philosophical community has happily welcomed. The systematic starting point of this movement (whose most remarkable protagonists are Pippin, McDowell, and Brandom) is an oft-quoted passage in Sellars's essay *Empiricism and the Philosophy of Mind*, in which he writes:

> In characterizing an episode or a state as that of knowing, we are not giving an empirical description of that episode or state; we are placing it in the logical space of reasons, of justifying and being able to justify what one says.[103]

Though our protagonists differently emphasize the consequences of this thought, Pippin, McDowell, and Brandom all agree that epistemic intentionality, that is all truth-apt or objectivity-directed reference to objects/facts, must have a normative and therefore social basis. The normativity of intentionality is not some secondary feature of intentionality or something that could be accounted for after we get clear on the structure of our epistemic relation to objects, as if our thoughts were primarily directed to objects in solipsistic sense-data theaters and only later and occasionally got caught up in the social world. Qua reference to specifically determined objects or states of affairs, that is qua thinking with some minimally distinct yield or grip, thinking is always already related to justification, and therefore is bound to historically variable practices of justification. To determine something as something in judgment presupposes that one participates in the game of giving and asking for reasons. Precisely in this way every object-directed intentionality is subordinated to always already social conditions of operation and motivation.

The norms that constitute intentionality are rules of meaning and reference (which among other things determine a range of factors, i.e. relevance, salience, etc.) that allow us, generally speaking, to move beyond mere intuitional shadings [*Abschattungen*] and to reidentify objects in terms of their spatiotemporal variation for intuition. That is, semantic rules give us the possibility of keeping anything as such in view. If I assume, for example, that the clause "if I assume" means nothing other than *if I assume*, that is, if I am in a position to distinguish between type and token, between the expressing phrase and the expressed proposition, and so on, then there are already rules of meaning in play that I must follow. If I were to fail to follow said semantic rules, my behavior would fall somewhere on a scale from idiosyncrasy to semantic madness.[104] My words would no longer mean anything and would thus, properly speaking, no longer be words.

All post-Sellarsian Hegelians cull this semantic lesson from Wittgenstein's private-language argument, which has shown that intentionality cannot be logically private. Thus, if it is to mean anything whatsoever, even the monologue in one's own head is always already a dialogue with others.

Now, Pippin, McDowell, and Brandom also agree that even Kant's famous identification of thinking and judging implies an identification of judgment and rule following; one can, in fact, offer a plausible exegesis of Kant along these lines.[105] It becomes more difficult, however, and here I slowly approach my critical objection, if Kant's transcendental synthesis of apperception is reinterpreted not only as the ability to participate in the game of giving and asking for reasons, but further if judging is conceived as completely a matter of self-determination, that is, as freedom in the sense of autonomy. For Brandom, "commitment" already carries sufficient weight as the definition or conceptual determination of autonomy in the reputedly Kantian sense. Therefore, by Brandom's lights, one is an American citizen (or a "legal alien" or any other taxpayer), and so is a free man, if one is recognized as someone who can enter a bank and set up a mortgage, which one *commits* oneself to pay off.[106] This conception of autonomy has recently been refuted by world history itself, the event of the worldwide economic crisis being the culmination of the spirit of American mortgage-autonomy.

In what follows, I would like to spell out how Hegel's critique of the philosophy of reflection in *Faith and Knowledge* points to an eminently practical dimension that most contemporary readers of the transition from Kant to Hegel neglect. I will do so by considering McDowell's version of the old thesis of the move "from Kant to Hegel."[107] In Pippin's vein, McDowell puts Hegel's partial tie to Kant and his praise of the speculative yield of the concept of apperception at the center of his interpretation. McDowell thus assumes that Hegel's idealism is exhausted by the thesis "according to which the very idea of objectivity is to be understood in terms of the freely self-determining operations of a self-conscious intelligence."[108]

In Part 1 of the present essay, I will sketch McDowell's interpretation, in particular in his essay "Hegel's Idealism as Radicalization of Kant." In Part 2, I want to show that Hegel's critique of the philosophy of reflection is not merely a criticism of a certain *epistemological* conception, but is rather critically aimed at the *Zeitgeist* of an absolutization of finitude. In this context, Hegel responded to the objection of those criticizing his system with reference to the self-opacity of its finitude. He turns explicitly against a certain "relation of domination"[109] between the infinite and the finite, according to which the infinite will be referred to as a mere unknowable beyond, such that "the worth of each and every thing" will be calculated exclusively with respect to finitude, that is, "every idea will be subsumed under finitude."[110] By Hegel's lights, this results in "the domination of the Concept over what appears as the real and the finite—everything beautiful and ethical being here included."[111] This dimension of Hegel's critique is metaphysically underpinned by the notion of absolute identity, which Hegel levels against the philosophy of reflection.

Thus, the meaning of Hegel's position on the question of the interaction between *system building* and *criticism of the system* is easy to locate: Hegel's claim to systematicity is directed against a blind spot generated by a reflection that wants to understand itself as finite. Furthermore, Hegel furnishes proof that this blind spot also needs to be addressed with regards to its political consequences. By my lights, it is along precisely these lines that Hegel's thought deserves to be defended. Thus, I assume that Hegel's claim to systematicity is not what it is usually taken to be: what we usually get when discussing Hegel on systematicity is a most bizarre caricature. On the contrary, I will be discussing a different Hegel, one whose insight ought to be, but has yet to be, fully translated into our time. This is, moreover, a Hegel richer in ontology than "normativity Hegelians" are able to accommodate, for they, incidentally, still feed on a plate of one-sided criticism of the system. My overall aim is to show that there is some middle ground between a Neoplatonic reading of Hegel's metaphysics in terms of onto-theology and a deflationary view according to which the transition from Kant to Hegel can be made without recourse to any ontology.[112]

1. Kant's Most Revolutionary Footnote

McDowell reconstructs Hegel's idealism in toto as a radicalization of the Kantian method, which shows that all claims to objectivity are derivative of a constitutive act of subjectivity. Thus McDowell adopts the Kantian identification of thinking and judging, which Kant had formulated. Kant ultimately asserts that to think

> is to unite representations in a consciousness [. . .] The unification of representations in a consciousness is judgment. Therefore thinking is the same as judging or as relating representations to judgment in general [. . .] Judgments, insofar as they are regarded merely as the condition for the unification of given representations in a consciousness, are rules. These rules, insofar as they represent the unification as necessary, are *a priori* rules.[113]

McDowell's entire theoretical edifice emphasizes this fundamental point, viz. that judging qua rule following is connected to freedom, which is why he interprets the spontaneity of thinking from the outset in terms of our responsibility or answerability to the world. He writes,

> [J]udging is at the centre of the treatment of objective purport in general. And judging is making up one's mind about something. Making up one's mind is one's own doing, something for which one is responsible. To judge is to engage in free cognitive activity, as opposed to having something merely happen in one's life, outside one's control.[114]

According to Kant, in contrast to particular, empirical individuality, the anonymous and therefore universal dimension in which we can encounter anything *überhaupt*, is resultant of the transcendental synthesis of apperception. The transcendental synthesis of apperception is indeed the activity by virtue of which anything is set in relation with anything else. The energy of this setting-in-relation lies in repeatability: the reidentifiability of signs first and foremost consists in what Fichte had pointed out at the beginning of his 1794 *Doctrine of Science*, viz. that if $A = A$ is to be possible, $I = I$ must first be established. That is, the identifiability of something is only comprehensible against an anteriorly stabilized background by virtue of which we are able to entertain a relation to objects. This is the fundamental meaning of "absolute identity" in both Hegel and Schelling: the very *idea* of identity—not of anything particular with itself or with anything particular apparently different from something else—that is, identity tout court. Thus, no instance of identity (not even the formula $x = x$) is absolute identity. Even the formula of identity aims at a difference between universal identity ($x = x$) and some particular identity ($a = b$, $2 + 2 = 4$, etc.). For this reason, absolute identity cannot be reduced to any formula of identity, for it antecedes any determinate identity whatsoever.

Kant had already shown that the conditions of our relation to objects cannot be undermined, or better, cannot but be fulfilled, for without said conditions we would not be related to anything whatsoever. As Kant puts it in the principle chapter of the first *Critique*: "the conditions of the possibility of experience in general are likewise conditions of the possibility of objects of experience."[115]

McDowell accuses Kant of ultimately violating this principle, asserting that he fails to follow out the consequences of his own thought: McDowell first wards off an obvious objection against Kant in order to then defend a more advanced version of the same objection.

The obvious objection states that Kant is committed to an inconsistent form-content dualism with his two-stem theory of knowledge. This objection suggests that Kant despite himself already employs the energy of synthesis and thus conceptual spontaneity in identifying the supposedly pure (not yet conceptual) forms of sensible intuition, space and time. To be clear: it is simply the case that Kant already employs the conditions of unity and diversity, of coordination versus subordination, and so forth in the identification of space and time. If this were not permitted, he could not even begin to argue that space and time are intuitions and not concepts, for "intuition" is, naturally, already a concept; this is, after all, why Kant himself speaks of the "concept of space" and the "concept of time."[116] Because intuitions and concepts can only be distinguished conceptually, there can be no access to the merely and purely analytic, no way to determine pure forms of intuition in the medium of transcendental reflection, that does not eo ipso presuppose a synthetic unity.

In the revolutionary footnote to Section 16 of the first *Critique* Kant writes, in reference to "the presupposition of a certain synthetic unity" he has just introduced, that any "analytic unity of consciousness" must be anteriorly rooted in "the synthetic unity of apperception."[117] If we take this thought seriously here, we can no longer simply impute to Kant the assumption that the categories were defined in the sense of a simple external reflection on sections of space-time or some similar sensory episode. This version of "subjective imposition" (as the Anglo-American literature likes to call it) can indeed easily be ruled out in Kantian terms. The obvious objection against Kantian form-content dualism, therefore, comes up short, as McDowell correctly emphasizes.

However, this is not yet enough for McDowell. Siding with Hegel, he argues that Kant still defends a "subjective idealism."[118] He sees this in Kant's transcendental idealism, in particular in the thesis that, whatever it actually might be, space and time do not play a role in the not yet synthesized manifold.[119] First, McDowell complains about the facticity, the "brute-fact-character" of the forms of sensibility in Kant. Secondly, he complains about the consequent contingency of our forms of intuition in (content-fully indeterminate) view of other potential forms of intuition. He feels aggrieved that space and time are for Kant only "a mere reflection of a fact about us."[120]

Strictly speaking, McDowell criticizes not only Kant's claim that space and time are factical and contingent, but further insists that such assumptions are, under genuine Kantian conditions, ultimately inadmissible:[121] by McDowell's lights, such assumptions contradict Kant's own insistence that objectivity is resultant of the constitutive performances of subjectivity. When objectivity as such can only come about under these conditions (viz. that all identifiable, analytical units are resultant of a judgmental synthesis), then one can no longer assume that anything exists that our sensory registries, owing to their form, cannot represent. For example, on this line of thought, unknowable objects or unknowable aspects of objects cannot take place. This rules out the idea of space and time as contingent forms of intuition that might be in disagreement with the actual ontological structure of things in themselves or a pure analytic manifold anteceding synthesis.

At this point it is clear that McDowell has accepted wholesale Hegel's critique of Kant in *Faith and Knowledge*. Hegel asserts in precisely the sense of McDowell's complaint that the thing in itself qua not yet identical outside, which functions variously and for various reasons in Kant's philosophy (most notably in his practical philosophy), never amounts to anything more than a "formless lump."[122] Hegel expresses this polemically as follows:

> Objectivity and stability derive solely from the categories; the realm of things in themselves is without categories; yet it is something for itself and for reflection. The only idea we can form of this realm is like that of the iron king in the fairy tale whom a human self-consciousness permeates with the veins of objectivity so that he can stand erect. But then formal transcendental idealism sucks these veins out of the king so that the upright shape collapses and becomes something in between form and lump, repulsive to look at. For the cognition of nature, without the veins injected into nature by self-consciousness, there remains nothing but sensation. In this way, then, the objectivity of the categories in experience and the necessity of these relations become once more something contingent and subjective.[123]

Hegel's objection against Kant can be reduced to a simple systematic point: the opposition of a "unity of self-consciousness" and an "empirical manifold"[124] is a theory-constitutive decision and no theory-independent presentation of a truly existing fact of the matter. The opposition ought to be transcendental and that is to say: not about two objects, but rather about the way epistemic reference to objects is possible. Moreover, Hegel suspects that the merely formal theory of synthesis falls in blatant contradiction. If synthesis is taken to be an act performed on some ultimately *given* material, how are we to square this with Kant's revolutionary observation that analytic unity is only ever resultant of an abstraction, that is, resultant of a reconstruction of the moments of synthetic processing? Hegel argues, therefore, that Kant is ultimately committed to a variety of the myth of the given, viz. that he postulates given analytic units that are not yet belated abstractions in the medium of synthetic unity.

According to Hegel, Kant's theoretical edifice collapses under the pressure of this contradiction. He writes,

> there is an immediate contradiction in this: this infinitude, strictly conditioned as it is by its abstraction from its opposite, and being strictly nothing outside of this antithesis, is yet at the same time held to be absolute spontaneity and autonomy. As freedom, Reason is supposed to be absolute, yet the essence of this freedom consists in being solely through an opposite.[125]

Here Hegel's critique goes beyond McDowell's in a decisive manner. Ultimately, Hegel's criticism is not merely the assertion that the thing in itself, the manifold of intuition, or whatever remains outside the reach of synthesis in Kant's thought, generates an untenable form-content dualism. Above all, Hegel also offers the following critique, which applies equally to Kant *and* McDowell: in delineating and creating the space of "absolute spontaneity and autonomy," autonomy is ultimately transformed into heteronomy. For if spontaneous synthesis can itself only be conceived as a relatum of a relation, as something which is determined over against something else in a relevant logical space—and this means in this case: over against heteronomy—then it should be trivial to point up that spontaneity is thus higher-order heteronomous. No matter how carefully he qualifies this distinction or how desperately he would like to withdraw such a distinction, Kant, in justifying autonomy by setting spontaneity and receptivity in a defining opposition, automatically loses grip on the autonomy he sought to identify, rendering it dependent on receptivity. Thus, the infinite, that is, the indeterminacy of autonomy, is rendered finite, that is, determined in its being set in opposition.

What this means is that Kant never fully grasped the universal dimension in which determinacy, that is, all specificity and individuality, is possible in the first place. Transcendental thought itself is subject to the form of judgment: it is ultimately only a cogent form of thinking about thought if we draw a distinction, a judgment, in which a subject, which has not yet received the content of intuitions, is distinguished from the judging subject. So, we could hold on to transcendental thought only by virtue of this

distinction: the problem here is that such a thought is straightaway dialectically contradictory! Against this background, Hegel claims in his *Logic of
the Concept* that the universal is not determinate over against the specific
and the individual, as if it could be determined independent of specificity
and individuality, but shows instead that the universal is rather an internal opposition, that is, an inner difference which is to be understood as
that which engenders the very possibility of universality and relation. Once
more: to complete transcendental philosophy, it is necessary to go beyond
its methodological restrictions. An ontology of the subject is needed in
order to overcome its opposition to nature (to what is given).

2. Absolute Identity versus Reflection

What Hegel praises in Kant's transcendental synthesis of apperception
is not so much the constitutive power of autonomous subjectivity in the
medium of judgment, as McDowell, following Pippin's lead, would have it.
In precisely the other direction, what Hegel criticizes in *Faith and Knowledge*
is Kant's account of judging, insisting that it can only account for "the difference whose appearance prevails in the judgment itself."[126] What Hegel
actually says is that the logical form of judgments, that is, the understanding in a thoroughly Kantian sense, leaves us with a truncated image of
the total domain of intelligibility: all it delivers is totality as a catalogue of
binary oppositions, as mind and world, "as spirit and world, or soul and
body, or self and nature, etc."[127] In judgment, the dimension of the knowable—
and in this sense of the intelligible that Hegel will after Kant call "the
universal"—remains subordinated and hidden.

According to Hegel, judgment is still a presentation of "absolute identity,"
albeit one in which absolute identity remains unthematized: remaining in
the medium of judgment is tantamount to remaining "without consciousness," as Hegel has it, of absolute identity.[128]

Absolute identity as the mediating concept manifests itself, not in the
judgment, but in the syllogistic inference [. . .] Here [i.e. in judgment,
M.G.] the rational is for cognition just as much immersed in the
antithesis as the identity is immersed in intuition for consciousness in
general [. . .] What comes to the fore and enters consciousness is only
the product, i.e., the subject and predicate as terms of the antithesis.
Only these terms are posited as object of thought in the form of judgment, and not their being one.[129]

It is not by accident that thinking as judgment distinguishes between things and properties on the subject-predicate model: Hegel spelled out the difficulties of such a model in the "Perception" chapter of the *Phenomenology*, showing there that the unity of things with their manifold properties could not in this way be consistently thought.[130] Thinking as judgment can only lead, according to Hegel, to a concept of totality in which mind and world fall apart; modern forms of epistemological skepticism can be read as the apotheosis of this philosophical trajectory. Epistemological skepticism corresponds, thus, to the metaphysics of judgment; it results from a particular interpretation of the relation between form and content of a judgment. In light of this fact, Hegel recommends recourse to the arguably superior form of the syllogism, for on Hegel's interpretation the syllogism manifests the activity of thinking as the absolute dimension in which any truth-apt relation of subject and predicate can be established. That is, the form of judgment is not absolute, but rather supervenes on the form of the syllogism. When one judges, one makes claims to truth, that is, he who claims that Berlin is bigger than Pittsburgh apparently asserts nothing about the activity of thought, but rather merely makes judgments about Berlin and Pittsburgh. The objectivity of judgments thus prima facie contains no reference to objectivity-constitutive subjectivity. With syllogisms and inferences, however, we are presented with a far different case, for here the explicit relationships of thought are laid bare: with the syllogism, relationships of thought become manifest in the medium of logical truth. Relationships are always only resultant of an anterior process of thinking, a processual mediation: it is precisely this that the form of the syllogism reveals.[131]

Judgment holds together an identity of subject and predicate by repeating rules of meaning. Famously, Kant believes that there are a finite number of rules, which constitute all rule-following activity. These constitutive rules (categories in their application to the sensory manifold) can only be made explicit belatedly in "transcendental reflection"[132] after the fact of having been employed.

> At the same time in the judgment the identity extricates itself as the universal from its immersion in the difference, so that the difference appears as the particular; the identity confronts this immersion as its opposite. Yet the rational identity of identity as [the identity] of the universal and the particular is the non-conscious in the judgment, and the judgment itself is only the appearing of this non-conscious identity.[133]

In the activity of the "original synthetic unity," Hegel sees Kant offering a particular speculative contribution towards the overcoming of the form of difference, which is an inexorable feature of the form of judgment. For this original synthetic unity is an "absolute, original identity of opposites."[134] This reading must not be misunderstood as a reversion to a crude Neoplatonic metaphysics of the One, against which Pippin and McDowell are right to warn their readers; incidentally, however, none of the post-Kantian idealists regressed in this way, Schelling included.

To be clear, absolute identity is ultimately on Hegel's reading nothing other than a universal dimension, in which differences as such can be produced. In other words, it is the ground of all differences and relations, including that of sensibility and the understanding, subject and predicate, mind and world, and so forth. It performs a unifying function, being that in which subject and predicate are both differentiated and held together: absolute identity is, in Hegel's terms, the domain in which the very possibility of truth-value differences takes place.

Further, this possibility of truth-value differences is a necessary anterior condition of truth-apt thought: objectivity is only possible where fallible truth claims will be raised and collected. In order for this process to take place, the existence of logical space, of a universal dimension, must already be presupposed. Hegel in his Jena period calls logical space "absolute identity." Now, this absolute identity is absolute, therefore, not simply because it marks the dimension in which anything can be distinguished from anything else, but also because it cannot itself be distinguished from anything else. It is, in other words, nothing distinct, that is, no analytical unity, but rather—to put it with Wolfram Hogrebe—the "domain of distinctions," the synthetic unity. Hogrebe describes the "space in which the distinctions we meet in the world are cleaved" as

> the space of all possible differences, which we can call: the dimension of distinction. Any claim about fundamental distinctions takes this dimension from the outset as given and complete. It cannot be distinguished from other spaces and simply cannot be positively identified: nevertheless, we need it because otherwise we could not create a universe through our distinctions. It is the semantically completely diaphanous background or protoplasm of all semantic contrasts, the transcendental condition of their possibility.[135]

The dimension of distinctions can rightly be called a universal absolute identity. It constitutes the conditions of particular (therefore, self-identical) entities by being the domain within which they can be individuated over against each other. This very domain is thereby nothing particular, no entity that would be distinguishable by way of reference to its predicates. It is precisely what Hegel later will simply call "the universal" as one moment of the concept. At the same time it can be seen as an inheritor notion of Kant's "synthetic unity," insofar as it retroactively unites all entities, all analytic unities in the insight that they can only be distinguished over against each other in a domain, which cannot be individuated in the same way. This is what Hegel means by "absolute identity" and it is evident that absolute identity is not tied to any notion of a Cartesian/Kantian subject synthesizing empirical, albeit (in the Kantian case) already conceptually structured data.

Hegel objects to Kant's way of conceiving transcendental reflection as a whole, insisting that it is unable to think *the constitution of constitution*. Kant was no doubt thoroughly correct when he recognized objectivity as tied to a constitutive performance: Kant's great insight is, after all, that objectivity is an *achievement*. However, the speculative dimension of reflection, that is, that which Hegel recognizes and in so doing outdoes Kant's philosophical project, consists in taking a further step back, as it were: *while Kant thinks the conditions of the constitution of objectivity, Hegel focuses on the constitutive conditions of a theory of the constitution of objectivity*. It turns out that Kant operates under the assumption of supposedly well-established conditions, viz. the difference between what is given and what is thought, between sensibility and the understanding, between matter and form. As Dieter Sturma rightly remarks, Kant argues "with the difference between what is given and what is thought, not for it."[136] It is against precisely this assumption that Hegel argues, pointing out that the very difference between the given and thought is itself a thought difference: with this thought, Hegel departs from judgment as the medium of reflection, changing philosophical registers entirely and undertaking his own systematic reflection on reflection.

3. Absolute Identity as a Critical Notion

Hegel's turn to his speculative system is to be understood as critical of the general philosophical position of modernity. Thus, Hegel is a critic of the "hallowing of finitude"[137] and the corresponding concept of "subjectivity as absolute,"[138] which he sees as an effect of the hegemony of a "culture of common sense."[139] Though perhaps a revolutionary of sorts in the old Oxford locale, the Hegelian motifs that might be claimed as motivation for McDowell's recourse to Hegel remain stuck in just such a commonsense culture. The problem of appealing to common sense, as McDowell wants to do in his quasi-Hegelian criticism of Kant's idealism, is that such an appeal is really just an effort to fortify one's claims to power. If one insists that objectivity must be understood as always already the result of a certain rule-following activity, that is, that to refer to objectivity is implicitly to refer to the community, then one certainly implies or claims, in fact, a dominion of the finite over the infinite. This gesture brings in view the truly critical potential of Kant's and Hegel's thought, viz. the eminently practical dimension of Kant's critique and Hegel's metacritique of the philosophy of reflection. The categorical imperative, for instance, can be addressed to every single person only because it is not bound to or constituted by a specific empirical community or their common sense. The same holds for absolute identity as that specific dimension in which claims of any sort whatsoever can be registered: it exceeds all communities. Hegel's work is above all aimed at educating us to overcome our assumptions about epistemic finitude: this is the import of the late-Hegelian pedagogical insight into the "true infinite." The true infinite is not a relatum of a relation, but is rather the dimension of distinctions, the background of relationality as such, which can therefore never be fixed as a given and determinate moment.

With recourse to an original synthesis, Kant and Hegel point to a way in which we can put power claims or claims to sovereignty or absoluteness in question: for, if universalizable circumstances were constituted exclusively in empirical communities, this question could not arise. The duty of the Kantian-Fichtian-Schillerian hero to prefer death to dishonesty or immorality is incomprehensible under the conditions of common sense. Even less so is Hegel's absolute idea possible in an empirical community: hence in the context of Hegel's theory of objective spirit the foundations are laid for a historical concept of reason which is, nevertheless, grounded in a dimension which is not subject to the decision of communities to recognize inferences or commitments as valid. The whole dimension of the sublime, which Hegel sees as threatened by Kant's image of "a Reason affected by sensibility,"[140] falls completely out of view for the "normativity Hegelians." In favor of their own harmless therapy program, they neglect the truly critical aspects of Kantian and post-Kantian idealism, declawing speculative philosophy and forfeiting the significance of Hegel's verdict against the philosophy of reflection.

An even stronger objection against a merely deflated version of the transition from Kant to Hegel lies in the discovery of the *dialectic of enlightenment*: the alleged establishment of autonomy results in a heteronomy of sensibility. If autonomy did not turn into heteronomy, that is, if it were possible, as they wish, to preserve Kantian autonomy (to have one's cake) and be Hegelians (and eat it too), the "normativity Hegelians" could not, for the reasons I have sketched, succeed in overcoming norm-nature dualism. For them it is not norms "all the way down,"[141] because at some point said norms must again spring from nature in order to stop the regress of rules that would be triggered if everything were merely rule-governed behavior. To put it polemically: the problem is not so much that the spade bends back when one hits the bedrock, as Wittgenstein expresses it,[142] but rather that reflection is itself conceived as a spade.

With Hegel's concept of "absolute identity" (or with the successor concept of the "absolute idea"), we are able to understand nature and spirit, first and second nature, as various presentational modes of determinacy.[143] Hegel thus offers by way of his own critique of judgment a reasonable ontology, in which one is able to thematize the natural bedrock, as it were, the nonpropositional relationship of the subject and the world, while preserving the thought that these relationships are only retrospectively established in discourse and so normative in the Pittsburghian sense. Ultimately the "authority" of Hegel's concept of "ethical life" (*Sittlichkeit*) should be, as he says, considered "infinitely higher" and infinitely deeper and richer than all explicable rules which could be negotiated as a catalogue of norms.[144] Propositional or inferential explication is only ever done belatedly or retrospectively and can never fully succeed; this thought is, of course, what Wittgenstein spelled out as well in *On Certainty*.

Hegel succeeds in thematizing the deeper dimension of the natural soul and its disciplining in terms of social "institutions" in ways that the "normativity Hegelians" simply cannot grasp in terms of their understanding of normativity, because they conceive normativity as the glue of a given community, the hierarchical power structure in which the community has authority over the individual unless it grants the special status of an expert to one of its members or to a subset of itself. Yet, Hegelian *Sittlichkeit* is not just an aggregate of norms voted upon, as it were, by the community, but precisely the very background of our rule-bound negotiations. This background is given to us by the unfolding of history and it can only be described after the fact, at its dusk: "The owl of Minerva spreads its wings only with the falling of the dusk."[145]

Against the background of thinking *Sittlichkeit*, the space of politics is for Hegel not merely to be grasped in terms of judgment or thought as substantially or ontologically opposed to individuals, that is, as exclusively constituted as an extension of their egoism and self-interest: on this Leviathanesque model, universality and sovereignty are merely extensions of self-interest and, at best, result in a tyranny of self-proclaimed common sense over the possibility of truly committed (and, therefore, sometimes exceptional) agency. However, even civil society—the form of community held together by contingent, negotiated rules—refers necessarily to a universal dimension that stands as near to us as our self-feeling and our discursive, universality-constitutive practices and institutions. This dimension cannot, without further ado, propositionally or inferentially be rendered explicit without being lost along the way. It is precisely with this dynamic in mind that Hegel turns against the philosophy of reflection. Ultimately, Hegel's analysis of *Sittlichkeit* is grounded in his philosophy of subjective spirit and in the way the psyche structures itself before acquiring the capacity to participate in communal practices (and, therefore, in objective spirit).

III The Pathological Structure of Representation As Such: Hegel's *Anthropology*

What Hegel generally speaks of as "spirit" in his *Encyclopedia* can only be adequately understood in the context of his metaphysics of expression: everything that is, on Hegel's view, necessarily exhibits an expressive structure. This expressive feature of reality is precisely what Hegel investigates in the chapter of his *Logic of Essence* entitled "Actuality" (*Wirklichkeit*). Hegel's account in this chapter no doubt brings to mind Aristotle's claim to the primacy of ἐνέργεια, or actuality, over δύναμις, or possibility. However, Hegel's thinking on this topic has a consequence that Aristotle was at the most only implicitly aware of.[146] For Hegel, spirit needs an other for its actuality, upon which it is *ontologically dependent*: thus spirit's activity cannot be absorbed into the abstract thinking of pure thoughts. Without the sphere of sensuous concreteness, self-thinking thought would be damned, as it were, forced to stay in the abstract "realm of shadows."[147] Without the actuality of an other, which is not spirit, spirit could not attain any determinate being (*Dasein*), that is, it could not *exist*.[148]

As one might expect, this dialectical structure whereby spirit presupposes an other plays a decisive role in Hegel's conception of the mind-body or soul-body problem.[149] By making the presuppositions of this problem explicit, Hegel develops a solution that can be put rather simply: the soul should be understood as the expressive dimension of corporeality. There is therefore neither a soul without an animal body nor an animal body without a soul. This means that body and soul are not ontologically independent entities: hence, they could not be substances in the Cartesian, dualistic sense. In contradistinction to such a dualism, Hegel joins with Aristotle's *On the Soul* and develops its thesis in an original way.

As Hegel writes in his *Philosophy of Subjective Spirit*, in an introductory section called "What Spirit Is," the "determinacy of spirit [. . .] is *'manifestation.'* "[150] It is crucial to note here that by "manifestation" Hegel does not understand any kind of representational structure, that is, no manifestation *of* something that would be independent of and logically-ontologically prior to this manifestation. Spirit does not manifest "*something* [. . .] but rather its determinacy and content is this revelation itself."[151] Hegel calls this structure, in which something is manifested that is not independent from its manifestation, the "revelation in the concept [*Offenbaren im Begriffe*]";[152] he also speaks of "creation."[153] Spirit creates itself: herein lies its freedom.

Now, for Hegel, this self-creation is in no way presuppositionless. It is not some eternal *causa sui*, which—always already determinate—could function as a metaphysical principle according to which we could grasp the organization of the whole. For it is *nature* that spirit presupposes: spirit develops itself out of nature, out of that which is not itself already spirit. Indeed "nature" should be understood as the presupposition of spirit in precisely the terminology Hegel developed in his *Logic of Essence*, that is, nature as the presup*position* of spirit, is that which is "*set forth* [. . .] as *its* world."[154] The manifestation of spirit presupposes a natural development such that it can account for and appropriate this development *post festum*. Spirit discovers a world; it comes on the scene in its world only belatedly, appropriating for itself a nonspiritual nature anterior to its birth. This appropriation is, however, a "generation"[155] of the natural presuppositions of spirit in the sense that spirit's own account of its natural origin consists in a transsubstantiation of natural predispositions into spiritual presuppositions.[156]

This picture of spirit's genesis that I have just sketched—whereby spirit presupposes something other than itself in its account of its own development, which it can only belatedly appropriate—is what I would like to reconstruct in some detail in what follows: I will do so on the basis of Hegel's *Anthropology*, in the context of his treatment of subjective spirit in his *Encyclopedia*. I will begin in Section 1 by discussing Hegel's theory of corporeality. Then in Section 2, I will briefly outline Hegel's rejection of the so-called myth of the given. This rejection consists foremost in *the discovery of the pathological structure of representation as such*: for Hegel there is no subjective space of presentation, that is, no judgmental or logical space in which something can be distinguished from something else, without the psychic monad having moved through a process of a pathological splitting. Thus anything like intentionality—what Hegel simply calls "consciousness"—and thus all truth-apt propositional attitudes, take place only due to a pathological splitting, grounded in a blind drive, which is worked up out of the "life of nature."[157] For Hegel, the natural presupposition of thought is *feeling*, or better, a kind of *self-feeling*: this auto-affection must be understood as anterior to thinking in order to grasp how representation as such (free of any myth of the given) is possible. Thinking substance is conditioned by feelings that it must acquire through repetition and practice. Without this *askesis* in the literal sense, it would be impossible for natural feeling to develop to the level of the thinking individual gifted with semantic, expressive freedom.

1. Hegel's Theory of Corporeality in the *Anthropology* (*Encyclopedia* §§ 388–412)

For Hegel, the realm of the psyche lies between the physical and the spiritual. The psyche is an immediate "self-feeling,"[158] which is not to be thought of as differentiated from anything, especially not from a body qua corporeal thing.[159] Rather, the soul is a sentient monad that, in this initial state, encounters only immediate qualities. Hegel refers to this encounter with an etymological wordplay: he speaks of *sensation* with the German "*Empfindung*" (§§399–402) hearing *finden*, to find, in it. Yet, what it finds is already negated as found by it. *Empfindung* is, thus, as the word's etymology "reveals," implicitly *Ent-Findung* or "de-finding." The soul is, in the first place, say, in the form of the embryo, immediately identical with the immediate qualities it encounters: in encountering these qualities, it does not recognize them as something other than itself, but rather it finds itself immediately and completely identical with them. In order for these encounters with immediate qualities to become sensations proper, the soul must alienate itself from these immediate qualities, must go through a process of dis-identification (*Ent-Findung*).

> Sensation is the form of the dull stirring of spirit in its insensate and non-intelligent individuality, in which *all* determinacy is still immediate. In terms of its content it is totally undeveloped, the opposition of an objectivity over-against the subject has not been established: it should be understood as a *most peculiar,* natural *singularity*.[160]

The natural individual, that which is developed into the *animal rationale*, into a being that is able to have propositional attitudes and to obtain a shared, objective world, is originally present in the world in this "dull stirring." In this state, it undergoes a series of affections that it cannot yet identify in a classificatory manner. Given that it is not yet differentiated from its environment, it is "ideal,"[161] as Hegel says. The ideal is here the antithesis of the material. As Hegel defines the soul, it is "not only for itself immaterial, but is rather the universal immateriality of nature, its simple, ideal life."[162] The soul in its immediate form of finding itself is connected with the world through feeling. One of Hegel's examples for this is the feeling of the shift of seasons. When spring comes (in a climate where the seasons are distinguished), we feel that nature is changing, our attitude towards the world changes without our cognitions therefore changing too. This change of attitude testifies to our natural connection with our environment, a connection that, having developed out of nature, remains a part of nature itself. Thus, nature itself has an immaterial side, something that cannot be explained with mere recourse to the organization of matter or to spatiotemporal entities/relations/processes. In this sense, soul is the "universal immateriality of nature."

Hegel's discourse on the soul is not based on rational psychology or the psychology of ancient Platonism (it should be said that the former is a historical development of the latter). The immateriality of the soul is not a property of a particular substance, but is the soul's ontological structure as that which is capable of opposing nature from within. Hegel is concerned here to avoid understanding the soul as a thing with properties and practical abilities, which would entail falling back behind Kant's destruction of rational psychology. Instead, he consistently aligns himself with (and radically develops) Aristotle's functionalism.

Aristotle had objected to Plato that the soul was not some immortal, self-standing existent substance, but rather had to be understood as the "first entelechy of an organic physical body (ἐντελέχεια ἡ πρώτη σώματος φυσικοῦ ὀργανικοῦ)."[163] Aristotle explicitly expresses that "neither the spirit nor any parts of it, if it can even be separated into parts, is separated from the body (ὅτι μὲν οὖν οὐκ ἔστιν ἡ ψυχὴ χωριστὴ τοῦ σώματος, ἢ μέρη τινὰ αὐτῆς, εἰ μεριστὴ πέφυκεν)."[164]

Hegel interprets this thusly: the soul must be understood as the organizing form of the body in such a way that the living body is always already body and soul. Those bodies we recognize as organisms are distinguished by an ideality, which consists in the fact that such bodies have an expressive dimension, and, thus, are *bodies* and not corpses. Bodies express emotions and moods, because they all are always already body and soul. Now, when the soul has a sensation (*Empfindung*) of something, it finds (*finden*) this sensation in itself. In this sense, the soul feels what it feels "*inwardly*."[165] This internalization is the minimal psychic structure of reference. The soul absorbs something into itself, feels something inwardly, without, however, this something being an object different from itself. The soul finds before itself what it senses as something, which is part of it. The traditional name for that which is found before the human, for that which man has not produced, is nature, φύσις, which stands in conceptual opposition to τέχνη, as Heidegger has repeatedly emphasized. The soul thus finds and feels its own nature: Hegel calls the soul in this state the "natural soul."

It is crucial to note that at this stage in Hegel's developmental account the natural soul is not yet individuated. It is not the soul of this or that individual, but rather a universal element, which is differentiated in itself: Hegel calls this general soul-element "substance." Yet the natural, general soul is "not to be fixed as *world-soul*, nor as a single subject, for it is rather the general *substance*, which has its actual truth only as *individuality*, subjectivity."[166] Thus Hegel positions himself once again in precise opposition to the tradition of Platonic psychology. This tradition assumes a world-soul in relation to which individuals must be understood as derivative. Hegel turns, on the contrary, in a typically modern direction: the "infinite worth of the individual,"[167] as Hegel has it, is the constitutive discovery of the transition from the ancient to the Christian world. This discovery implies a radical methodological reorientation. With this discovery, the individual suddenly plays an indispensable role in the constitution of the universal. This idea, which is an essential mark of modernity, and which Kierkegaard, Heidegger, Deleuze, and others have all referred to in varying ways under the heading of "repetition," is prefigured here in Hegel's anthropology.

The natural soul is ultimately no existing world soul, but is rather a "dull stirring," a stupor from which the soul gradually awakens. This can only come to pass if the soul develops habits and renders its corporeality alienable in the form of a sign (§§409–11). "This self-integration of particular or corporeal determinations of feeling into the *being* of the soul appears as a *repetition* of the same and the generation of habit as a *practice*."[168] The natural soul only becomes actual, that is, it can only present itself as soul, if it has internalized and integrated its corporeality. The soul only comes to itself by overtaking or appropriating its corporeality and instituting it as the organ of its expressive freedom. Without the mastery of corporeality in the medium of *askesis*, that is, of disciplining repetition and practice, philosophical thinking would not be possible. Subjective spirit's ability to discipline itself belongs, on Hegel's account, among the conditions for possibility of absolute spirit.[169]

> Thinking too, however free and active in its own pure element it becomes, no less requires habit and familiarity (the impromptuity or form of immediacy), by which it is the property of my single self where I can freely and in all directions range. It is through this habit that I come to realize my *existence* as a thinking being.[170]

Hegel's thought here is obviously aimed against the Cartesian dualism of thinking and extended substance. According to Hegel, thinking is not a substantial "ghost in the machine" (Ryle), but is rather a corporeal reality, which is primarily exhibited as feeling and sensation. This corporeality, which feels and senses, must become self-feeling, if thinking wants to come to itself in the individual.[171] By relating to its feelings, it is already implicitly self-feeling. Feelings are not objects in the same way as the classical object-type considered by modern epistemology, that is spatiotemporal causal entities, typically referred to as "physical objects." Feelings are not physical objects; they are not objects at all, if "object" designates something independent of being referred to. Feelings do not go unnoticed, even though they might be repressed. In this respect, feelings are prototypes of self-reference, of subjectivity. They are objects, which intimately belong to a subject; they are self-objectivations of the subject.

Hegel's theory of subjective spirit begins with feeling, which is inextricable from corporeality. Thus, from the very outset Hegel's theory does not set spirit and nature in opposition. The epistemological subject-object dichotomy is a secondary splitting of the psychic monad, which its natural anchoring, that is, corporeality, presupposes. In this way, it is impossible to delimit thinking substance from the feeling soul: this thought renders the central question of modern epistemology ("how can we be sure that our immaterial representations correspond to material states in the world out there?") plainly ridiculous, because our ideas simply are not immaterial in a dualistic sense. And while our feelings (and not only our thoughts) are ideal and immaterial in the sense that they originally develop in the dimension of what will become interiority, this does not therefore imply that they do so without corporeality. The body is above all a tool of the organism, the organon of its expressive freedom; thus, in a distinct way, Hegel's account is of an idealized body, for there is a certain ideality at the heart of bodily life. This expressive freedom presupposes an appropriation of feelings through repetition and practice, through which classificatory patterns are engendered, that turn feeling in general into specific feelings, say emotions.

2. Hegel's Rejection of the Myth of the Given

The decisive insight of Hegel's philosophy of subjective spirit is the genetic primacy of feeling and sensation over thought. In fact, Hegel only later treats thought under the general heading of "psychology." The psyche is "neither merely bodily nor merely spiritual,"[172] but is rather a "form of *immediacy*, in which subjective and objective have not been distinguished, in which intelligent personality has not been determined against an external world, in which any finite relations between such terms are non-existent."[173] Hegel insists that this relationship has not received due attention because the modern mind-body problem has, since Descartes, presupposed an uncrossable limit between the subjective (our mental states) and the objective (the world): thus, Hegel criticizes the "assumption" of "the absolute spatial and material externality of one part of being to another."[174] That is, modern dualism presupposes a *substantia extensa* and thus loses sight of the real (really ideal) relationship of body and soul.

With its assumption of an extended substance, modern philosophy presupposes that thinking is not in the world and thereby introduces a split within a larger unity (the whole) it does not refer to at all. If mind and world exist, they have to exist within a domain they have in common. Otherwise they could not even be distinguished. However, this domain is the world, and so we need to understand the world as capable of an internal splitting into spirit and its other. In modern epistemology and metaphysics, the spatial and material world *out there* is made absolute as self-existent substance. The individual is thus conceptualized as if it were always already among other individuals, always already related to them and to the world in the mode of a classificatory observation, standing over against an "objective world"[175] that is ontically-ontologically antecedent to and independent of its being referred to. Under the conditions of such a subject-object dichotomy, no sense can be made of what Hegel speaks of as a "feeling totality."[176] This consists in that originally "oceanic feeling," which psychoanalysis later investigated: the psychic monad begins its life in the mode of immediacy, in a feeling totality. The child is united with the mother, a condition described by Hegel as "genius."[177] "In immediate existence this is the relation of the child in the mother's womb, a relation that is neither merely bodily, nor merely spiritual, but is rather *psychic*, a relation of the soul."[178]

It is clear from this passage that Hegel is totally undeserving of the charge of intellectualism, which he all too often suffers. In discussing the mother-child relationship, Hegel characterizes it as a "*magical* relation" and points out that "sporadic examples and traces of this *magic* tie appear elsewhere in the range of self-possessed conscious life, say between friends, especially female friends with delicate nerves (a tie which may go so far as to show 'magnetic' phenomena), between husband and wife and between members of the same family."[179] The condition of the infant is that of a "monadic individual"[180] who has not yet internalized its world of feeling and who has not yet arrived at the position modern philosophy presupposes as original and absolute, viz., that of the closed subject set against the objective, mechanical world. In order to be set in relation to such an objective world, the natural soul in the state of feeling totality must become differentiated in itself. In order to arrive at the position of a subject that stands in relation to an objective world, a pathological splitting of feeling must take place in which the soul projects its natural side *ad extra*. The soul must present what it finds inside itself *as if* it were outside of itself: only through this dynamic can the soul penetrate into the domain of its expressive freedom.[181]

In order for the soul to have sensations proper, it must dis-identify with the feeling totality by learning to present these feelings as other than itself: the internal must be alienated as internal and taken to be other. Only in this way is what Hegel calls "consciousness" in his *Phenomenology of Spirit* possible: with this complex dynamic of the self-feeling soul alienating that which it feels (itself) from itself so as to engender, through this splitting, an other to which it refers, Hegel is simply accounting at a deeper genetic level for the very structure of intentionality he spells out in the *Phenomenology*.

Whereas the 1807 *Phenomenology of Spirit* begins with an analysis of consciousness as intentionality along the lines of Reinhold's *proposition of consciousness*, in the philosophy of subjective spirit intentionality as a relation to an external world begins on a more fundamental level, possessing its own genealogy. Reinhold's proposition famously reads: "In consciousness the representation is distinguished by the subject from the subject and the object and is related to both."[182] Yet, in order for this structure to be established, the psychic monad has to be opened up to an object, to something it can distinguish from itself. The first distinction is not one between a subject and an object, but rather an internal division of the feeling totality. For this reason all accessible objects are emotionally invested, they all result from a splitting of emotional energies. Even those objects we regard as correlates of purely theoretical observation are emotionally apprehended with the emotion of the pleasure of cognition and knowledge acquisition.

In this sense, there is nothing external on the level of the feeling soul; the idea of an externality has to be gained and sustained. For this reason, sober consciousness is not a stable item, it is always threatened by a regress into what the Jena Hegel called the "night of the world."[183] In the night of the world, the subject is not sufficiently differentiated in order to conceive of itself as intentional consciousness. However, the epistemic career of the subject begins with an overcoming of its primary narcissism, which is why Hegel in the *Encyclopedia* adds a genealogical account of the object of phenomenology, that is, of consciousness in the realization of its paradoxes.

Hegel's objection to the modern formulation of the body-soul or body-mind problem is this: all propositional attitudes, all modes of consciousness, that is, all truth-apt, epistemic relations are rooted in a pathological dimension.[184] This dimension must first of all become differentiated within itself, that is, the soul must become determined as a domain that excludes the objective world from itself, if we are to be able to stand in any relation to objects other than one of immediate identification (feeling totality). If such identification were not ruptured, no epistemic economy would be possible. Hegel describes this originary differentiation (*Ur-teil*) as judgment (*Urteil*).[185] With this move, Hegel offers an original interpretation of the Aristotelian analysis of κρίσις, which claims that perception has a judgmental structure. It is crucial to see, however, that the soul's judgments are not only the common judgmental acts whereby the soul determines something as something in the differential sphere of truth-value, the sphere of truth-apt representation, in which claims to true *or* false perception are possible. The soul's judgments also and primarily consist in the initial differentiation of the soul in itself, which enables it to discover its natural side and to express itself in this other order: through this process what Hegel calls the "actual soul" is realized. Hence, the soul's judgments are not only truth-apt judgments which refer to objects in a predicative ambience, but function also on a deeper level: by way of an originary differentiation, the soul engenders the possibility of a truth-apt sphere. A truth-apt sphere for the soul presupposes an internal split (which produces the relation of the inner and the outer in the first place).

In this context, Hegel anticipates one of the central philosophically relevant insights of psychoanalysis: all intentionality is resultant of a fragile pathological splitting, and this fragility can only be remedied by way of repetition and practice. The soul comes to be actual only by virtue of the fact that it imagines and presents its corporeality as a "sign"[186] of itself. This idea also lies behind Wittgenstein's dictum: "the human body is the best picture of the human soul."[187] Only as embodied is the soul able to be inner: the distance between body and soul necessary for inner experience to take place only exists through splitting. For only through this internal differentiation between the inner and the outer can the soul come to be for-itself over-against its natural dimension, nature in-itself. Without the ultimately pathological institution of the in-itself within itself, the soul's natural side, the soul could not be for-itself. The soul is thus nothing but its relation to nature, a relation that is not another natural item and that cannot be construed in terms of full-blown intentionality either.

In this way, Hegel replaces the Cartesian conception of the soul as a thinking "ghost in the machine" by asserting the genetic primacy of feeling. This move has remarkable consequences for his theory of knowledge. Modern Cartesian epistemology is often charged with being committed to a mental representationalism susceptible to skepticism. In this tradition, the subject is conceived as primarily thinking, not always already embodied substance. This raises the question of how the nonspiritual, nonconceptual, merely vast expanse of the outside world can ever come into relation with the mind: how is it that spirit's immaterial world of representations can ever be transcended in the direction of the material world outside of itself? Whence the classic *dream problem*, which asserts that we have no criteria at hand to secure the claim that we are awake and not dreaming. Hegel rightly observes that when we are faced with the dream-problem, the situation into which we have maneuvered ourselves is based on an empty abstraction, namely, is based on a false concept of (the primacy of) representation. Hegel argues against the assumption that we relate to the world primarily by means of our representations and that this world is out there behind the "veil of perceptions," insisting that "the world of understanding consciousness is something quite different from a painting of mere representations and pictures."[188] With this assertion, Hegel does not simply and superficially beg the question against Cartesian skepticism. Instead, he offers a developmental account of consciousness, that is, of all propositional attitudes and intentionality, which demonstrates that a nonpropositional presupposition of an originary emotional relation lies at the heart of consciousness as such, by virtue of which it is naturally intertwined with the world itself. The world is thus not a mechanical, merciless machine, but is rather a totality differentiated in itself, into which we enter on the basis of primary feelings: after all, the feeling soul belongs to the world itself, or rather the world and the feeling soul are originally undifferentiated in feeling totality. Once only **feeling** souls, we have become accustomed to and capable of thinking and abstraction through repetition and practice. However, only belatedly does this end up leading us into a solipsistic impasse from which we, like Wittgenstein's "fly in a fly bottle,"[189] desperately seek a way out. While Descartes still needed a God as the mediator between self and world in order to free himself from the predicament of skepticism, Hegel reminds us of the fact that, as *feeling* souls, we needn't worry whether or not we are truly connected with what there is.

Hegel's innovation in epistemology in the narrow sense of the term thus lies in the introduction of a notion of feeling totality. Our connection to what there is and to other people is not primarily that of propositional attitudes or truth-apt cognitions, but is rather one of feeling. The gap between mind and world is only opened up retroactively, as the result of a pathological splitting. Yet, this pathological splitting presupposes a unity, a feeling monad, and, hence, can never really result in the possibility of a purely Cartesian spiritual realm shut off from the external world.

From the very start, Hegel's account of the soul is aimed against the intellectualization of the soul. In fact, Hegel insists that philosophy itself, so-called pure thinking, is bound by the conditions of subjective spirit, which by absolutely no means may be satisfied without corporeality. Hegel reminds us that our freedom is an expressive freedom, which is to say, a freedom that is only possible because it can be manifested through our bodies in the world. What it would mean to be deprived of this expressive freedom has recently been explored in Julian Schnabel's movie *The Diving Bell and the Butterfly* and in the 1971 classic *Johnny Got His Gun*. The protagonists of these movies are both paralyzed and locked in, almost completely deprived of their resources to give expression to their interior. If Descartes's picture of the spontaneity of thinking were adequate, the locked-in person would enjoy a state of pure spirituality. Yet, spirit without an expressive body is horrible precisely because spirit is nothing but a certain being there of bodies, a mode of a particular kind of body.

Hegel clearly sees, therefore, that the myth of the given must be brought to an end. It is, after all, the epistemological keystone of solipsism. This myth assumes that an unsurpassable gap exists between what is given and what is thought, and that what is given somehow comes to perception from across this gap; it thus repeats the ancient distinction between αἰσθητόν and νοητόν, which had already led the theories of perception of Plato and Aristotle to paralyzing impasses. Hegel insists that the ideality of the soul, the mind, and the spirit simply does not take place without materiality: "nowhere so much as in the case of the soul (and still more with spirit) is the ideality determined: it must be noted that for understanding it is essential that ideality is the *negation* of the real, but a negation in which what is negated is preserved [*aufbewahrt*], virtually retained."[190] The soul and spirit cannot therefore be separated from corporeality and the symbolic interaction with others in the objective world. For souls are essentially manifestations, and as such rely on the expressive medium that they appropriate. In place of an ontological gap between body and soul, Hegel reveals their interpenetration in feeling, which is differentiated in itself. This differentiation is developed through habit and practice, and in this way a pathological splitting is produced in the psyche that at its apex expresses itself as the opposition of subject and object. The subject-object dichotomy is certainly no absolute, given fact, but is rather the result of a theoretical operation loaded with presuppositions, not the least of which is manifest in the often unquestioned and totally contemptible obliviousness, dismissiveness, and forgetfulness with which philosophers treat the *feelings* of human beings.

Chapter 2

Schelling's Ontology of Freedom

Schelling rightly points out that Kant tends to identify the thing in itself with freedom.[1] However this might be interpreted in detail, Kant indeed needs to draw a line between the phenomenal world—constituted as a domain of reference for finite thinkers—and the epistemically inaccessible "domain" of the thing in itself/things in themselves. Otherwise he could not account for the possibility of freedom given his thorough commitment to a mechanistic understanding of natural laws. Schelling approaches this distinction with his recourse to the problem of phenomenalization: how does the phenomenal relate to the noumenal, given that the phenomenal is precisely the appearing of the noumenal? If every appearance is an appearance of the noumenal, freedom has to lie at the ground of appearances. With this intuition in mind, Schelling develops an ontology of freedom as the project "of making freedom the one and all of philosophy."[2]

In order to defend this ontology, Schelling sets off with an ontology of predication. Just like Kant, he works on the assumption that determinacy has a judgmental structure. Whatever is determinate, is determinable in judgments as being such-and-so in opposition to other possibilities ruled out by our commitment to things being such-and-so. Yet the judgmental domain of our answerability to the world is not opposed to the world. It exists itself. This is evident, once we judge that the relation between judgments and the content judged is such-and-so. In this case, judgments themselves exist; they belong to the very domain about which we judge. Now, if it turns out that that very domain can legitimately be described in terms of freedom, an ontology of freedom is justified via the theory of predication. This is exactly the form of Schelling's overall argumentation, in particular in the *Freedom Essay* and onwards in his development.

In the current chapter, I reconstruct Schelling's theory of the potencies, that is, his ontology of freedom, in terms of a theory of predication. This leads me to a reconstruction of the relation between Schelling and Heidegger in terms of their respective understanding of being and judgment. Also,

Schelling and Heidegger both suggest that we turn away from subjectivity as a universal dimension of commitment and move towards the particularized notion of a person or a self. Yet, in order to motivate this transition, it is necessary to show the limits of our self-understanding as subjects of judgments prominent since Kant.

I Unprethinkable Being and Event: The Concept of Being in Late Schelling and Late Heidegger

There are no doubt many points of connection between Schelling's late philosophy and Heidegger's own late work: consonances of which Heidegger himself was aware, though only to a certain degree. Heidegger's judgment of Schelling's thought oscillates between, on the one hand, the high approbation of Schelling as the first philosopher to overcome onto-theology and, on the other hand, the opprobrium of Schelling as a necessary station on the onto-theological path from Hegel's idealism to Nietzsche's will to power, the latter of which Heidegger sees as an explication of Schelling's famous formulation "Will is primal Being [*Wollen ist Urseyn*]."[3] In other words, Schelling appears as a problem for Heidegger: Schelling's philosophy seems to represent a possible escape from the tradition of onto-theological metaphysics, though it nevertheless remains by Heidegger's lights one of onto-theology's central stations.

In this essay I will attempt to bring Schelling and Heidegger in conversation by demonstrating the ways in which these two thinkers respectively transform the traditional concept of Being. As I see it, Schelling and Heidegger both call the classic, ancient concept of Being into question: both thinkers insist on a transformation of the classic metaphysical conception of the question of being, according to which any given question of "being" (ὄν) must instead be understood as a question about "determinacy" (τι).[4] According to a central theory of determination, dating back at least to Plato, determinacy can only take place in a whole, in which everything determinate is so only by virtue of its being predicatively comprehensible and distinguishable from everything else. For Plato, being and logos thus belong together, are inextricably linked; he makes this plain in the *Sophist* in particular. While Plato was the first to clearly formulate this theorem, the same thought arises in modern philosophy with Spinoza's famous formula according to which *omnis determinatio est negatio*. In what follows I will speak of this concept of being under the banner of *the logical concept of being*.

Schelling and Heidegger set a *historical concept of being* against the logical concept of being, a move that is grounded in a revisionary analysis of the idea of judgment and of the "apophantic *as*" in Schelling and Heidegger, respectively. Schelling and Heidegger identify the historical concept of being as a presupposition or condition of the logical concept of being; thus, a limit is set to the latter, which is not and cannot be brought within its reach. That is, upon realizing the import of the historical concept of being, it is clear that the limits of the logical concept of being can no longer be presented as *logical* limits: in a word, all reasoning and justification, all grounds, have an "abyss [*Abgrund*]" (Heidegger) or a "non-ground [*Ungrund*]" (Schelling) as their limit. In his late philosophy, Schelling demonstrates that this thought reveals the contingency of being as such.

In what follows, I will begin by turning, in Section 1, to Schelling's text *Another Deduction of the Principles of Positive Philosophy* and sketching the way in which Schelling attempts to overcome the purely rational, logical concept of being, which he assigns to what he calls *negative philosophy*. In this section we will bring Schelling's central concept of unprethinkable being in focus. Next, in Section 2, I will turn to Heidegger's late concept of "being" as "event." Finally, in Section 3, I will briefly compare the two thinkers, emphasizing that both make remarkable headway in establishing the relation, even the fusion of being and self, bringing into view the idea of a *personal sense of being*.

1. The Limit of Negative Philosophy: Unprethinkable Being

According to a longstanding tradition that begins with Plato, the world can be understood as the whole of beings. Against Parmenides's ontological monism, Plato had argued that all beings are determined by the fact that they are different from all other beings. Every thing is ultimately everything it is not, for any determination is defined as what it is by virtue of its place in the totality of all relations of inclusion and exclusion, that is, the relations it maintains with all other determinations therein.[5] According to Plato, "being" (ὄν), "determinacy" (τι), and "the whole" (ὅλον) are ultimately equivalent terms, for the whole is constituted by means of a universal and continuous difference or differentiation, what Plato simply calls "the Other" (θάτερον).[6] The whole as a form of totality is therefore present in each individual being, and each individual difference in turn participates in the whole. Yet, totality is only ever present in the mode of negativity: totality is in each case "nothing" in the sense that it is always other than that which it is determined to be. Given that it is nothing determinate, it is not a determinate thing.

Plato's ontological holism thinks being therefore always as determinacy, so that being exists ultimately as thinking in the sense of νοεῖν: being is to be recognized in our thinking. In our thought of being, that is, in philosophical *epistêmê*, being thus encounters itself, because thought is only thought of something. Plato takes this insight from Parmenides and modifies it: genuine thought is an opening of being to thought and not some arbitrary invention of contents. Genuine thought knows itself to be being revealed to itself precisely because all contents of thought are presented within an open space. Through the mediation of a long Platonic tradition, Hegel eventually comes to think "being" in its relation to "determinacy."[7] Clearly, the first dialectic of his *Science of Logic* is a modern repetition of Plato's *Parmenides*, and the conclusion is the same: the difference between being and nothingness is necessarily nullified, for being cannot be determined against nothing, without nothing itself ex hypothesi becoming something determined through this operation. For this reason, being has to be determined as something determinate, as determinacy. In this sense, Hegel inherits Plato's concept of being, that which had already led Plato to conceive the whole of beings as something, which should be understood (and which expresses itself) essentially through its logical character, as a "network of pure determinations (τῶν εἰδῶν συμπλοκή)."[8] Thus the whole must not be conceived as opposed to thought, for everything determinate can be thought; we should be careful here, for this does not imply straightaway that everything determinate is actually known. On the model of the Platonic concept of being—wherein being, determinacy, and totality are understood as inextricably linked—one can ipso facto reckon that it is not the case that when reaching out to the whole the whole escapes, for instance, or that being is something which is opposed to thinking as such.[9]

Now, late Schelling famously introduces a much-discussed and controversial distinction between *negative philosophy* and *positive philosophy*. What I have sketched above as Plato's logical concept of being will suffer harsh scrutiny from Schelling in his negative philosophy, which he himself describes as "purely rational philosophy." The content of Schelling's negative philosophy is his own enquiry into that which he calls the "idea of being," the "figure of being," or the "blueprint of being."[10] Clearly, Schelling here alludes to Plato's "idea of being (τοῦ ὄντος ἰδέα)," which is discussed in the *Sophist*.[11] "Idea" here signifies for Schelling the totality of determinations from which all knowledge results, that relative to which the endeavor of capturing determinate beings and completely distinguishing them from one another takes place. Therefore, Schelling goes on to identify the idea of being with the Kantian "transcendental ideal of pure reason," which by his own measure is *the* essential theme of post-Kantian idealism.[12]

Negative philosophy operates, therefore, with a determinate concept of being, which one can refer to as the logical concept of being, which with Schelling and later with Heidegger can be distinguished from the historical concept of being. For Schelling, the most important representatives of the logical concept of being are Parmenides, Spinoza, Hegel, and finally his own philosophy of identity. In Plato and Aristotle, however, Schelling sees the development of something like an alternative concept of being, what he finds especially strongly pronounced in Plato's *Timaeus.*[13] Without this other, historical concept of being, which Schelling elucidates and justifies in his text *Another Deduction of the Principles of Positive Philosophy*, the project of a positive, that is essentially "historical philosophy,"[14] cannot even begin. In order to grasp in full Schelling's positive philosophy, we must first take a detour through his theory of judgment.

The logical concept of being depends ultimately on a certain conception of judgments, according to which all beings are necessarily and consistently determinate, and each being or determination holds a certain functional position in the contexture of the whole, such that any determination is recognizable by virtue of its differential relations. Presumably, all the relations of a given thing may not be readily available to our finite thinking: for no single thing are we able to explicate by way of thorough predication the totality of its determinations. Nevertheless, an absolutely complete knowledge in the logical sense cannot be ruled out. Negative philosophy aims, therefore, to articulate a view of the whole, setting it apart from all individuals in order to thematize the All in the horizon of a proper whole. The key gesture of the project of negative philosophy lies ultimately in a reaching out to the whole, toward the general and universal—or as Schelling says, again with Plato— toward the "highest species," that which Schelling refers to as "the highest and most general modes (the *summa genera*) of being."[15] The individual is hereby understood as eo ipso nothing more than a moment of the whole, a conception which Hegel, in particular in his *Logic of the Concept*, has given voice to: the individual is a self-determination of the concept, which itself comes to be as universal, single, and particularly determinate only through this self-determination, and which is known as such in its diremption. Indeed, this is the logical concept of being par excellence in high Hegelian style.

This thought implies at the same time that the philosophizing individual can himself be understood exclusively as *atomon eidos*, that is, as a moment of the self-explication of the idea. However, and this is crucial, this conception of the thinker fails to account for the thinker's own *existential position*: in mobilizing this point against the logical concept of being, Schelling is rightly recognized as a forerunner of so-called existentialism.[16] According to Schelling, in order to grasp ourselves as the creatures we truly are, that is, to resist retreating from ourselves and comprehending ourselves only under the banner of pure apositional thinking, we must reckon with the fact that the idea of being itself is an effect of our contingent position in the whole of beings. In other words, we must begin to take into account the ontological significance of our thinking *personality*, if we are to succeed in giving a philosophical account of ourselves that can be distinguished from the thought according to which we are the impersonal instantiation of pure thought, in which God's essence can be glimpsed, as Aristotelian onto-theology has it. Thus Schelling sets out to think the audacious thought that being itself is contingent; this thought naturally has great, if not devastating consequences for all onto-theological perspectives.

"Contingent" should here be understood simply by way of Aristotle's definition: "that which could be otherwise (ὃ ἐνδέχεται ἄλλως ἔχειν)."[17] Thus, Schelling begins his *Another Deduction* with the question of whether it is possible to think being itself as *contingency*. Were being itself a matter of contingency, it would have to be possible ex hypothesi that both being and thought could be otherwise (given, of course, that thought belongs to being, i.e. that thoughts exist). For Schelling, "the question is, hence, whether this unprethinkable Being absolutely does not allow for a contradistinction, which could alter it, over against which it would, therefore, prove to be contingent."[18] This "unprethinkable being" that Schelling speaks of here designates merely that whose determinate being (*Dasein*) is necessary for thought, that is, that which it would be impossible not to think. Unprethinkable being is therefore merely "that which, no matter how early we come on the scene, is already there."[19] It signifies therefore the always-already as such: if anything whatsoever is, then unprethinkable being is always already there. It is crucial to note, however, that this does not in any way offer insight into the *essence* of unprethinkable being. The unprethinkability of being merely implies that all thought always already finds itself in being, in a situation that it has not itself set up in advance.

When approaching the thought of the unconditioned in the traditional way, it is prima facie impossible to think that it could be otherwise: in the traditional way of thinking the unconditioned we are confronted with pure necessity or, in Schelling's own terms, with some *"necessario existens."*[20] The question is thus: how, in contradistinction to traditional philosophy, could being be contingent and in what sense?

Schelling's answer is as simple as it is striking: the necessity of the *necessario existens* is itself contingent, because it depends on the existence of chance, the being-there of contingency, such that it can be determined over against contingency in the first place *as* necessity as such. For the *necessario existens* is necessary properly speaking only once the ontological modalities are distinguished. This means that the "possibility of another being,"[21] and therefore the possibility of being's own contingency, cannot be excluded from unprethinkable being. Yet, even stronger than this impossibility of excluding contingency, without this other and therefore contingent being, the *necessario existens* would not itself be necessary: contingency is thus shown as a logical-ontological condition of necessary being. The necessity of the absolute origin of all beings cannot therefore outstrip the fact that when something arises, it does so only by virtue of being always already in relation to something else. That is, anything that has originated is thus contingent, because it cannot exclude the fact that it has originated; the very structure of coming-to-be-determinate necessitates the contingency of determinacy. Yet, the most challenging thought of Schelling's work here is this: this dialectic opens up the further possibility that even unprethinkable being itself, that which affords all determinacy its being-there, could be a fortuitous, contingent being, since its own necessity is contingent, for it is determinate as necessary only through its difference from the possibility of another being.

The always-already of unprethinkable being is ultimately at the same time always already related to the not-yet of another being. From the vantage of any origin, that which originates is not yet. The origin is therefore, according to an ancient Platonic tradition, essentially "not yet of the same kind as that whose origin it is."[22] The absolute necessity of the origin must therefore be compatible with the contingency of everything that originates. Thus the necessity of the origin is contingent because it depends on the existence of a contingent being, which cannot be ruled out a priori. Whatever originates from the origin must be compatible with the origin: thus the contingency and necessity of the origin must both be possible. Schelling puts it this way:

> [F]or the very reason that the potency [possibility, M.G.] did not precede the unprethinkable Being, it could not be *overcome* in the act of

this unprethinkable existing. But thereby an ineliminable contingency is posited in this very unprethinkable existing.[23]

We can reconstruct Schelling's reasoning here by following a famous passage from the twelfth book of Aristotle's *Metaphysics*, to which Schelling is surely alluding. "Actuality" (ἐνέργεια) must necessarily be antecedent to "possibility" (δύναμις), for otherwise nothing actual would take place. If, ultimately, possibility were antecedent to actuality, an initial and initiating act would be needed to lead possibility over into actuality. This initiating act, however, would be actuality, so that again actuality would have come before possibility, such that the latter could come to be determined as actuality.[24] Actuality or the "Actus," as Schelling says, cannot rule out possibility, because it cannot maintain any relation to it without eo ipso becoming something determinate and therefore possible, that is, something that could be otherwise. But since we are looking for an alternative concept of being, we would be ill advised to always already determine unprethinkable being over against possibility: this move would, of course, be tantamount to reverting back to the logical concept of being. The "possibility of another being" can therefore not be grasped from unprethinkable being. In this way, we can make sense of the question: "why is there anything at all and not rather nothing?"[25]

Schelling repeats this question for a variety of reasons throughout his thinking. It must be understood as the question of the ultimate and originary ground of determinacy, and therefore as the question of why anything at all, that is, anything determinate, takes place. That which is something determinate is, according to Schelling's theory of predication, that which could always be something other. In a famous passage from the *Philosophy of Mythology*, Schelling offers his own critique of judgment, as it were, which shows that judgment as such is the assertion of the possibility to be otherwise.

> Because the true meaning of the expression: *being* something is precisely this. When speaking of Being *cum emphasi*, the expression *being* something = the case of being this something's subject. So, if the copula in each phrase, e.g. in the phrase "A is B" is meaningful, emphatic, if it is the copula of a real judgment, then "A is B" means as much as: A is B's subject, i.e. it is not itself and by its nature B (for if the latter were the case the phrase would be an empty tautology), rather: A is also that which cannot be B.[26]

The question of why anything at all takes place rather than nothing can therefore be construed with recourse to the question of the origin of judgment. Now, the origin of judgment cannot be sought merely in subjectivity, for subject and object, thinking and being, cannot be presupposed as always already separated. At the origin of judgment, there cannot be a judging subject in opposition to a world in the sense of a set of ready-made referents. This idea is itself part of a particular way of thinking about the world, which presupposes the successful establishment of judgments. Schelling is thus from the outset clearly engaged in opening a path of departure from a certain Cartesian conception of subjectivity. For Schelling, being must not be assumed as the other of the self, since this separation cannot be presupposed if what we seek is the origin of judgment through which all separation is in the first place possible. Therefore we find ourselves asking the question of the origin of judgment in a domain "where the laws of thinking are the laws of being,"[27] which, according to Schelling, is the domain of logic in the Aristotelian sense. Thinking and being alike are subject to the elemental conditions of determinacy that become clear in the structure of judgment, the dynamic by which something is determined *as* something. The question of why anything at all takes place, therefore, is not merely an ontological issue (and certainly no cosmological or ontic quest for the actual origin of the universe), but is rather the logical-ontological *ur*-question.

Schelling answers this question with his doctrine of the potencies, which I will now reconstruct grosso modo. To begin: determinacy and therefore something, anything whatsoever, presupposes that something be determined. Schelling calls this *the first potency*, the determinable. Schelling refers to this first potency in a variety of ways, for example, as the "originary subject"[28] or as "pure being without any 'could,' without any capability."[29] This first position of judgment is itself not yet determinate: it cannot yet be a singular term in a judgment, nor something to which we can ascribe predicates, for we are dealing precisely with that which makes all of this possible. We experience something ultimately through those predicates which belong to it and by which we are informed what it is. However, the first potency does not have predicates yet, it is like a raw element of predication. To be precise, it is not yet even an element of predication, because there is no complete judgment yet. It is the very beginning of a determinate thought, a beginning, which cannot be a determinate thought yet. Thoughts have to be processed, and the beginning of thought processes is never the full thought.

According to Schelling, the second position of judgment, that is, *the second potency*, features what he refers to as the "originary predicate,"[30] or as "pure 'could' or capability without any being."[31] Now, predicates are general in the sense that they can be applied to many things. Whatever predicates apply in any given case cannot be known by our acquaintance with the predicate alone. Whomever is in a position, for example, to be informed that and to pronounce that the predicate "X is *yada yada*" might apply to something, has no information at hand with which to determine whether or not there is, in fact, anything to which this predicate applies, and if so, what it would be. The figure of the predicate opens, therefore, a logical space of possible instances, without there being eo ipso a determinate instance to sort out. Therefore, any predicate is pure "could," pure capability, without any being: it is not a priori decidable if the predicate applies to anything whatsoever. Subject and predicate must therefore be coordinated: this is what the third position of judgment, that is, *the third potency*, accounts for. Thus, Schelling refers to the third potency as the "originary synthesis of subject and predicate."[32] The third potency is thus the copula, or "spirit," as Schelling tends to say.

Wolfram Hogrebe has succinctly described the three potencies as "elemental predicative particles," further characterizing them as "pronomial being," "predicative being," and "propositional being," respectively.[33] For in every judgment there is something or other to which we can initially relate only in a pronomial manner, and which, with the help of a predicate, we can then identify *as* something and so differentiate it from other things. Through this move, a logical space is constituted, in which something or other can be differentiated from other things. As soon as this minimal determinacy is given, the identity of being and determinacy is established, and with this, the logical concept of being. The latter, however, is already an interpretation of fully established judgments and therefore has no grip on the originary subject of judgments before it is determined by predicates. As long as the *ur*-subject is not yet determinate, it is as a matter of fact not yet a potency; it is "pure being without any 'could,'" or as we now can say, it is unprethinkable being. Unprethinkable being is the first potency in its initial independence from judgment. It is not always already determinate as potency and therefore as a position of judgment, because it must first in effect become determined as the originary position of judgments. That unprethinkable being becomes determined and that thereby a "dimension of distinction" is established means that we should not attempt to make it comprehensible with recourse to the already fully established structure of judgment, since it takes place essentially as a presupposition which is not yet itself a judgment. To attempt to think unprethinkable being in this way would simply be to employ a certain logical-ontological anachronism.

> Against this Being which, no matter how early we come on the scene, is already there, I have often heard the following objection: such a reality, which precedes all possibility, is unthinkable. And indeed it is unthinkable for a thinking, which precedes Being and therefore for the kind of thinking to which we are accustomed. Thinking posits this Being as its point of departure in order to attain that which it deems as most worthy to and for knowing and thereby as the most desirable thing in knowledge, in order to attain it as a reality. And actual thinking only comes to pass when departing from this point—but just as the *terminus a quo* of a movement, in which, actually, the movement itself does not already exist, still belongs to the movement, so every Being through its progress, by its setting off from itself, becomes a moment of thinking [sc. namely the first potency!].[34]

That being, which no matter "how early we come on the scene, is already there," is unprethinkable being: that which thinking cannot get behind or before, that which cannot be anticipated or anteceded by any thought whatsoever. Unprethinkable being is therefore to be understood literally, in the sense that it is precisely that about which no thought whatsoever can be presupposed. This means that this being cannot be presented in any thought, since all thought is always already predicatively mediated sense, in the sense determined by the logical concept of being. Yet *that* there is a logical space that is opened by and through the fundamental structure of judgments and the potencies cannot be explained or understood with recourse to judgment. The existence of logical space is therefore contingent, because no ground can be given to account for the fact that it exists. Unprethinkable being can therefore not be understood as the *ground* of logical space, because the very concept of ground already presupposes the successful constitution of logical space. Unprethinkable being is consequently the paradoxical "ground of ground" in the full-blooded Heideggerian sense, what Heidegger also speaks of as the "abyss."[35] Schelling himself had suggested the expression "non-ground"[36] in his *Freedom Essay*, a term which in his later philosophy is replaced by unprethinkable being.

Unprethinkable being should thus be understood as the actuality of all possibility, that is, all determinability prior to its becoming anything determinate as such. This means that it takes place prior to any and all "*as*."[37] It cannot exclude the possibility of being otherwise, and thus the possibility of the potencies, as it cannot take place in a setting where relations of inclusion and exclusion are at play, that is, it is antecedent to the logical concept of being and all relationality as such. Thus, the belatedly diagnosed immediacy of the beginning is not related in any way to mediation.

It is with this insight into belatedness that we can, with Schelling, assert the ineradicable contingency of all existence. For everything that exists is something and is therefore determinate. That anything whatsoever exists cannot be justified with reference to a determinate ground and therefore cannot be grounded in any manner whatsoever. Thus there is no *ratio determinans* for the existence of logical space: that a predicative ambience exists in which we can acquire knowledge is a fact that can neither be grounded in nor excluded from unprethinkable being. Logical space could have not come to be: it is sensu stricto contingent, because its other, that which it would be were it otherwise, that is, the eternally indeterminate, cannot be a priori ruled out.

While negative philosophy examines only the constitution of logical space, and thus in all of its claims assumes the logical concept of being, positive philosophy sets out from the insight into the contingency of logical space as such. In this way, Schelling opens onto a novel possibility for philosophical reflection, viz. thinking the transition from actuality to possibility, what Schelling calls "potentialization"[38] as the essential act of freedom: that is, as an activity that can be understood as taking place without any sufficient reason, as absolute spontaneity, or as that which, in contradistinction to the Kantian identification of freedom and autonomy, cannot be brought under any rule.

This groundless, excessive freedom is, according to Schelling, nothing more than the specific ontological status and role of *personality*. Who we ultimately are at any given time depends on our freedom, since we are only what we make of ourselves (which includes what others make of us), what we take ourselves to be. We are held accountable for our personality, for the way in which we see the world and our position in it, because we are the very open region in which fields of sense appear as such. Thus Schelling anticipates the foundational thought of existentialism, in particular Sartre's concept of freedom, with, however, the following important difference: Schelling develops a concept of being that is *a limine* logically and ontologically compatible with our groundless freedom. While Sartre owes us an answer to the question of how the *en-soi* and the *pour-soi* are ontologically compatible with one another, Schelling attempts precisely to understand freedom as the coming-to-be and coming-to-itself of unprethinkable being (of the *en-soi*). In order to understand how being and freedom, that is, personality, can be compatible with one another, Schelling needed to give voice to an alternative concept of being.

The project of positive philosophy, which Schelling simply takes to be the philosophy of a "person seeking person,"[39] crucially corresponds to and necessitates the establishment of a historical concept of being. Being itself is to be considered historically and in such a way that it is made transparent as a process of the constitution of self-relations. To explicate this thought, positive thinking must turn to history in order to show this constitution of self-relations as a transformation of being itself; this is the task Schelling undertakes in his *Philosophy of Mythology* and *Philosophy of Revelation*. The resultant positive philosophy thus contains a history of the self, a developmental account of the self that comes to itself; thus the late-Schellingian effort can indeed be thought of as a continuation of his earlier project of a "history of self-consciousness."[40]

To this end, personality as such must be conceived as the meaning of being. Specifically, this means that Schelling is trying to trace a history of Being, which goes from unprethinkable being to the establishment of a self, which Schelling refers to as "absolute spirit."[41] This would be a "pure self,"[42] which, unlike our own factical, contingent selves, would be necessary in a not yet to be anticipated sense of "necessity." The possibility or actuality of an absolute spirit is, however, not yet proven or provable, for the history of being has not come to an end. Had it come to an end, we would already be "beyond being"[43] in the Platonic sense. Yet, "beyond being philosophy can only find what will be."[44] Here Schelling alludes to the name of God in *Exodus* 3.14, which he consistently renders in the future tense, in precise opposition to the onto-theological tradition. "The starting point of philosophy is, therefore, what will be, the absolute future: it is hence our duty to penetrate into the essence of the absolute future."[45]

Despite some major obscurities in the text, Schelling's point can be summarized as the discovery of ontological future. In the tradition, Being's eternity has either been associated with a pure presence (as in the case of the eternal present in propositions such as "It *is* the case that $2 + 2 = 4$") or, as Hegel does, with a logical past. In this sense, essence in Hegel is "timelessly past Being."[46] This corresponds to Hegel's analysis of presupposition, in which Being turns out to be a presupposition of reflection. Schelling, on the contrary, insists on the fact that whatever originates from Being, in whichever way it is determined, that which originates is an ontological future from the vantage point of "timelessly past being." Therefore, the ontological structure of any given world as it presently is, is the realized future of its origin. This also allows for the possibility of change in the actual ontological structures presented to us, because they have as much a future as they are themselves realized futures of their origins or conditions. There is, therefore, an ontological temporality, which arguably lies at the ground of any other form of temporality.[47]

The diagnosis of the history of being serves human interests inasmuch as it helps us understand this history as the transformation of being to self, which creates space for hope for a pure self, which would be consistent with and is the final aim of our deep and deeply human search for sense, for meaning. As Schelling puts it,

> [T]he dead body has enough in itself, and only wants itself. The animal, as everyone can see already at the level of the living plant's hunger for light, wants something outside itself, the human wants something above itself. The animal is through its will pulled outside itself toward something and the human in its truly human will is elevated above itself.[48]

The question of whether something above the human will be achieved, whether there will be a pure self, however, cannot yet be regarded as settled. For this reason, Schelling conceives of his positive philosophy as "a proof, self-strengthening with every step, of the actually existing God."[49] The historical concept of being here is thus a handy diagnostic tool for grasping history as revelation. Yet, as long as this history goes on, "the realm of actuality is not yet closed, but is rather one which constantly moves toward its completion," such that "the proof is *never* [!] complete and thus this science remains only philo-sophy."[50]

The historical concept of being is thus the *conditio sine qua non* of a philosophy of hope, which for Schelling is the crucial difference between positive philosophy and classical onto-theology: for positive philosophy, hope lies in (its emphasis on) a future which is to take place *within* being itself, that is, a future which is to be thought of as history, not as eternity. On the basis of the logical concept of being, however, history can at best be grasped as a caricature of "eternal being (ἀεὶ ὄν),"[51] as the tradition of Platonism has made plain. Unlike this tradition, Schelling thinks *being as time*: with this move he comes into direct contact with Heidegger.

2. The Event

Famously, Heidegger had himself studied Schelling's *Freedom Essay* in great detail, finding in Schelling a properly congenial thinker.[52] Yet the proximity of Heidegger's late thought and the late Schelling has been insufficiently exposed: despite Schelling's (ostensibly) onto-theological vocabulary (the talk of revelation, of God, eternity, etc.), his late work is far more Heideggerian than Heidegger himself would have expected. For, as we have seen, Schelling limits onto-theology in the classical sense to the logical concept of being, and thus to negative philosophy, which he takes to have been given its most direct formulation in Aristotle's concept of God.[53] In contradistinction, positive philosophy thinks being as the historical transformation from being to self, which cannot be anticipated by thinking, because it is structurally not a possible thought, for all possible thought comes after this event. Thinking is thus on a structural level referred to its own historicity: upon having this self-referential, historicizing insight, thinking cannot overcome or outstrip the fact of its historicity. For even the insight into the historicity of thought is itself a historically conditioned thought.

The presupposition of classical onto-theology is in fact its concept of being. The identification of God and being is ultimately grounded in the eternal character of the ὄv. God, as the principle of everything, is identified with the eternal origin of everything that exists, which has sometimes been called the One or sometimes being itself. Classical metaphysics is certainly ontology, in that it poses the question of essential being, or οὐσία, that is, the question of what, as essential being, lies at the ground of all changing phenomena, that which above all affords all beings their being. Classical metaphysics thus climbs out above all that exists in order to grasp that in which the total organization of reality is grounded, that is, what the one true being (οὐσία, ὄντως ὄν) is. Thus, as its essential orienting principle, metaphysics assumes that "being lets itself be found in beings—and in such a way that thinking goes beyond beings."[54] Metaphysical transcendence in this way determines what the being of beings is, in that it recognizes that being-ness (οὐσία) essentially is the being of beings. God is understood in this context as a name for the original ground of all beings. Therefore, metaphysics since Plato and Aristotle has been understood *expressis verbis* as theology, as θεολογία[55] or θεολογική,[56] which one should understand as the name for any and all theories which lay claim to the highest principle or original ground of all reality.

Going back to Greek philosophy, the traditional metaphysical talk of God is always fundamentally onto-theological in that in all cases God and being are identified such that beings are to be thought as relative to or derivative from this substratal God-being. Metaphysics exceeds what is, that is, the world of phenomena, drawing a distinction between essential being and the here-below. The essential being (say, of God) distinguished from all beings is in no way changeable or historical. Rather, it is conceived as the a priori immutable and eternal, that which grants being and form (εἶδος) to all changeable entities. In this sense, Aristotle speaks of essential being (εἶδος) as "cause of being (αἴτιον τοῦ εἶναι)."[57] Essential being is determined ultimately as comprehensive, inasmuch as it is what gives recognizable shape and structure to the evanescent beings of the phenomenal realm, given that this realm is in itself devoid of and awaiting said form and structure. Classical metaphysics therefore sets in opposition "eternal being" (ἀεὶ ὄν) and the "eternally becoming" (ἀεὶ γιγνόμενον).[58]

It is precisely in this opposition that Heidegger recognizes the blind spot of metaphysics. By going beyond the manifoldness of beings to the origin in which they are ultimately unified, metaphysics always already opposes being and beings: however, metaphysics presupposes this ontological difference without reflecting on this fact or reflecting on how this fact emerged. The ontological difference must be taken as given and must fall into the background and out of view such that metaphysics can take place. This corresponds to the identification of Being's time as eternity. Being therefore appears as timeless givenness (and in this sense, paradoxically, as an existing thing). Only at the end of a long history of metaphysics can Heidegger see retrospectively that the being of beings has been determined differently in each historical case: idealistically as the spiritually imbued, interconnected totality; materialistically as the spatiotemporally extended system of particles; as class struggle or will to power, and so forth. From this vantage, Heidegger concludes that the history of metaphysics is to be understood as the history of being. The history of being appears as the history of the prevailing concepts of being, which can be seen most clearly in those texts of the metaphysical tradition in which being itself is the concept in question: this is why Heidegger's late archaeology of the history of being takes place as a confrontation with the tradition. Thus Heidegger's effort should not be understood as some kind of classicism, and his voice should not be heard to speak with nostalgia for some truer past; on the contrary, Heidegger reconstructs the genealogy of a certain concept of being, which, in a variety of forms since antiquity, behaves *as if* it were an ahistorical representation of pure facts. Clearly, Heidegger's goal in all this is to develop a critical instrument to be used against ideology in general and the technical-technological concept of being in particular.

Being is therefore historical, because it is what is given to knowledge in the sequence of concepts of being, that is, as that which cannot be brought under any *single* concept. Heidegger determines the new grounding question of the historical thinking of being as the question: "how does being essence [*wesen*]?"[59] Asking after "being" with this new question (which only appears similar to the classic ontological question), Heidegger addresses ontological difference as such, to show through a reading of the tradition that the ontological difference itself shifts and transforms and is thus itself

articulated as history. Insofar as this history is a history of the concepts of
being and insofar as the concepts of being belong to our particular understanding of being, the history of being can be brought in view as being at
the same time the history of our self-understanding. For being does not
take place outside of self-understanding. It simply is not the eternal, originary ground of all beings. He who conceives "being" in this latter sense
is committed ipso facto to a *determinate* concept of being, and thus misses
the historicity of "being"; Heidegger insists that to proceed in this way is to
grasp nothing about being.

For him, being is therefore to be grasped through what can be characterized as its "finitude and uniqueness,"[60] for being is always supervenient
on our understanding of being and thus on *Dasein* in Heidegger's technical sense. Yet, *Dasein* is in turn dependent on being, for it understands
the being of beings differently in each of its historical figurations. *Dasein*
is as such caught up in a historical interpretation of the being of beings,
or, more drastically expressed: *Dasein* is *thrown*. This "thrownness" means
nothing more than this: *Dasein* is subordinated to a certain economy
of meaning or sense, which conceives of being in a certain way. Given
that *Dasein* does not exist independent of this thrownness, and given
that *Dasein's* self-understanding (on which the determination of being is
dependent) takes place only through thrownness, being and *Dasein* are
inextricably linked.

The self is in this way subordinated to the world, although the world, and
thus the whole, does not exist without *Dasein's* conceptual effort. *Dasein's*
foreconceiving of the world, what Heidegger calls "transcendence," determines the being-there of the world as such, and thus determines what
can happen in this world. The self is thus paradoxically subordinate to
an economy of sense that, though of its own making, is experienced as
imposed on it by how the being of beings appears in each of its historical
shapes.[61] As a result, the being of beings appears to the self first and foremost in the light of a *determinate* concept of being, so that being appears
to it as given or as the world, that is, as that into which the self has been
thrown for no reason whatsoever and which she must take as given. The
history of being can thus also be read as the history of the world. There is
no such stable and well-defined entity as the world. The world as the all-
encompassing field of sense is only manifest in sense making. Contrary to
ordinary things, it does not exist independently of sense making. The way
sense is made changes and the concept of the world covaries with the way
sense is made. The history of Being is therefore world history in the literal
sense of a history of the world.

Given that the being of beings has been interpreted differently in each case of its historical guises, what Heidegger intends to show in his various sketches of an archaeology of the history of being is that "being" itself cannot be determined and distinguished from the historical process of the determination and displacement of the senses of being. "Being" is rather the variable taking place of the difference between being and beings. Since this would not be possible without *Dasein* qua self-understanding, which sunders being and beings through its transcendence, being and self belong together in *the event of being*.

"Event" has therefore at least two meanings or two moments. *First*, it refers to a process, the *taking place* of difference, in line with the typical meaning of the expression "event." *Secondly*, it refers to a "selfing" [*Verselbstung*], which is evident in the German word for event, "Ereignis," which can be parsed as "Er-Eignis" or "en-owning," as the standard translation has it, in which being and self come to be and belong together. The event is therefore nothing but the coming together of being and self: this is what we can refer to with Schelling as personality. Personality is the coming together of being and self, a self's confrontation with its own facticity and the ensuing contingency of its self-conception. Being comes to itself or owns itself in our own personal sense of being, that is, our self-understanding personality. Heidegger never tires of inculcating his readers with this second aspect. *Dasein* is ultimately

the turning point in the turning of enowning [*Ereignisses*], the self-opening midpoint of the mirroring of call and belongingness, the ownhood or "*own-dom*" [*Eigentum*], understood as the king-dom, the mastering midpoint of en-ownment [*Er-eignung*] as the belonging-together to the event [*Ereignis*] and to Dasein at the same time: becoming-self.[62]

Dasein and Being therefore belong together in the process of self-becoming, of becoming oneself where self is not reducible to the subject or the I as a synthetic function in judgments. Heidegger conceives of the transcendence of *Dasein* as groundless freedom because it makes grounds or reasons possible in the first place. This transcendence belongs to the event itself, because the event is the groundless deferral of sense making. The event does not take place like an ordinary event in the objective world (that is within an already established order), but rather occurs such that it changes the very setting within which entities appear and ordinary events occur. The event does not simply take place, but is rather eventuated in the language of *Dasein*, which, as Heidegger's oft-quoted dictum tells us, is "the house of being."[63]

In addition to these two aspects of the event, what one might call the "historical" and the "reflexive" aspects, Heidegger draws another, original meaning from the etymological sense of event. "Ereignis" in German originally is "Eräugnis," the passing in front of one's eyes, "Augen," what Heidegger in his lecture "The Turning" renders as the "insight into that which is."[64] Again, this insight (*Einblick*) should be understood as an "Einblitz," that is, as the explosive suddenness or the "in-flashing" of the "clearing" in which we are positioned because we are selves constantly coming into being. According to Heidegger, *Dasein* is ultimately "the *open place*,"[65] in that it brings measure and self-understanding to the scene of the taking place of the difference between being and beings.

Truth-apt thought is possible by virtue of standing at a constitutive distance from beings; it presupposes the clearing of an epistemically accessible world. What takes place for *Dasein* appears to it always only in the horizon of its world, that is, against the background of a determinate interpretation of being that in turn determines what can be understood as a possible or actual being in this world. *Dasein* thus subordinates itself in every case of its being to a determinate norm of truth, by which thought and action are oriented.

This norm of truth is just as historical as the meaning of being. Therefore Heidegger does not uncritically return to Parmenides, as is too often incorrectly assumed, conceiving truth as ἀ-λήθεια in the sense of unconcealment, and thus in the sense of a nonrepresentational self-transparency. Heidegger is not so naïve as to interpret being as eternity in the sense of a metaphysics of presence, that is, as pure ἔστιν. On the contrary, Heidegger insists on the historicity and, in this sense, the finitude of being itself, since only in the taking place of differentiation is the ontological difference shown. In other words, ontological difference takes place only as the taking place of differentiation in our self-understandings.

In this way Heidegger transforms the very question of metaphysics, as he himself points out. Across the *Contributions* and in other texts from the same period, Heidegger distinguishes his own questions—what he calls "*grounding-questions*"[66]—from the "guiding-question"[67] of metaphysics. While the recurrent guiding-question asks after the relation of "being and thought," grounding-questions ask after the problem of "being and time,"[68] what could also be called the relation of being and self, or personality.

The entire Western tradition and conception of Being, and accordingly the fundamental relation to Being that is still dominant today, is summed up in the title *Being and thinking*. But *Being and time* is a title that can in no way be coordinated with the divisions we have discussed. It points to a completely different domain of questioning.[69]

Parmenides had already discovered a nonrepresentational sense of being. Thus he famously understood the belonging together of being and thought in the sense of νοεῖν, in that the pure transparency of thinking belongs to being itself. Being and thinking are therefore equally eternal, immutable. Heidegger, however, thinks being from time, asking after the history of metaphysics as a history of the concepts of being. This question therefore breaks with the classical conception of onto-theology, according to which being itself, like God, is displaced from the realm of becoming and is thus presented as pure self-equality and self-identity, which in this tradition is given the name of God translated as *"ego sum qui sum."* For Heidegger, by contrast, neither being nor thought are conceived as eternal occurrences; rather, in a central move of his destruction of the foundations of classical ontology, both being and thought are located *within Dasein*, the self in time or personality, a move Heidegger had worked on since *Being and Time*.

3. The Personal Concept of Being

Schelling and Heidegger thus both develop *a historical concept of being* that is to be understood through its difference from *the logical concept of being*. Both break with the tradition of thinking "being" as the determinacy of judgment. For Schelling, the logical concept of being is restricted to the purview of negative philosophy. For Heidegger, the analysis of the *apophantic as* leads to a hermeneutics of facticity and the discovery of the *hermeneutic as* (aspect-seeing from the vantage of personality), which pierces through and breaks out of the logical concept of being; Heidegger makes this plain in his reading of Aristotle in particular. In a properly Schellingian move, Heidegger asserts that the historical concept of being is a presupposition of the logical concept of being, so that understanding in the sense of orientation is given priority over objective knowledge.

Our interpersonal understanding and orientation is indeed always already before and beyond any secured knowledge. Personalities are always closer to us than things: thus the asymmetry assumed as the first premise of the problem of other minds is reversed. In order to show that the possibility of a personal sense of being follows from the original primacy of the person, the limited logical concept of being must be displaced. In this effort, Schelling and Heidegger both turn to the concept of "ground" or "reason," pointing out its "abyss [*Abgrund*]." This "abyss" is for Schelling "unprethinkable being," while for Heidegger it is "being" in the sense of the "event." The network of inferential relations established in the game of giving and asking for reasons is itself groundless, there is no halting point, reference to which could prove that the game is more than the ideology of the powerful. As a matter of fact, what can "authority" in this game mean if not "power"? Reasons in the sense of the backbone of decisions to judge that *p* (rather than *q*, *r*, *s* . . .) are ultimately groundless, they refer us to personality, to groundless agents who see the world and their position in it in a particular way. Of course, this ontological situation seems to justify a blind adherence to given power structures. Philosophy seems to deprive itself of its critical edge. However, quite the contrary is the case! Pointing out the contingency of all particular orders within logical space due to logical space's constitutive contingency opens up the space for an ontological future, the event, or the absolute self (as Schelling has it).

Schelling and Heidegger are well aware that transcendence, that is, an excess over the given ontological structure, is difficult to achieve. For how are we to decide that their contributions to philosophy are more than but another power claim disguised as critique? What guides them is contingency as part of the mythology of modernity. The very mythology of modernity is committed to reason as the glue, which is to hold communities together. Yet its apotheosis of reason represses the genealogy of reason not only in order to cover up the irrational and violent origins of modern rationality, but also in order to make it look necessary despite its contingent history. Rationality could not have taken place and it could cease to be, it is inherently threatened by the way it came to be. Therefore, we have to face the truth of contingency in order to create an opposition to ideology's efforts to naturalize the contingent and thereby to deprive us of our freedom of groundless decision. In this context, it is remarkable how TV shows like *Mad Men* celebrate the threat of a return to the ideology of the 1950s. It looks as if we are moving towards a naturalization of the current state of affairs, to an "atonic universe" in Badiou's sense.[70] Against this, it is sufficient to point out that the event constantly takes place as that which withdraws in all structures.

Contrary to Badiou, though, we should not postulate a Platonic, heroic ideal of destruction of the order in order to create points of decision. The event is not some extraordinary event as the *Commune de Paris* (to pick up Badiou's favorite example), because our transcendence, that is, our reaching out to the whole, belongs to being itself. Schelling expresses this thought by asserting that being comes to itself in the self-understanding of positive philosophy, opening itself to the hope of a final transformation of being to self. Heidegger again thinks being as "becoming-self"[71] or as becoming oneself, that is, as the event and thus also as the unity of being and self, which is understood only in the being- and self-understanding of *Dasein*.

For Schelling and Heidegger, being and self constitutively belong together: with this insight both rightly attempt to combat the alienation of epistemological reflection, which presents mind and world as ontologically different and differentiated, opening up at the heart of epistemological theory a gap that is impossible to bridge. For as soon as the world is conceived as a given and necessarily spiritless and thoughtless whole of particles organized according to natural laws, a world in which man is no doubt even less than a stranger, the grip of the "historical" as well as the "personal" sense of being (along with hermeneutics, which asserts that being and language are inextricably interwoven) disappears. Today, the reduction of the meaning of being to a cheap materialistic explanation is unquestionably widespread: our understanding is to be reduced to given material conditions, conditions whose history and whose coming to be are not often well understood. If we want to think about this reductive tendency critically, that is, if we want to reflect on the conditions and history of this widespread theoretical tendency, we must put ourselves in a position from which we can see a history that does not unreflectively assume the truth of reductive naturalism and ontological homelessness. This will require a sustained and repeated reflection on the predominate metaphysical predispositions of our time, what Heidegger in "The Age of the World-Picture" described as "reflection" (what has otherwise been translated into English as "mindfulness") and conceptualized as follows: "reflection is the courage to put up for question the truth of one's own presuppositions and the space of one's own goals."[72]

II Belated Necessity: God, Man, and Judgment in Schelling's Late Philosophy

Thus far from man and his endeavors making the world comprehensible, it is man himself that is the most incomprehensible and who inexorably drives me to the belief in the wretchedness of all being, a belief that makes itself known in so many bitter pronouncements from both ancient and recent times. It is precisely Him, the human, who drives me to the final desperate question: Why is there anything at all? Why is there not nothing?—[73]

Why there is anything at all and not rather nothing? As we have already seen, one must understand Heidegger's famous and oft-quoted determination of the fundamental question of metaphysics with Schelling as a question about *determinacy*.[74] What comes into question here, then, is the determinacy of something *überhaupt*: so, in asking why anything whatsoever *is*, the question asks why something is *determinate*. Schelling spells this question out as a theory of determination, a theory that poses the problem of how determinacy altogether is logically-ontologically possible. Schelling's solution to this problem is his theory of the potencies, which he reconstructs in his theory of predication. He describes the potencies *expressis verbis* as "the originary subject," "the originary predicate," and "the originary synthesis of subject and predicate,"[75] and founds his theory of predication on his analysis of the dynamic of these originary potencies.

Schelling's reflection ultimately leads to the following conclusion: it is man who judges and not the merely abstract structure of the logical I or the Hegelian concept. What comes into question then in the fundamental metaphysical question can be understood as the question of how it has come to pass that we have gotten caught up in a predicative ambience, in which one thing can be distinguished from another; the subject of this question is indeed the subject as *the human person*. There exists by Schelling's lights an essential connection between determinacy, that is, intelligibility, and God: for the late Schelling, man, God, and judgment cannot be negotiated as elements separate from one another, but must be thought together.

For Schelling it is crucial to note that "God" refers to nothing more or less than the incessant and polymorphous becoming of intelligibility. God is sense, the almost trivial fact that the ways we access the world (our sense-making practices, which generate fields of sense) belong to the world itself and cannot be empty projections onto a meaningless domain of geometrico-physical extension.[76] For this reason, it is a mistake to construe ontology along the lines of the existential quantifier, for any such ontology winds up with a merely referential, senseless set of entities defined by our ontological commitments. Thus, when Schelling talks about God as a person, he is far from defending any kind of ontic, pseudoscientific nonsense, such as contemporary North American moronic creationism. "God" and "creation" are names that Schelling assigns to ontological structures that are not in our hands: Schelling uses a quasi-theological register in order to refer to a constitutive thrownness, to the essential heteronomy of autonomy, which consists in the historical facticity of autonomy. Beings, who consider themselves modern autonomous persons, have not chosen the worldview in which this choice is possible. In this respect, autonomy is contingent upon a process, which is not yet autonomous. "God" in Schelling is the name for a process we as persons depend upon in the sense that a person's reaching out to the whole can only ever be understood in terms of a "person seeking person."[77]

It is with this thought in mind that I seek in what follows to formulate the relation of man and God in Schelling's late philosophy. The fact that I begin again with Schelling's predication-theoretical reflections is crucial, because I am convinced that therein lies the key to Schelling's entire late philosophy. This holds true in particular for understanding the significance of the relationship between creation and predication: God, in order to be God, depends on *our* predication of him *as* God. For the late Schelling, man and God reciprocally determine one another. On the one hand, God as creator, as the "lord of being" comes to be as God only through man. *Without the will of the human being there would be no God.* However, this structure should not be misunderstood as a kind of incipient pronouncement of the Feuerbachian projection thesis. For Schelling, it is rather the case that in order to think the autonomy of self-positing, subjectivity as such must be compatible with an originary theonomy; Walter Schulz's idea of "mediated self-mediation"[78] comes to mind here. Unlike so many other philosophers, Schelling insists that this figure of a mediated self-mediation does not entail the total self-empowerment of reason and the total elimination of the thought and significance of creation. To wit, this connection of God and man is for Schelling a critical tool for motivating the self-restraint of idealistic reason, that is, Schelling reconstructs the relation of autonomy and theonomy with an eye to articulating the critical self-limitation of autonomous reason.

I will proceed in three steps. First I will investigate the relation between *judgment and being*. Here I present the thesis that Schelling is a thinker of *an evolutionary account of logical space*: his account begins with unprethinkable being as the abyssal domain of distinction and from there opens onto a future overcoming of necessity. This overcoming of necessity consists in the insight that all necessity is belatedly established and is thus supervenient on a moment of radical and contingent freedom. In the second section I will investigate the thesis that *judgment and existence* are absolutely, inextricably linked in the *réalité humaine*. Cosmogony, that is, the very production of order as such, is for Schelling ultimately a matter of anthropogony: this event is repeated in every single judgment. Finally, in my third section, I will articulate the relation of *God and man* and spell out how this relation has massive consequences for Schelling's concept of an eschatological future.

1. Judgment and Being

Something can become established as something determinate only by becoming distinguishable from all other things that it is not. Determination and difference are thus intractably linked. All determination is an act of differentiation, in which something as something is established and set apart from all other things. When we claim that a given x is F, we claim that it is distinguishable from everything else by its predicates, and thereby we at least implicitly bring into play both the set of all non-x in our application of the predicate F to x and the set of all other predicates that might apply to x. Schelling expresses this thought thusly: when we claim that x is F and, say, not G, through this operation we let G shine through, ἐμφαίνεσθαι. F renders G visible—ἐμφαίνειν—when it is *claimed* that x is F.[79]

He who claims that x is F and not G, claims, as Schelling has it, that x *could have been* G, but has instead turned out to be F. Hence, a simply, merely categorical judgment is not the same as an "empty tautology." A noninformative claim would not be a claim at all, would be nothing we could understand. Frege thus stands in unintentional proximity to Schelling when he writes:

> It is only in virtue of the possibility of something not being wise that it makes sense to say "Solon is wise." The content of a concept diminishes as its extension increases; if its extension becomes all-embracing, its content must vanish altogether.[80]

Every rule of use establishes a predicate and thus a domain of objects, in which something is F, something else is G, H, or whatever else. Being without otherness would remain, therefore, utterly indeterminate, that is, if there were a being without another being there would be nothing there on which, in distinction from something else, the existential quantifier could get a grip.

Our predicative being-in-the-world is such that in every moment of our conscious lives we are confronted with fully new configurations that we evaluate and handle by way of distributing a range of predicates: $F(x)$, $G(y)$, and so forth. Presently I sit in front of my laptop, editing my manuscript on a beautiful Sunday morning. I register all of this such that my consciousness, which could also be otherwise, that is, "somewhere else" as we say, or up to something else, can become directed today towards editing this text about God and man. The fact that $F(x)$, $G(y)$, and so on, is in this sense *contingent*: I am able to understand the "possibility of another being"[81] when I *claim* that $F(x)$. Whatever is the determinate case *as* something, could always be otherwise. This contingency is at least epistemic, because we can confuse almost everything with almost everything else. Whether everything is also metaphysically contingent is another question, which for the time being does not interest us in our analysis of our predicative being-in-the-world. For metaphysical contingency itself would need to be *claimed* in some way or another and thus both differentiated from epistemic necessity and set apart from other claims. Insofar as metaphysical contingency would be asserted in a judgment and predicated in some way, it would itself be an *F* that lets some *G* shine through. The claim of metaphysical contingency would also let its opposite shine through, if it is different from other claims, if it is in fact a genuine claim. Given that our access to existence is mediated through predicative determinations, reality is thus only available to us in judgment and therefore only ever in the medium of contingency.

For Schelling, judgment and the logical concept of being cannot be separated, for it is in *judgment* that *we claim* that *x* is *F*. We do not claim that *x seems to be F* or that we represent *x as if* it were *F* (save in solipsistic scenarios, in which the world is only our representation). When we claim that *x* is *F*, we set ourselves in relation with *x* (and not with our representation of *x*), such that *x* should befit the quality of properly being *F*. The determinate being of things reveals at every moment the "possibility of another being." Against this predication-theoretical background it is clear why Schelling takes this possibility as equivalent to difference as such, as accounting for the first difference that makes a difference, that is, the difference between what he calls "unprethinkable being" and everything else.

Unprethinkable being is the "starting point" that exists "before all thinking."[82] Unprethinkable being is unprethinkable in the sense that it is precisely that which we cannot not think, that which is at play in all thought but about which no grounded or groundable thought can be presupposed as possible. Unprethinkable being is thus only the name for the very structure of presupposition of all determinations, and not some transcendent **je ne sais quoi**.

> Anything that enters the world and becomes actualized for and in the world needs a presupposition, a beginning, which is not what is true or what ought-to-be. But it is not instantly recognized as such. In order to be firmly rooted, this beginning has to consider itself as being for its own sake. Therefore, a higher potency is needed to liberate the development from its presupposition.[83]

When we determine *x* as *F* we automatically place *x* as the subject (ὑποκείμενον) of a judgment. In any judgment we place a to be determined subject before us from which we want to "depart" "in order to arrive at the idea," as Schelling puts it.[84] In order for us to stand in relation to an object, in order to refer to anything at all, we must place it in a field of sense, that is, we must define it as something. Before this judgment of the object comes to pass, we deal only with some x that is given to us and that retreats as soon as we determine it as J or G or K, and so forth. Schelling expresses this in a scholastic manner by asserting that every x is or actually was an *Actus*, while he refers to J, G, K, and other possible determinations of x as *potency*.[85]

> So evidently, this still unglimpsed "what," this x of unprethinkable being remains a mere "what," for it only ever appears as the antecedent or *a priori* of some being. But nothing prevents that even this unprethinkable being, that which is antecedent to beings, becomes that which it is able to be afterwards or *post actum* (as one should actually say).[86]

For Schelling, it is crucial to heed the fact that nothing can be, without thereby revealing the anterior or at least concomitant order of potentiality, that if x is F, then G and so on shine through. However, the motivation for the transition from being to potentiality, which Schelling describes as the transition from unprethinkable being to the Idea, cannot be understood simply by way of an analysis of the concept of x. For nothing follows from x, it exhibits no qualities, consequences, or reasons, so long as it is not determined. Without being bound by F, G, and so on, x would not even be the subject of a judgment, that is, it would not be an object in the Fregean sense. For objects as such are first made available only once a predicative setting has been established, in which concepts and objects can be distinguished. For this ontological reason, our relationship to objects is *constitutively fallible*. Objects and concepts do not simply stand in relation, but rather must be brought in relation: to wit, any conceptually established link between a concept and an object in no way guarantees a necessary relation to a particular nonconceptual thing.

Because the transition from unprethinkable being to any predicative setting in which our intentional relation to objects takes place cannot be accounted for from within the predicative setting, a "non-excludable contingency is unassailably constituted in precisely this unprethinkable being."[87]

Schelling's reasoning for this is again easy to follow: all judgments reveal a paradoxical structure of presupposition that we cannot in principle get control over through predication. That is, the taking place of judgments reveals a pure dimension of distinction, which is nothing determinate in its own right. It is that which always already is necessarily presupposed as being-there as soon as something as something has been set in place. Therefore any act of determining generates an area of latency, which is logical space itself, in which nothing definite, nothing determined as *F*, *G*, or *H* has yet been marked. Unprethinkable being qua presupposition of thought cannot be thought: yet, once we attempt to think it, it is determined as withdrawal. As a presupposition of understanding determinacy, unprethinkable being turns out to be at the very least epistemically necessary. But it is also metaphysically necessary, because every single thing that exists is distinguished from everything else it is not. Otherwise, something could take place that could, potentially, not be itself. This condition cannot be satisfied by unprethinkable being that is thus paradoxically "unequal to itself."[88] For this reason, "unprethinkable being" is not a proper concept, because everything determinate that takes place, that is, everything that can be conceptualized in any manner whatsoever, must at least be itself, not anything else. Self-identity presupposes negation and therefore relationality. *Relation and difference determine existence.*

However—and here is the crucial move—this ontological axiom does not apply to unprethinkable being itself, to the unknown *x*. The ontological presupposition of determinacy is not itself subject to determinacy, but rather can only be brought under any determinate criteriology belatedly. There could not have been a determinate reason for the taking place of determinacy: the reason for reason(s) as such can only be proffered.

Judgment and being, just as the epistemic and metaphysical necessity of unprethinkable being, can only be differentiated retroactively. For even if we want to distinguish between its metaphysical and its epistemological necessity, its metaphysical necessity would be determinate over against its epistemological necessity. An epistemically relevant difference, which cannot be external relative to the things being differentiated, is always already at play. Unprethinkable being is thus logical-ontological, which means: epistemically *and* metaphysically necessary. It can neither not be, nor not be thought. And yet, and this is Schelling's decisive point, it is contingent. For, it is presupposed for all determinate thought, that is, the set of all assertorical judgments *F(x)*, *G(y)*, and so forth. It is, however, only first established *as* a presupposition when a predicative ambience has been constituted.

For the very reason that the potency [possibility, M.G.] did not precede the unprethinkable being, it could not be *overcome* in the act of this unprethinkable existing. But thereby an ineliminable contingency is posited in this very unprethinkable existing.[89]

We cannot discuss *x* in any manner without establishing a predicative ambience. That is, before the establishment of a predicative ambience relation as such does not take place: *x* is on this side, as it were, of the unfolding of the modalities. At point zero of determination, nothing can be ruled out, because rules are not yet there. To rule something out presupposes a grip on something determinate, but there is no traction in the area of latency. Before something comes to be, *x* is what it is "without choice,"[90] that is, it cannot decide for or against its coming to presence in predication, which Schelling refers to as "potentialization."[91] The mere being-there of a dimension of distinction as such still has no relationship to a differentiation in judgments and is therefore indeed a necessary presupposition: *yet* it is only a contingently necessary presupposition. It is a necessary *pre*supposition; however, it is so only "post actum" or "a posteriori,"[92] as Schelling says, that is, only as a presup*position*.

Positing, that is, determination, takes place only within a predicative ambience. The necessity of the presupposition is, therefore, only determinate in contradistinction to the contingency of our positing and therefore supervenient on contingency, or resultant of an accident. In other words: *necessity is belated* and is, for this reason, contingent. Further, in the presupposition as such no reasons can be found, for it is from this very contingent ground that reasons as such come to be. Thus the reasons for the original decision or presupposition only come to be retrospectively, only after "I have decided between +a and –a [can it be said that] my 'being +a' is not resultant of a mere, blind whim, which would always and necessarily require thinking its contingency. Now it is not seen as a contingency because it is an intention, something willed."[93]

Unprethinkable being makes it such that the potency can "*possibly* appear in the first place."[94] The reason for this is that unprethinkable being cannot in advance rule out any consequences whatsoever, which opens up the "possibility of another being." This is, of course, merely possible, that is, it can happen or not. However, it does indeed come to pass and is repeated in every single judgment. Thus, the process of potentialization is incessantly repeated: unprethinkable being is transformed into idea in every judgment and in every determinate act in which something is differentiated from something else. Our predicative being-in-the-world is the potentialization of our presuppositions, or in other words: *determination is repression.*

This logico-ontological structure of repression lies also behind Schelling's groundbreaking thesis: "will is primal being [*Urseyn ist Wollen*]."[95] Schelling's thought here is this: the transition from *x* to *F(x)* has the peculiar double aspect of having established determinacy and yet lying outside of determinacy. For this reason the transition must be *willed*: the transition is resultant of an act of decision that leads to the very idea of a distinction. Insofar as beings are determinate, all such determinations and therefore all beings must be willed, for otherwise the very dimension of sense would never have become established. This fact lets itself be stated *belatedly*, but not conceptually anticipated. Thus, our thinking comes after an unprethinkable being and not before. Likewise, unprethinkable being *as* such comes to us only as that which is posited also only as *x*, as possible subject of a judgment. That unknown *x* is then also a belated *x*—an object variable that can be determined in possible judgments.[96]

2. Judgment and Existence

In its self-relation, the human being surely always encounters existence as that which has not been set in place through its own self-relation. The human always comports itself towards something which it has not posited. When man comports himself thusly, he comports himself to his own unprethinkable being, that behind or before which no thinking can grasp anything in order to justify thought. In this self-relation we can see the dynamic by which the freedom of self-consciousness is constituted and in terms of which this freedom should be understood. The freedom of self-determination has to "go beyond"[97] the actus of an unadorned *that*. All consciousness of something is thus always in a certain respect free, insofar as this consciousness is differentiated from its object and must comport itself to this object. The self, which is in this way determinate, is therefore an act of freedom: however, paradoxically, only through this comportment, which is a restriction of freedom, is the self possible. The paradox is this: freedom lies only in transcendence, yet without something given, transcendence would have nothing to go beyond. Human freedom is in this sense necessarily finite, for if it did not have a limit, which it could exceed and to which it comports itself, it could not possibly be. Without the presupposition of unprethinkable being we could not go beyond anything and our freedom would thus be null. Nevertheless, we are not bound to this necessity, for we only belatedly posit it and do so always already according to the dynamic of potentialization we have sketched above. This thought is the existential(ist) purchase of Schelling's theory of the potencies.

His theory of the potencies reveals a repressed contingency in every aspect of our lives. Insofar as man decides to be himself, and thus undertakes an existential project, he must constantly negate the actualization of other possibilities, with which he is thereby ipso facto confronted. Insofar as we are able to decide, a range of options must first of all present themselves as possibilities *as* such, that is, as possible ways for a self to be, if this self's mode of existence consists in the decision to be itself. Finite freedom, that is, the human, whose existential projects go beyond all that is given, only becomes itself relative to and over against the given and orients itself to the whole it anticipates. It cannot exist without the possibility of another being, nor can it exist without unprethinkable being itself, which only takes place *as* unprethinkable being, that is, as the indeterminate x anterior to all determination, if it is possible that F or G or H, and so forth.

The finite self is therefore an instantiation of being. Just as being turns out to be only Idea in the mode of possibility, that is, that its starting point does not exclude its coming to be presented in the mode of the idea, likewise our existence cannot at any moment exclude the fact that it could be another possibility, that our life could take another form than that which is presently accepted. Being a person is the constant negotiation of and confrontation with other forms of life. Who we are depends on who we *want* to be, which itself is always being negotiated: we determine our position in the whole of the world and in our self-relation, a self-determination, which cannot be imposed on us from outside. The project-like character of human existence is therefore not an ontological impossibility, but is rather grounded in the fact that, as an effect of the comportmental structure of its intentionality, the human brings a project to the whole. This is how Schelling translates the Judeo-Christian thesis of an *imago dei* into a philosophical language.

Schelling expresses this thought also with reference to the Aristotiean primacy of ἐνέργεια over δύναμις, by highlighting that the potencies are not established in any *actus purus*, but also cannot be denied a priori. Through this unprethinkable being makes "it *possible* in the first place for potency to appear."[98] In order for freedom to exist, pure actuality and ungroundable facticity must potentialize themselves, must be transformed into the material of freedom. "Contingently necessary existence"[99] must therefore be able to be thought such that it can enter into self-relation, such that it can be made a "necessarily necessary existence" (SW, XIV, 339), which can only ever belatedly take place. As we have seen, the necessary being-there of unprethinkable being in no way eliminates its own contingency (for example, it cannot be conceptually eliminated), as it does not consist in any way whatsoever in a relation with other things. Necessary existence, that is, the ground of the whole, cannot be related to anything contingent, because it is pure necessity. In this way, then, it should not be understood as excluding contingency, for this relation would render pure necessity *a* possibility among others and so only contingently necessary. The existence of the actually contingent and differentiated world in which we live is proof enough that the necessity of unprethinkable being is only contingently necessary. This is, however, one world, that in which *we* live and that *we* must decide on, since there are no judgments without willing, without desire. The contingency of the idea in view of unprethinkable being testifies to the possibility of unprethinkable being coming to mediate itself, coming into self-relation. Its necessity therefore also does not exclude that it can belatedly be seen as the origin of a contingency. The original necessity itself is therefore a matter of contingency: indeed, it is by way of an "*ur*-contingency"[100] that we stand at a distance from something and that we are able to determine something as something.

Unprethinkable being, when brought to language and thus eo ipso gone beyond, is of course not God or the absolute in some glorious sense. At best it could be said to be the absolute in the literal sense of that which is "unrelated." Further, unprethinkable being is not some *causa sui* or absolute I in an idealistic sense. It is itself nothing, and even this is incorrect: it is nothing that could be said to be identical to itself; thus it is not even nothing. Rather it is an unmarked and unmarkable state before all difference, a being that manifests itself in the world as the world's always-already. Once we find ourselves in the world, the world is always already there. Yet, what is always already there is not so much the differentiated world, because we trivially change the world through our thoughts and actions. What is always already there is rather unprethinkable being, the uncanny real, which precedes the imaginary and symbolic structure we bring into being. Unprethinkable being is, like the Lacanian real, not an entity or a set of extant entities, as the most naïve ontology of things has it, but rather that which cannot be gone beyond under the current conditions. It is experienced as a limit in manifold ways, for it is not even identical with itself. There is no such thing as the singular, individuated real, which manifests itself in one particular shape, but an endless variety of withdrawals related to the manifold ways we relate to what there is.

The *actuality* of the world, that is, the predicative ambience that we at each moment determine as such-and-such cannot be seen a priori as the necessary starting point, for nothing as such follows from the actuality of the world, not even the thought of actuality as the necessary starting point. The possibility of the world as well as the presupposition-structure I am trying to make explicit is ultimately only graspable *post festum*, through our actuality. For Schelling, the importance of encountering the truly unthinkable cannot be overestimated, for to come closer to such a delicate speculative thought brings us in a definitive measure closer to the human, to ourselves.

> One must at times imagine such a being, i.e. in the case of productions, deeds, actions, whose possibility is conceivable only through their actuality. No one would call original what comes into existence according to a preexisting concept. An original is: that, the possibility of which one only grants after having its actuality in view.[101]

The possibility of any determinate arrangement of things, elements, or states of affairs, and in this sense the possibility of the world, cannot be anticipated a priori, before it has become actual. Any world is in this sense an original, something that has an origin (*origo*) to which it refers and which does not stand in any necessary relation to it. Otherwise the world's actuality would follow from its possibility. Yet, the network of the modalities is only retroactively established, once conditions for consistency can be retrojected out of a determinate field of sense. Retroactively, the conditions for consistency of a given field of sense are necessary for the field to be consistent. Consider Kant's version of creation: the world of appearances as a particular field of sense (albeit the only one available to human finite cognition) originates out of a determinate set of constitutive and regulative rules. Those rules are necessary in the face of the contingent tribunal of experience. Once experience is established as a fact, a set of rules is retrojected. Independent of any relationship between origin and originated, the conditions' necessity would not be in place. In this sense, the conditions are an instance of unprethinkable being having become intelligible in terms of a particular set of conditions for a particular field sense (the field of experience in Kant's sense). The origin's necessity can only be determined over against the contingency of that which originates.

It is impossible to go *behind* the necessary existence of an origin, to get to the nonconceptual being of the whole and to find there a motivating reason or ground that makes sense of this being itself as world. *That* anything whatsoever is, that is, that there is anything determinate, that being in the sense of determinacy *is*, is wholly groundless, resultant of a transition Schelling coins "willing." Thus we encounter at every turn an ineliminable groundlessness, in particular known to us in decision making.

In general, the being of subjectivity—*that* subjectivity is or *that* subjects exist—is conceptually underivable and therefore ungroundable. Even if "subjectivity" designates a field of sense particularly prominent in modern thought about intelligibility, it has an origin. It is not always already there, it comes to be, a movement, which cannot be conceptualized by the subject and therefore generates the sentiment of uncanniness.

"Groundless being"[102] is, like Spinoza's *una substantia*, only thinkable as being, as "that of which the nature is only conceivable as existent (*id, cujus natura non potest concipi, nisi existens*)" (E1Def1). Groundless being, which is in the first place unreflected, comes to be confronted with the not a priori excludable possibility of it's being not only *actus purus*, but also self-performance, self-possession, or lord of its being and in the final instance "lord of being."[103] That means that "that which is beyond being"[104] is not always already beyond being, but only comes to be so through self-mediation; here, Schelling offers a counter position to the traditional, static concept of transcendence.

The "lord of being" is Schelling's name for the event's manifestation as the contingency of any ontology. Once the event will have taken place, it will be the case that everything turns out to be contingent, and therefore subject to change. As Wittgenstein puts it from the vantage of the event: "Everything we see could also be otherwise. Everything we can describe at all could also be otherwise. There is no order of things a priori."[105] However, this presupposes an insight into the becoming of a world, into the becoming of intelligibility. Here, Wittgenstein is not radical enough, because he notoriously still presupposes *ur*-objects, the arrangement of which might be contingent. Schelling, on the contrary, is aware of the utter contingency of the original being itself (whatever might be accepted as an instance of original being). The lord of being is like Badiou's subject: he only comes to be as a thorough commitment to the event of truth. However, the event of truth is not just a momentary rupture in the ontology of set theory, possible through the split between being and being-there, but rather the contingency of ontology itself, the world's possibility to be otherwise. Once this possibility has become the very focus of existence, necessity begins to be overcome in a movement of transcendence over what is given.

Schelling's philosophy is meant to contribute to this overcoming and can, therefore, be read as an attempt to realize the lord of being. The lord of being is, thus, not the Christian God in a naïve sense. He is closer to the "last God" of Heidegger's *Contributions*, who in my understanding names nothing but the event of the event, the grounding of our self-understanding in the event, that is understanding ourselves as constituting being by being beyond everything that is given. This transcendence, however, is being itself. Being or the lord of being, for that matter, are no entities philosophical discourse might try to represent. Heidegger is clear about this point:

> It is no longer a case of talking "about" something and representing something objective, but rather of being owned over into enowning [*Er-eignis*]. This amounts to an essential transformation of the human from "rational animal" (*animal rationale*) to Da-sein. [. . .] This saying does not describe or explain, does not proclaim or teach. This saying does not stand over against what is said. Rather, the saying itself *is* the "to be said," as the essential swaying of be-ing.[106]

God as the lord of being is therefore transcendent only by way of a reflexive appropriation of his unprethinkable being, his absolute *Prius*. This appropriation, what Schelling calls an "increase in selfhood [*Erhöhung in Selbstheit*],"[107] takes place as our becoming ourselves, that is, in our predicative being-in-the-world. When we judge that $F(x)$, $G(y)$, and so on, we produce a distance between us and something and so presuppose the dimension of distinctions. Without this dimension coming to pass, God also could not be himself, that is, could not go beyond his own unprethinkable being. God's transcendence is thus dependent on our transcendence. God is not a transcendent entity, but a name for the event.

3. God and Man

Positive philosophy investigates the *historical* evolution of logical space. This evolution can be called "God," insofar as we understand "God" to mean an autoepistemic process of reflexively becoming transparent. "God" is simply the name for a "pure self"[108] beyond all being, that is, a self that goes beyond all being *as* something. God is thus the name for an ultimate excess—excessive over all being *as* something—that which Schelling calls "absolute spirit,"[109] "absolute personality,"[110] or, in a word, "freedom."[111]

God's freedom is in this sense finite, for he, too, is not a transcendent being before his being: he only *comes to be* the lord of being by appropriating a posteriori his *prius*, that is, by going beyond his being. Only therein lies his freedom, which for this reason does not precede necessity. For God is "*a priori* actus" and not already freedom. Freedom as the result of a reaching out to the whole only comes to be via the establishment and differentiation of the modalities.

> If God has his *prius* in *actus*, then he will have his divinity in the potency, in that he is the *potentia universalis*, and as this that, which is above being, the *Lord* of being. But for precisely this reason—in order to actually reach

God, that is, to prove as far as it is possible the actual existence of the divine, we must proceed from that which I have called that, which *just* exists: from the immediate, simple necessary being, which necessarily is because it precedes all potency and all possibility.[112]

For Schelling, the decisive point here is that the freedom we attribute to God is *our* highest moment, something that we want. Therefore, positive philosophy does not begin with a mediated insight, but rather with the exclamation: "I want that which is *above* being [*Ich will das, was über dem Seyn ist*]."[113] We must recognize that which is beyond being as an excess over any ontology. It is only belatedly, that is, in the reconstruction of the genealogy of order, the very reason of order. And this reconstruction is, too, resultant of and bound to a choice, a decision, which can only take place against the continuation of a beginning without alternative. For this reason, Schelling defines the human being as "natura sua God-positing consciousness."[114] Only through human acts, the determination of *x* as *F* or *G* or *H* and so on—which is a free act because as the first predicative act it cannot yet be bound to a determinate order—is God posited *as* God. Therefore, according to Schelling, man, not God, is the creator of this world. "Man can call this world his world—he has posited the world outside of God—*praeter Deum*—by positing himself in the position of God."[115] The human itself expresses the "possibility of another being," another being in which God is seen, where the human wills God as a person beyond being. Schelling expresses this in the transition from negative to positive philosophy with his famous dictum: "person seeks person."[116] The belated necessity of a free origin of all determinations comes into the world only through the human being. This is necessary, of course, if unprethinkable being is to raise itself to the level of the pure self.

Because no thought, and therefore no dimension of sense, can anticipate or preempt being, being itself is, in a determinate sense, senseless. Being goes before all sense and is therefore the unassailable presupposition of all sense: only in this way does being as such have a meaning, that is, it can only be captured under a determinate description as that which is included as excluded. What is given is always given in a certain way. It is against this background that Schelling poses the problem of the meaninglessness of the *existence* of God. For this existence is not yet caught up in the form of the dimension of sense. Being the fundamental being-there that is presupposed by all determinate being-something or being *as*, it is not itself something *as* something. This does not lead, however, to any kind of irrationalism: thinking and its sense-making efforts are not therefore set against an irrational world. For whomever would claim that the discovery of the sense-making activity of subjectivity entails that the world in itself, that is, the world without subjects, must be senseless, subordinates the world once again to a category of sense, namely that of senselessness. The sense-lessness of existence itself comes into existence only belatedly, that is, only through and as a moment of the self-mediation of subjectivity as a field of sense. The starting point of self-mediation can itself be called senseless only from the vantage of self-mediation and its sense-making activity.

If no reason exists for the existence of sense and determinacy, then every passage to the order of sense must itself be senseless, as Joseph König has put it.[117] And there is, in fact, no reason that sense exists: there is no reason for reasons as such, no sense can be made external to sense-making itself. The always belatedly diagnosed immediacy of the beginning is ultimately seen to have no relation whatsoever to mediation, otherwise it would not properly be the immediate beginning. Herein lies the irremediable contingency of all meaningful, justified existence, around which Schelling centers his entire philosophical project.

The work of positive philosophy lies, then, in the proof that groundless being is itself mediated in the idea, that it is ultimately to be *as* absolute self-mediation; this, however, can only occur in the eschatological future. Schelling's reconstruction of the history of being and of consciousness, therefore, is aimed toward opening onto the possibility of another being, that is, the possibility of a future. Positive philosophy ultimately investigates the establishment of the *as*, given that it is necessarily and essentially absent at the beginning: this effort is aimed at making room for an eschatological hope, precisely that which sets a limit to philosophy—the end or aim of philosophy that philosophy itself cannot determine from within itself as its end or goal, an end that cannot be transcended by philosophizing itself. The object of positive philosophy is therefore the self-mediating movement of "blind eternity, eternity that merely exists" to "eternity of essence, the eternity of the idea"[118]: the thought of such development opens up as a prospect a modality of the future that cannot be anticipated in any way.

So Schelling's argument goes "precisely in the opposite direction of the ontological argument"[119] and is consequently *the reversed ontological proof.* For Schelling's account charts the movement "from being to essence,"[120] whereas the ontological proof begins from essence and seeks through its conceptual explication to prove the necessary existence of this essence.

Time and thus the possibility of an eschatological future in which God *as* God would come to be, that is, a future in which an absolute transcendent freedom would be, is only first a possibility once a predicative ambience has become established. Judgment and time are thus interdependent. But if the first judgment can be made, a detachment must have taken place, which from the perspective of the beginning could not have been anticipated. This detachment is, according to Schelling, the fall of man, his self-determination, which he achieves as determinate over against the unknown x, that which precedes him as being. Given that the intrinsically contingent individual is an x to itself and remains an x to itself, and given that only contingent beings ask questions, every concept of the whole which is incompatible with the contingency of the questioner has to be inadequate: for the questioner is surely herself part of the whole. Schelling's revolutionary thought, which has been vindicated in the history of philosophy most notably by Kierkegaard, can be understood as an incorporation of the fundamental thesis of existentialism into a theory of totality, the result being a reconciliation of metaphysics and human existence.

God and man are allies in the constitution of order. God is a *terminus reduplicativus* through man, because God as God is himself only by virtue of taking a certain distance from his original being by being **as** God. Yet, on this definition, a certain inextricable possibility can be glimpsed: God is not only necessity, but rather also possibility. This otherness, as it were, cannot be excluded, for if there were only the One, there would be nothing: for what could this One, related to nothing, not even to itself, be? For if any One consists at least minimally in a self-relatedness, a difference is already in play that makes this self-related thing something as such. Something is always differentiated from something else: thus Schelling asserts that eternity without *as* would have to be some kind of pre-predicative being, or "primordial being"[121] as he has it. This pre-predicative being is necessarily present in all predicative acts, without thereby being able to be predicatively explicated. The One cannot therefore exclude the being of another, for if it were to do so it would affirm the being of others: to assert any relation of exclusion with the other would be to cease to be the One.

Primordial being is placed at an unsurpassable distance from us through an originary possibility, viz., the possibility of predication. This distance is the possibility of creation, that possibility which is actualized through the establishment of a dimension of sense. Only insofar as a world is possible as that domain, in which the distinction of something from others is actualized, does the human take place. And only so far as the human takes place, willing something determinate, does the transition from x to $F(x)$ come to pass. That is, the human is the establishment of the distance from primordial being and so sense or predication as such. Thus, just as anything else determinate, God can only become established as God through this distance taking, that is, through the passage to determinacy that the human being brings to being. This is precisely what Schelling means with his theory of *natura sua* God-positing consciousness.

As far as we know (as of 2010) the human is the only creature that is capable of or interested in developing and deciding on a theory of totality. The human is thus the theory-agent par excellence, the concept-mongering creature that asks itself how it is possible that there is such a thing as recognizable being, that is, why and how there is intelligibility *überhaupt.* The human plays, therefore, a decisive role in the reflection of the whole, that is, in the establishment of a divine self-relation. In this way Schelling builds the human into the self-constitution of the whole, in that he identifies the human with the possibility of another being, that is, with the "originary possibility"[122] through which a process of self-knowledge can be initiated in the first place. Man is installed in the process of creation as the God-positing being: the whole can only observe itself by and through the constitution of a groundless difference in the whole. The human being is thus to be understood as the original observer of God, that is, of the whole, insofar as it is that creature which relates the whole to itself, that moment in the dynamic of creation which brings the whole to itself and so constitutes the whole.

One can support Schelling's no doubt bizarre sounding theory of creation as follows. That we observe the world is a rather uncontroversial fact. Yet in order to observe the world, we need to establish a difference, at least the difference between us as observers and everything else. "When one wants to see unity, difference appears."[123] The difference between an observer of the world and the world itself must, in the case of a theory of the world as world, be able to be thought as the immanent differentiation of the unity, since the observation of the world as a whole is at the same time the self-observation of the world from within. For is not the observation of the world, after all, located in the world? Thus the world carries a fundamental differentiation within itself, viz. the distinction between observer and observed. For this reason its unity is always already passé as soon as it can be observed. The observed metaphysical starting point is therefore always a paradox, for its unity sensu stricto cannot be observed without there already being a difference in play. The task of Schelling's theory of the potencies is ultimately the temporalized resolution of the paradox that the unity observes itself in a theory of totality and thus differs from itself. This resolution is achieved by the combination of predication and willing.

Resolving the paradox of a self-observing unity is the common program of all German idealist systems and remains at the center of Schelling's late philosophy. The structure of totality must at all times instantiate the form of "unity of unity and opposition,"[124] as Schelling has it in the *Initia*. Only thus can it be guaranteed that the unity can remain a unity, while at the same time consisting in an unmistakable difference between the unity itself and the theory of unity. The presence of the unity in difference must therefore be thought as a differentiation of the unity itself. The difference between the origin and that which originates or springs forth, between *principle* and *principled*, does not go from the former to the latter, for the former takes place in the first place only belatedly, only belatedly coming to be presupposed *as* the origin or principle. There is thus no logical anticipation of existential decisions, for, conversely, the very existence of logical space depends on a decision. The continued existence of logical space is at every moment the result of the repetition of a decision to see x as F and thus to actively exclude G. In the final analysis, an absolute freedom hides itself behind the supposed "hardness of the logical must." This freedom only makes itself understood as given through decisions, though it is never reducible to a particular decision.

Schelling's theory of creation originates in the question of "how the world is set up such that it can observe itself, such that it can break itself up into a difference of observer and observed."[125] Therefore, the theory of creation is a theory in which the conditions for the possibility of a theory of totality are reflected. It turns out that a theory of totality is only possible when we ourselves decide to set being in place as determinacy. The totality, which would remain utterly indeterminate without its thematization, requires our decisions in order to be as such. This decision is made by man, only inasmuch as he wills something beyond being and thus determines being as such-and-so and in this very act determines being contingently. The creation qua God's taking a distance from himself presupposes the possibility of another being, that over against which our act of differentiation, our decision, is actualized.

The primary object of positive philosophy is the human, because God is only accessible, ontologically speaking, by and through the human. Schelling clearly expresses this in the first lecture of his *Grounding of Positive Philosophy* when he writes: "the sole object of the final science which answers all questions, the sole object of philosophy, is the human."[126] The originary possibility, the human, is the very possibility of the world. Now, man alone lives in the world because only the human exceeds the given in the direction of totality. The human is thus the only (known) world-being. The world exists in its inexistence only in the human transcendence over the world. The original possibility of the world is therefore the originary possibility of the human, that is, that transcendent being without whose transcendence things could not be things in a world. Thus Schelling reiterates once more the great lesson of Kant's Antinomies chapter in the *Critique of Pure Reason*, in which Kant pithily asserts that "the world does not exist at all (independently of the regressive series of my representations)."[127] The world as the whole is already for Kant no thing that could be given to intuition, that is, which could be given as an object: rather, for Kant, the world is only that ideal at which the synthetic activity of the search for knowledge of finite epistemic beings aims. The world is always only the ideal of a world-whole. On Schelling's translation of this thought, this means that the world is not a thing, but is rather the place of the determinacy of everything that exists as a process of the constitution of determinacy for finite epistemic beings. The human and totality refer therefore to one another, for the totality does not itself exist as an independent thing (for it is not some spatiotemporally extended universe).

The *Logos*, that which reveals itself as logical space (as predicative ambience), in which we exist, and that only exists inasmuch as we synthetically establish and perpetuate its structure, was in the beginning with God. This famous starting point of the *Gospel of John* is read by Schelling as indicating that the possibility of another being, say, the *logos* of the three potencies, as *natura sua* God-positing consciousness, cannot be excluded a priori. The human being as the possibility of God-positing is always already in play in the constitution of being as God: the world-being *intelligibilizes* being. As soon as the human has established God, that is, as soon as it becomes the case that being is determinacy, he has established himself as the son of God, for he recognizes God as the starting point and in this sense as the Father. Whence the precarious position of mediator between the son of God and the son of Man, as Schelling repeatedly points out.[128] Schelling infers from what he sees as the progressive movement of the history of being and of consciousness (from no intelligibility to progressively more intelligibility) that together they move towards an eschatological future, which cannot be anticipated by inspecting the ontological structure of the world. Thus, positive philosophy must create space for a future, a space that it itself could no longer occupy. Our being beyond the world, which in the first place allows us to determine *this* world, opens the horizon of an eschatological future. Whether or not a God, who alone could save us as Heidegger's dictum has it, will meet us on this horizon, cannot be said, for we could not guarantee that such an event would even be *thinkable*. All we can do is work to open the possibility of a decision for a logical space in which, in the future, God would be possible. This position of the transcendence of reason, which confronts reason with its controlled failure, is the situation of the son, who alone through man is posited as someone who is not only man, but *Übermensch*. To repeat Schelling's anthropological formula:

> The dead body has enough in itself, and only wants *itself.* The animal, as everyone can see already at the level of the living plant's hunger for light, wants something outside *itself,* the human wants something above *itself.* The animal is through its will pulled outside itself toward something and the human in its truly human will is elevated above itself.[129]

The human *will* therefore goes beyond the human. Whether the human will ever reach the position of a fully established lord of being who has surpassed his precarious, historical existence once and for all cannot be considered a decided fact. In this sense, Schelling's thought of the modesty of reason is a crucial part of a philosophy of hope, one which, in view of the progressive form of history, places a bet on philosophical reflection contributing to the future being a future in which God shall be.

Chapter 3

Contingency or Necessity?
Schelling versus Hegel

The crucial difference between Schelling and Hegel can be tied down to
their modal ontologies. Generally, they agree in their analysis of the second-
order relation between contingency (Hegel actually speaks of "chance,"
Zufälligkeit) and necessity. As Hegel has it, necessity presupposes contingency, because it can only be made intelligible as the oscillation between
actuality and possibility. The reason for this can be summarized in the
following manner. Actuality or "reality," as contemporary language tends
to call it, is divided into two aspects. On the one hand, we have the way the
world is, a set of facts, while on the other, we have our potentially distorting
visions (judgments, thoughts, hunches guided by affect, emotional attach-
ments, imagination, etc.) about the way the world is. Yet both, the way the
world is and our forms of registration of this way, belong to one and the
same world. The world as the domain, which encompasses both facts and
references to facts (which, of course, are also facts, albeit facts about facts),
is what Hegel calls "actuality." Now, actuality is opposed to possibility in
that possibility is Hegel's name for the domain of all occurrences within
actuality. Actuality in its contingent relation to whatever occurs is possibility. Thus, the relation between actuality (the being there of a space of
distinctions) and possibility (the various occurrences or entries within that
space) is contingency. The particular determinations, or ways the world
is, are not anticipated in the simple thought of a space of distinctions. In
this respect, they are contingent. Now, this oscillation between actuality
as the very domain within which possible occurrences become actual and
actuality as an occurrence within that very space is a conceptual necessity.
It is necessary that the space of distinctions be distinguished even though
the very distinctions are not entailed by it. Along those lines, Hegel argues
in the chapter on "Actuality" in his *Science of Logic* that the only "absolute
necessity" is that of the oscillation of (and therefore relation between)
actuality and possibility.

Against Hegel, Schelling maintains the contingency of this thought. According to him the higher-order modality of the second-order relation between actuality and possibility is not necessity, but itself contingency. In this chapter, I will first discuss Hegel's moves toward the insight into a necessary immanence of what he calls "essence." There are not two worlds which are contingently connected (be it by the will of a transcendent being or by the laws of nature), but only one world. Where Schelling differs from Hegel is in the determination of the modal status of this all-encompassing structure. Whereas Hegel argues that necessity even governs contingency in that the very logical form of contingency is a necessary logical achievement, Schelling insists on the contingency of even that operation.

In this context, I cannot fully argue for both options. In order to prepare the systematic presentation of contingency, it is first necessary to work through some of the fundamental operations of a transcendental modal ontology. Schelling's and Hegel's ways of thinking about the modalities are too far away from contemporary modal logics to be presupposed by a systematic revival of their insights. For this reason, in this chapter I will only defend a reading of Schelling and Hegel on the modalities along the lines of transcendental ontology. The next step will be to defend the claim to a higher-order contingency in its details.

The central tenet of this chapter is that the modalities qualify framework internal relations between elements. For example, if it is necessary that $2 + 2 = 4$, then the elements 2 and 2 are related via the addition function in such a manner that the outcome 4 could not be otherwise. Yet, the very operation on elements defined by "addition" is only determinate in a context, which is not reflected in the axioms of number theory, set theory, or arithmetic. Mathematics does not mathematically distinguish itself from other operations on elements. This is why it could be otherwise than $2 + 2 = 4$, even though we have no grip on this possibility, because our surrounding beliefs are arranged in a manner that is not itself an object of mathematics. If I claim that the necessity of $2 + 2 = 4$ could be otherwise, and even that any logical necessity could be otherwise, I am not saying that it is *arbitrary* to believe that $2 + 2 = 4$ rather than $2 + 2 = 5$. I am only claiming that the possibility of revision is built into every belief system. And even if mathematics were the attempt to map an eternal realm of laws (whatever that might mean), it would have to map it, and that is to say it would have to consist of claims. Claims are finite, because they are determinate, and determinacy entails higher-order contingency, as I hope to make plausible in this chapter against Hegel's claim to a closure of the indeterminacy of determining.

As should be obvious by now, this is neither skepticism nor a claim to transcendence. The very point I emphasize with Schelling against Hegel is that closure cannot be achieved. Ontological thought remains finite, which only threatens its possibility if we presuppose a transcendence over finitude.

I The Dialectic of the Absolute: Hegel's Critique of Transcendent Metaphysics

Heidegger famously criticized Hegel's philosophy for being an onto-theological system. The snag Heidegger finds in onto-theology is that it hypostatizes a first principle on which, to quote from Aristotle, "the universe and nature depend."[1] According to Heidegger, Hegel presupposes an absolute in the form of an absolute subjectivity from the very outset of his system; an absolute principle, which accounts for the teleology in the various histories Hegel subsequently reconstructs. Heidegger attacks Hegel because he believes that Hegel draws on a determinate version of the ontological difference which, eventually, defines being as an absolute, self-transparent *Geist*, and beings as its spiritual manifestations.[2] If Heidegger were right in his interpretation of Hegel, Hegel would actually be defining Being as Spirit and would, therefore, be determining it as a hyperbolic kind of thing, instead of understanding it as the process of alterations within the ontological difference that Heidegger envisages with his concept of Being.

In order to reassess this criticism, one needs to first look at Hegel's concept of the absolute. In what follows, I shall argue that Hegel's conception of the absolute is based on a detailed exposition of the dialectical failure of transcendent metaphysics. Hegel denies that there is an absolute beyond or behind the world of appearances. The world we inhabit is not the appearance of a hidden reality utterly inaccessible to our conceptual capacities. But this claim does not entail any kind of omniscience on the part of the philosopher, as many have suspected. It rather yields the standpoint of immanent metaphysics without any first principle, on which totality depends. Moreover, Hegel does not claim to finish the business of philosophy once and for all; on the contrary, his conception of the absolute entails that philosophy is awarded the infinite task of "comprehending one's own time in thought." Hegel himself conceives of the absolute as of a process, which makes various forms of conceptualizing totality possible.

Unlike Heidegger, I do not believe that the concept of the absolute in post-Kantian idealism entails a denial of the finitude that looms large in

Kant's own system, as Heidegger acknowledges in his *Kant and the Problem of Metaphysics*.[3] One possible way of interpreting the overall internal development of post-Kantian idealism is to regard it as an extended commentary on Kant's concept of the "unconditioned" in the first *Critique*. In fact, one could easily argue that the whole post-Kantian movement ought to be understood as a development of the Kantian exposition of the "transcendental ideal of pure reason."[4] The epistemological and metaphysical enterprise that is awakened by Kant's analysis of the dialectical consequences of the transcendental ideal primarily depends on a theory of determinacy. Given that determinacy cannot be restricted to being a property of concepts, such a theory of determinacy must ultimately be both logical and ontological. Determinacy must be in some way out there, in the things themselves, because even if we denied the determinacy of the world, this would still presuppose its intelligibility qua undetermined or unmarked something. Indeed, being an unmarked something is as much a determinate predicate as being a particular something.[5] There is no way to oppose mind (concepts, consciousness, and what have you) and the world without, at the same time relating them to one another. Both, mind and world, that is, the logical and the ontological order, have to be determined, at least over against their respective other. In this sense, they depend on each other, a principle Putnam explicitly concedes to Hegel in claiming that "the mind and the world jointly make up the mind and the world."[6] The logical space in which mind and world are both distinguished and interdependent can be called the "unconditioned," the "absolute," or the "infinite." It is in this respect that we can consider post-Kantian idealism to be a commentary on the Kantian "unconditioned."

A broadly Kantian theory of determinacy is the key to the development of Fichte's, Schelling's, and Hegel's thought ever since their Jena period. One of the characteristic moves in the post-Kantian critical evaluation of Kant's system at that time was the standard claim that Kant did not clearly identify the principle upon which the whole architectonic of his system was based. In the eyes of the post-Kantian idealists, the alleged absence of methodological self-consciousness led Kant to his misconception of the thing-in-itself as a hidden reality behind or beyond the appearances. Post-Kantian idealists believe that Kant himself drew a distinction between mind and world, form and content or, in their words, between the for-us and the in-itself. But such a distinction is for-us and therefore, the in-itself is in some yet to be determined sense in-itself-for-us. This dialectic lies at the base of Hegel's dialectic of the absolute, which is not incompatible with finitude and immanence, as Heidegger suspects. It rather renders finitude intelligible and unavoidable, including the finitude of any determinate conception of the absolute as a determinate principle.

If we were to search for the absolute in Kant, there would be many candidates: the transcendental apperception in the *Transcendental Deduction*, the Categorical Imperative, the ethico-teleological unification of theoretical and practical reason in the *Third Critique*. This spurned the later Fichte's criticism according to which Kant postulated three absolutes without ever identifying their common ground as the real absolute, which would have to be the monistic principle of disjunction in its three manifestations.[7] Hegel makes a similar observation in the *Difference Essay*, where he famously attributes a "subjective subject-object,"[8] that is, a subjective absolute, to Kant and Fichte, which he claims was later corrected by Schelling's "objective subject-object"[9] in his *Naturphilosophie*, and finally synthesized in Hegel's own master-concept of "identity of identity and difference."[10]

If we ask the question, "what corresponds to the absolute in Hegel's mature system?" we will barely get a clear-cut answer. Is it absolute knowing, the absolute idea, or absolute spirit? Before we can even try to answer the question concerning the absolute in Hegel, we shall have to fix a criterion for singling it out. In full awareness of this problem, Hegel himself presents his *Science of Logic* as a sequence of "definitions of the absolute."[11] Yet, none of the definitions make the grade but one. In this sense the whole enterprise of the *Logic* can be read as an attempt to define the absolute, an attempt whose success cannot be guaranteed from the outset. And the essential outcome is that the absolute cannot be defined, lest it were understood as a distinct and distinctive object. As we shall see, the absolute can only be attained as a *process of manifestation* which Hegel calls (among other things) "actuality" (*Wirklichkeit*). This process manifests itself as a history of being à la Heidegger, that is, as a history of transcendental signifieds, which transform the absence of the absolute into the presence of its manifestations in various disguises.

In what follows I shall first argue, in Section 1, that this is the result of the dialectic of the absolute in the chapter on "the Absolute" in the *Doctrine of Essence*. I shall reconstruct the argument of the chapter in some detail in order to show that Hegel unveils the underlying dialectic of all concepts that define the absolute in opposition to the relative. I shall thereby show how Hegel rejects every theory of the absolute that tries to define it within the range of the inaccessible in-itself or the beyond. Secondly, in Section 2, I shall sketch an interpretation of the relation between the absolute idea, which I understand as the process of elucidation which is the *Science of Logic* itself, and the absolute spirit at the end of the *Encyclopedia*.

1. The Dialectic of the Absolute in the *Doctrine of Essence*

The general aim of the *Doctrine of Essence* is to spell out the ontological difference between appearance and being insofar as this difference is constitutive of any metaphysical system that defines its principle, its absolute, in opposition to a world of appearances.[12] It is obvious that the primary target of Hegel's dialectical analysis of the absolute is Platonist metaphysics broadly construed.[13] As Hegel puts it, Platonism draws a distinction between "*two worlds*."[14] In its classical versions, the realm or world of forms, which are objects of the intellect, is opposed to the realm or world of the sensible objects, which are objects of perception, an idea essential to Plato's epistemological remarks in the *analogy of the divided line*.[15] The relation between the two worlds is interpreted as an asymmetrical relation of participation (μέθεξις) such that every item in the sensible world is what it is only insofar as it is the deficient appearance of an item in the intelligible world. In this sense, the two worlds add up to "*two totalities* of the content, one of which is determined as *reflected into itself*, the other *as reflected into an other*."[16]

This relation is *essential* in Hegel's terminology: it is a relation of appearing, in which one relatum is defined as being and the other as appearance, one as eternal and unchangeable, the other as finite and mutable. However, Platonism is not aware of the role reflection plays in the constitution of this ontological difference that has been characteristic of classical metaphysics from the time of the pre-Socratics onwards. The relation of appearing is blind with regard to the reflection that motivates its formulation. Every metaphysical system that draws a distinction between two worlds is forgetful of this very operation of reflection and hypostatizes it in the "form determination"[17] of two worlds which build but "*one* absolute totality,"[18] namely the totality of metaphysical reflection. The two worlds only come to be opposed *in* metaphysical reflection, which is not reflected in Platonism. Therefore, the ontological difference between the world as it is in itself and the world as it appears to us amounts only to a simple negation which has to be supplemented by the negation of the negation implicit in metaphysical reflection. The simple negation, which establishes an essential relation between the two worlds must become the object of a further reflection in order to make its dialectic explicit.[19]

This movement of the negation of negation is precisely what takes place in the chapter on "The Absolute" in the *Logic*, the introduction and first subchapter A, which proceeds in three steps. First, the absolute is determined as absolute transcendence, or as absolute identity, which outstrips our conceptual capacities. It can only be paradoxically determined by the

negation of all predicates. Second, this movement—which is really a movement of reflection—is made transparent *as* reflection. In order to steer
clear of the problem of absolute transcendence, the finite is determined as
an image of the absolute, which has being far more than any finite being
due to its pure positivity, a position Hegel ascribes to Spinoza. However, this
threatens to dissolve the finite into the absolute. Third, this whole movement is presented as a process, by which we eventually arrive at the form
determination of the absolute form, where form and content of reflection
coincide in the "self-exposition" of the absolute, that is, in the reflection
of reflection.

Before we can approach the text in the light of this sequence, it is important to bear in mind that "the absolute" is a concept that is used to define
the totality of relations of determinacy and, hence, all actual and possible
worlds, *as* worlds, that is, as relational networks. According to the famous
principle of determination, namely that determination is negation, the
world *as* world can only be posited if we determine it by negation. The
absolute is, therefore, introduced as the negation of the world, of the world
we try to determine *as* such. This is why any given totality of relations refers
us to something that is not part of the relational network in the same way
that the relata are. The world is defined in its opposition to the absolute
precisely because the absolute functions as a *concept of contrast*: we come to
see the world *as* world only if we define some unmoved mover, some fixed
point towards which everything aspires and on which everything depends.[20]
Whatever the absolute is, it serves as a foil for making us aware of the fact
that our conceptualizing the world as such is conditioned.

Various forms of defining this absolute have been recorded. One of the
most general ways to distinguish metaphysical systems is to divide them
up into *transcendent* and *immanent metaphysics*. Transcendent metaphysics
defines the absolute as entirely different from totality and therefore as transcendent. The absolute is categorically not part of this world. Immanent
metaphysics, on the contrary, understands the absolute as a totality diffe-
rentiating itself. Neoplatonism is perhaps the most prominent example of
transcendent metaphysics, whereas Spinoza and Hegel are the most reso-
lute defenders of immanent metaphysics. This is why Hegel joins Spinoza
against transcendent metaphysics in the chapter on the absolute, aiming
however, at the same time, to surpass Spinoza in his methodology.[21]

(1) Given that transcendent metaphysics conceives the absolute as the
entirely other that transcends the totality of determinations, it cannot characterize it through any positive predicate.[22] For this reason, the transcendent absolute is traditionally dealt with in terms of an absolute oneness or

absolute identity which cannot positively be described, as this would make it something determinate and, hence, part of the world, part of the network of determinate beings. As Hegel has it,

> The simple substantial identity of the absolute is indeterminate, or rather in it every determinateness of *essence* and *Existence*, or of *being* in general, as well as of *reflection*, has dissolved itself. Accordingly, the process of *determining what the absolute is* has a negative outcome, and the absolute itself appears only as the negation of all predicates and as the void.[23]

It is obvious that the negation of all predicates cannot be a reflection performed by the negative absolute itself. Otherwise we would have to ascribe some sort of self-determining activity to it, a move that would contradict its alleged absolute identity. Hence, it is our own reflection that accomplishes the negation of all predicates. However, this entails that the absolute is already determined in opposition to our reflection as that which does not accomplish the negation itself. This in turn implies that our reflection has merely been an "external reflection"[24] up to this point. Reflection opposes itself by positing an absolute: it posits the absolute as if it were not posited by reflection. Yet it is, hereby, already determined by reflection.[25] This motivates a countermove.

(2) If it makes sense to talk about the absolute at all, we cannot define it in opposition to reflection, lest this opposition relativized it. Reflection must not "stand *over against* the absolute identity of the absolute."[26] This is why the absolute needs to be understood as the "*ground*"[27] of totality, with no determinate content but that of grounding. For his reason, the correct determination of the absolute has to be "the *absolute form*,"[28] which is in and for itself "the absolute content,"[29] as Hegel puts it. It is nothing but the name for the grounding relation, by which the finite becomes intelligible as such. Yet, this grounding relation does not have a content apart from that of being a grounding relation, it is no particular relation, which would hold between two relata and, therefore, between two entities. An absolute, which satisfies this prima facie weird condition can only be the movement of pure thought performed by the *Science of Logic* itself. The *Logic* itself is the unfolding, the exposition of the absolute. The absolute is both the form and content of the *Logic* and is, hence, not something prior to its manifestation in logical thought.

No transcendent absolute could possibly satisfy the logical demands of an absolute form as long as it is opposed to reflection. But the negation of all predicates, which is the method of the classical negative dialectics of the One, is already a process of reflection. According to Hegel, this implies that the absolute is posited as positivity out of reach, the "beyond"[30] of the movement of negativity revealed as the movement of reflection. The second, "*positive* side"[31] of the dialectic of the absolute is, thus, triggered by the insight that the absolute is pure positivity, the ground of the movement of negation, an insight which reflection had somehow in view all along without ever having been able to attain it.

This motivates another standard move of transcendent metaphysics: everything, every determinate being, is related to the absolute. The absolute is the absolute substance, that which does not change because it transcends time and finitude altogether. In order to avoid the trap of absolute transcendence, the transcendent metaphysician introduces the further determination that every determinate being is only a partial manifestation of the absolute, which constantly withdraws in this very manifestation to the beyond. Finitude is thus determined as an appearance of the infinite. But again, if we determine the infinite as the pure void, as the negation of all predicates, the only thing we come to grasp in determining finitude in opposition to the negative absolute is nothing. If the totality of being which is our world is determined as "illusory being,"[32] it is ipso facto related to the absolute by being its reflection, its appearance. Hegel asserts, "this positive exposition thus arrests the finite before it vanishes and contemplates it as an expression and image of the absolute."[33]

The strategic withdrawal to positivity does not solve the initial problem of transcendence. If we circumvent the trap of transcendence, which posits an unattainable absolute beyond our conceptual grasp, an indeterminable something-nothing beyond logical space, we do not make any progress in relating the finite to this vacuity. By relating the finite to the unspecifiable transcendent absolute, we rather destroy the finite. Everything vanishes into nothing once it returns to its origin, the absolute Oneness, which is nothing determinate at all:

> [T]he transparency of the finite, which only lets the absolute be glimpsed through it, ends by completely vanishing; for there is nothing in the finite which could preserve for it a distinction against the absolute; it is a medium which is absorbed by that which is reflected through it.[34]

The apparent positivity gained by determining the finite as an image of the absolute vanishes once we realize that we have transposed the negation of all predicates from the absolute to the content manifested in finite determinations. Those determinations cannot preserve any determination against the absolute. The determination which now determines the absolute as pure positivity beyond our conceptual grasp and the finite as its inane manifestation stays once more "external to the absolute."[35] The absolute, "which is only *arrived at*"[36] in the movement of reflection, remains essentially "imperfect."[37] For, once again, "the absolute that is only an *absolute identity*, is only the *absolute of an external reflection*. It is therefore not the absolute absolute, but the absolute in a determinateness, or it is the *attribute*."[38]

(3) Hegel's dialectical critique of transcendent metaphysics results in the necessity of Spinozistic monism and, hence, of an entirely immanent metaphysics. The absolute determines itself as attribute in Spinoza's sense, that is, as one of the infinite manifestations of the absolute positivity of substance.

In subchapters B and C, Hegel sketches the dialectic of the absolute in Spinozistic immanent metaphysics. Immanent metaphysics sets out to determine the absolute identity in its manifestation. Spinoza famously argues that the two Cartesian substances are, in fact, nothing but aspects of the one substance that has infinitely many attributes, only two of which are (contingently) known to us: thought and extension.[39] Again, the totality of manifestations or attributes is only conjoined in one absolute, in the one substance, by a "*reflective movement*."[40] This reflective movement is the very thought that relates the substance to its infinitely many manifestations as ground of their unity. The opposites themselves—say extension and thought—are in themselves "*without the return into itself* [i.e. into the absolute, M.G.]."[41] They remain external to the absolute and are never fully identical with it. In this sense, they do not return to the absolute. They are only related to it in our reflection, which is a reflection in the mode but not in the attribute.

Hence, the absolute identity of the absolute is contingent upon its manifestations that are related to the absolute in *our* act of reflection. But this reflection only takes place in the mode of the absolute, that is, in our thought that conjoins the manifestations and returns them to their unity. Hence, totality is only established in thought. This fact is not reflected in Spinoza's theory of the absolute, for Spinoza's substance is precisely characterized by "an *immediate* subsistence of its own":[42] it is what it is by simply being what it is. In Definition 6 of the first part of his *Ethics*, Spinoza unmistakably asserts that God's absolute infinity "does not involve any negation (*negationem nullam involvit*)."[43] Hegel's trouble with this explanation is that

it cannot account for the particularization of the infinite so long as negation is not intrinsic to the very totality, that is, God or Nature.[44] If negation
is external to the absolute, then why is there anything finite at all?

The supposed immediacy of substance is only determined as "simply
affirmative"[45] over against the "reflected immediacy"[46] of reflection. It is
the very essence of substance to be what it is independently of its accidental determinations. But this opposition between substance and accidents
is an essential relation established in reflection. Therefore, the substance
depends on the reflective movement shining through in its mode, in our
thought. It is the reflecting subject which posits the absolute in opposition
to its positing it. This very act of "determining"[47] is thus what retroactively
generates the absolute substance. The substance, therefore, is a presupposition of the reflective movement in the terminological sense of the *Doctrine
of Essence*: it is a *pre*-supposing which posits the substance as that which is
grasped in the reflection of the absolute.[48] Contrary to the merely negative
approach to the absolute other of transcendence, immanent metaphysics
resorts to "a determining which would make it [sc. the absolute] not an
other but only that which it already *is*, the transparent externality which is
the *manifestation* of itself, a movement *out of* itself."[49]

At this point, Hegel makes use of Spinoza's construction of the *amor dei
intellectualis* that he interprets from a dialectical vantage point.[50] The
intellectual striving to see everything *sub specie aeternitatis* is the absolute's
movement itself and not a process of external reflection. The absolute
determines itself in our determining it. Every dialectically consistent form
of determining the absolute has to be compatible with this self-referential
insight, which reflects on the conditions of possibility for grasping the
absolute. Hegel's label for this self-referential structure is "absolute form,"
a form that is the content of itself. The content of the exposition of the
absolute is, thus, the exposition itself. There is nothing beyond this exposition, beyond this manifestation. Hence, form and content coincide in the
absolute. "Or," as Hegel suggests, "the content of the absolute is just this, *to
manifest itself.* The absolute is the absolute form, which, as the diremption
of itself is utterly identical with itself, the negative *as* negative [. . .]. The
content, therefore, is only the exposition itself."[51] The absolute does not
manifest anything, which outruns our conceptual capacities. It is nothing
but the sheer manifestation, the fact that there is something rather than
nothing. The "absolute is manifestation not of an inner, nor over against
an other, but it *is* only as the absolute manifestation of itself for itself. As
such it is *actuality*,"[52] or as Hegel sometimes puts it, "self-manifestation."[53]

The absolute is, to be exact: the manifestation that something is manifest, that there is something rather than nothing. Without pursuing this correspondence here, one could even argue that the absolute's self-manifestation corresponds to Heidegger's concept of ontological truth, that is, of the facts' unconcealedness (*Unverborgenheit*), which antecedes propositional truth. For Hegel, the absolute is a means of reflection in a twofold sense. On the one hand, it is a moment of the movement of speculative metaphysical reflection. On the other, it functions like a mirror (*speculum*), which reflects our fundamental ways of conceptualizing totality vis-à-vis the unconditioned. All of this means that the absolute is an indispensable notion of metaphysical reflection. But it must not be interpreted as any special sort of object or as a transcendent being. *Hegel's absolute is a rather deflationary concept, a harmless, yet necessary presupposition of metaphysical reflection insofar as it aspires to unfold the concept of totality implicit in the important and utterly indispensable notion of the world.*

We do not need to go into Hegel's further development of actuality here, the line of reasoning issuing from the thought that the distinction between form and content collapses into the immediacy of actuality, which generates another opposition, namely possibility. We do not have to follow Hegel's whole dialectical path to the *Doctrine of the Concept.* In order to give an answer to the delicate question concerning what the absolute in Hegel's system is after all, it is sufficient to state the important fact that it has to satisfy the conditions of absolute form without collapsing into an immediate unity of form and content, into another entity. Given the exposition of the concept of the absolute so far, it is evident that the absolute can only be the totality of the self-exposition of the Concept as it appears at the very end of the *Logic.* There is but one dialectically consistent definition of the absolute, which is the *Science of Logic* itself.

2. Absolute Idea and Absolute Spirit

There are at least three prominent candidates for a closure of the Hegelian system and that correspond to the three possibilities of the Hegelian absolute: absolute knowing, the absolute idea, and absolute spirit. Apart from the intricate historical question regarding the degree to which Hegel might simply have changed his view during his development, I believe that for systematic reasons, the absolute idea qua "absolute method"[54] has to be the adequate candidate for the Hegelian absolute. While absolute knowing implodes, as it were, into the indeterminate being of the beginning of the

Logic, absolute spirit is, after all, the self-referential insight that the whole of nature and spirit is an exposition of the self-determination, the *Urteil* of the absolute idea.[55] The absolute idea, therefore, discloses itself in absolute spirit, which is not a "super-mind" endowed with the power of omniscience. Absolute spirit is, rather, the concrete, realized self-awareness of the absolute idea in its actuality, that is, philosophy.

If we try to address the problem of the relation between the absolute idea and the totality of nature and spirit, we must not undermine the logical standards of the *Science of Logic*. One violation of those logical standards would be the Neoplatonic conception of emanation, which Hegel explicitly rejects in the chapter on the "Absolute idea":

> [T]he advance is not a kind of *superfluity*; this it would be if that with which the beginning is made were in truth already the absolute; the advance consists rather in the universal determining itself and being *for itself* the universal, that is, equally an individual and a subject. Only in its consummation is it the absolute.[56]

This consummation ultimately takes place in absolute spirit, which is present as the finite individual subject thinking logical thoughts. This subject has to become aware of its position in the concrete totality of nature and spirit in order to exhibit the absolute idea, because its exhibition can only consist in its self-awareness in finite thinkers.[57]

Absolute spirit is, after all, the unification of subjective and objective spirit: individual subjects have to perform the reconstruction of the absolute idea. But they can only do so in the wider context of objective spirit and its social reality (i.e. mutual recognition and, hence, normativity), which transcends natural immediacy. This again presupposes the existence of nature as the backdrop for the self-establishment of the realm of freedom. This whole story is told from the standpoint of absolute spirit, which grasps its own activity in the medium of the absolute form. The self-referential comprehension of the absolute idea qua concrete individual reconstructing its position in totality can only be realized if we attempt to determine the absolute as such. But, as we have seen, this act should not be one of external reflection. The determination of the absolute *as* absolute must be its self-constitution, a constitution that displays itself in the process of the exposition of the absolute. This exposition is carried out by individual thinkers reconstructing the conditions of their being there at all. For this reason, this reflection is bound by historical conditions, the wider conditions of finite, subjective thought laid in out in the *Philosophy of Objective*

Spirit. Therefore, it could not occur that the exhibition of the absolute ever came to an end in such a manner that there were no further content of its actuality to be made transparent by finite thinkers. Even the *Science of Logic* has to be its "time comprehended in thought."[58]

However, this should not lead to a thorough reduction of absolute to objective spirit. Absolute spirit refers us to an even wider context, contextuality as such, that is the content of ontology. Hegelian ontology lays out the conditions for determinacy, and it turns out that reflection is an ontological structure constitutive of what there is, insofar as the whole depends on reflection. What there is or that there is anything whatsoever can only be made sense of in the medium of thought. In this respect, thought and being are one and the same, which again does not entail ontic nonsense according to which there would be no objects at all if there were no finite minds apprehending them. Yet, balancing the tendency towards rampant idealism should not force us to deny the almost trivial truth that mind-independence is generally mind-dependent. Even if for a very large class of classes of objects it is obviously not the case that they are mind-dependent, this very insight is itself qua insight mind-dependent. We cannot make sense of mind-independence without higher-order mind-dependence. Thus, our conceptions of the whole—to which the class of classes of mind-independent objects naturally belongs—has to account both for mind-independence and for mind-independence's higher-order mind-dependence. The former—ordinary mind-independence—is called "nature," while the latter comes under the heading of "spirit" in Hegel. I believe that this thought is the entire content of the "absolute idea," a content, however, which can only be grasped at the end of the process of failing to think about the world otherwise (say in terms of a universe of spatiotemporally extended mind-independent objects, minds excluded).

If the absolute idea "contains *all* determinateness within it,"[59] we have to give up determining the absolute "only as a sought-for beyond and an unattainable goal."[60] The Hegelian absolute is rather always already with us insofar as we determine it in reflection. It is reflection's determining itself, because reflection cannot be opposed to the absolute. If the absolute idea is the unfolding of logical space, and if the *Science of Logic* displays this evolution, there can be no absolute beyond the absolute idea.[61] Hence, nature and spirit "are in general different modes of displaying *its being there*."[62] Consequently, the absolute idea does not exist outside of its finite manifestations as a given logical order ready to be discovered by finite thinkers who aim to reunite with their origin. This is the very essence of Hegel's absolute idealism and of his thoroughgoing antirepresentationalism.

The relation between the absolute idea as absolute form and its exposition, its being there in the modes of nature and spirit, cannot be an essential relation, to wit a metaphysical relation of being and appearance. Therefore, nature and spirit are not mere appearances of the absolute idea, but rather modes of its exposition. The "emergence of *real difference, judgment*, the *process of determining* in general"[63] is not an external manifestation of some hidden metaphysical realm of forms, but a self-exposition of actuality. There is nothing beyond or behind the manifestation of the absolute in its attributes: in nature and spirit, and its modes, that is, finite beings. In this sense, Hegel is a Spinozist of absolute subjectivity. Whereas Spinoza determines nature and spirit as attributes of the *una substantia*, Hegel sees them as form determinations of the absolute idea, which is absolute subjectivity or, as Hegel says, *"pure personality."*[64]

The crucial point of Hegel's dialectic of the absolute is that metaphysical reflection must not be external reflection. We cannot determine the absolute as absolute substance ontologically anteceding our conceptualization of it. Otherwise we would fall victim to the dialectic of the absolute in the *Doctrine of Essence*. Therefore, reflection has to become absolute, that is, self-referential. Only in the mode of self-reference can we determine the act of determination as self-constitution. For this reason, the relation between the *Logic* and the *Realphilosophie* has to be a conceptual relation, namely the relation of judgment captured by the notorious German wordplay on *"Urteil,"* which Hegel famously "translates" as "the *original division* of the original unity."[65]

The absolute idea is only grasped in the context of a theory of self-constitution of logical space, that is, of *the* concept in an eminent singular. This is why Hegel is perhaps the most astute critic of any variety of Neoplatonism. Neoplatonism posits some paradoxical nothing, a pure unity beyond being without reflecting on its very act of positing it. Its absolute is posited as if it were not posited, a dialectical contradiction exposed by Hegel—whence emerges his conception of the absolute as a *result* of metaphysical enquiry.[66] Hence, even if there were transcendence, it could and should not be shaped by any determining reflection or, to stick to Hegel's terminology here, by external reflection.[67]

> The answer, therefore, to the question: how does the infinite become finite? is this: that *there is not* an infinite which is first of all infinite and only subsequently has need to become finite, to go forth into [*herausgehen*] finitude; on the contrary, it is on its own account just as much finite as infinite.[68]

Hegel's point about infinity is basically the same as the one employed in the overall dialectic of the absolute: the true infinite must not be determined over against the finite.[69] If the question is "*how [. . .] the infinite becomes finite*,"[70] then this question cannot be answered by presupposing an infinite, which is in-and-for-itself, that is, always already the infinite, for such infinity would be indeterminate and as such determined over against the determinacy of totality. For this reason, Hegel conceives the infinite or absolute as an ongoing process of self-constitution, which is not determined over against anything external to this very process.[71]

The overall end of the Hegelian system in the *Encyclopedia* is the absolute idea in its actuality, that is, the reflected connection of the absolute idea in its yet to be determined universality with its manifestation, its being there. As Hegel writes, "this notion of philosophy is the self-thinking Idea, the truth aware of itself (§236)—the logical system, but with the signification that it is universality approved and certified in concrete content as in its actuality."[72] It is crucial, for any reading of Hegel, to recognize that the self-thinking idea needs approval by concrete content. Otherwise it would be reduced to the abstract structure of logical space, the "realm of shadows,"[73] as Hegel calls it, thereby inverting the Platonic hierarchical order. In order to attain actuality, the idea is strictly speaking dependent on nature and spirit. It has to form a system, which can only occur in the historically bound situation of finite thinkers. In this manner, Hegel avoids determining the abstract structure of logical space over against the totality of realized determinations. Logic is not opposed to concrete content, since it is not a purely formal business. For if we oppose form and content, we already invoke a logical distinction in Hegel's sense: namely, the distinction between form and content that is itself one of the categories of Hegel's *Science of Logic.*

Hegel orients this whole line of thought toward his notoriously obscure doctrine of the three syllogisms of philosophy.[74] Without pursuing the technical question of which logical forms underlie the three syllogisms of philosophy, I suggest that Hegel's use of syllogism should be understood in the literal sense of a gathering together (συλλέγειν), of a *Zusammenschluß*. The three terms of the syllogisms correspond to the three parts of the system: logic, nature, and spirit. The simplest way of understanding the form of the three syllogisms renders them as follows:

(1) Logic, Nature, Spirit
(2) Nature, Spirit, Logic
(3) Spirit, Logic, Nature

Setting aside exegetical questions, I suggest understanding the three syllogisms as follows.

(1) The first syllogism corresponds to the standard way of interpreting the sequence of Logic, Nature, and Spirit as a succession. It seems as though the logical, absolute idea in some way or other emanated into nature that then progressed towards mind.

(2) The second syllogism is already more reflective. It is based on the insight that the first syllogism is an activity of the mind penetrating nature with regard to its logical foundations, its being structured in an intelligible way. Spirit (in the form of mind) becomes aware of the fact that it presupposes the logical categories as principles of the intelligiblity of natural processes.

(3) Eventually, the third syllogism draws on the self-referential insight that the very reflection of the second syllogism presupposes the logical form of the absolute idea, since this expresses the highest formal standard of metaphysical reflection according to the *Logic*. Therefore, it is the absolute idea that returns to itself in our penetrating nature with regard to its intelligibility. In this sense, nature and spirit are manifestations of the absolute idea. As Hegel has it,

> [T]he self-judging of the Idea into its two appearances (§§575, 576) characterizes both as its (the self-knowing reason's) manifestations: and in it there is a unification of the two aspects:—it is the nature of the fact, the notion, which causes the movement and development, yet this same movement is equally the action of cognition. The eternal Idea, in full fruition of its essence, eternally sets itself to work, engenders and enjoys itself as absolute spirit.[75]

Here, absolute spirit does not refer to any transcendent entity or teleological guarantee concealed by the potentially misleading appearances. It is nothing but the activity of putting the system together. In other words, there is no absolute God-like mind, in which finite thinkers might participate once they reach the status of enlightenment. Any Neoplatonic story of this sort is incompatible with Hegel's dialectic of the absolute and his conception of absolute form, the truly infinite.

The idea behind the three syllogisms of philosophy is the absolute idea insofar as it is the absolute method. It is the method that construes itself in such a manner that it finally grasps itself as the actuality of the system, as that which does the job of conceptualizing totality. The activity of conceptualizing displays itself in the form of nature and spirit, that is, in the form of the absolute idea's being there. According to Hegel, everything that there is, is intelligible, for everything is determined in the overall conceptual network of logical space.[76] Since there can, in principle, be nothing outside of logical space, the reflection of logical space on itself is the only absolute available. Given that this absolute reflection takes place in the *Science of Logic*, Hegel can claim to expose the absolute, to make it explicit. The exposition of the absolute does not represent the absolute in the potentially distorting medium of language. On the contrary, it deconstructs language's reference to a given world order external to reflection. There is no absolute beyond the absolute form, which is the form of language becoming aware of its speculative role.[77] Therefore, the system gathers together the totality of form determinations belonging to the absolute form, which necessarily leads to a self-referential insight into this very activity. Hegel's claim to totality does not hypostatize the absolute. The absolute does not stand still, but continues to manifest itself as that which performs the shifts from one determinate conception of the absolute to another. This very insight, however, does not change in the same way as the definitions of the absolute change. Hegel thus tries to secure the critical position of philosophy by, at the same time, subjecting it to the very patterns of change that it discovers in critical self-reflection.

II The *Spielraum* of Contingency: Schelling and Hegel on the Modal Status of Logical Space

To begin again, let us recount the *credo of physicalism*: "the world is a big physical object."[78] On this credo, the world is an object alongside others—say, alongside my massive new American refrigerator or a skyscraper—to be spoken of in the same breath as the *Big Apple* or the *Big Mac*. Of course, the world is significantly larger than all these other big things. It is, nevertheless, *a big physical object*.

At least this is how David Lewis has it on the first page of his book *On the Plurality of Worlds*. While his book does indeed say something about the plurality of worlds, he is obviously not referring to a plurality that would consist of the world of the happy, the world of twenty-first-century, late-stage capitalist Times Square, the world of Hinduism, the world of a movie, or anything like that. Rather, Lewis speaks of an in principle countable collection of "big physical objects" in the plural, which he calls possible worlds. His hypothesis of a plurality of worlds is explicitly intended to protect against any kind of higher spirituality, and he develops and offers his vision of the world as a "big physical object" in direct opposition to the idea of "entelechies or auras or spirits or deities or other things unknown to physics."[79]

It could not be more obvious how Lewis sees things: the world is the extended totality of all objects in space-time, which one might grasp or grope.[80] Further, according to Lewis there are countless other worlds, in which everything possible is also a physical event-thing in space-time: this is his thesis of modal realism.[81] Further, Lewis announces in earnest certainty one definitive fact that holds true for all these worlds: "the worlds are not of our own making."[82]

Now, Lewis's position leans on a diverse range of metaphysical background assumptions, viz. that every world is a physical object; that the world is not made by us; not to mention his assumption without argument that there are heaps of worlds, all of which are absolutely spatiotemporally and causally isolated from each other. Even if we are thoroughly charitable, these metaphysical background assumptions are suspicious at best. Hardcore physicalism and indeed all claims to the total quantifiability of the world (the former being the latter's almost parodic apotheosis) succeed only by virtue of disguising their own theory-constitutive decisions. In Lewis's case we can surely say: *his* worlds are "of his own making."

Contemporary modal logic, which operates with a semantics of possible worlds, displays a shocking confidence in the possibility of a complete and completely lucid *mathesis universalis*. With such confidence, concepts such as "world" and "logical space" may be used safely without any reflection being brought to bear on the theory-constitutive semantics of these concepts. The real impetus and aim of contemporary theories of the modalities articulates itself as *the demand of quantification*: "modality turns into quantification."[83] And it is thanks to the elaboration of a formal semantics of the modalities (actuality, possibility, necessity, etc.) on the exclusive basis of quantificational definitions and standards that physicalism, for instance, is apparently justified in its metaphysical assumptions, even if such assumptions have not been specifically investigated or argued for.

Besides its metaphysical obscurities, another problem with modal logics modeled along the lines of an unclear notion of possible worlds (which, by the way, is closer to science-fiction B movies than to Leibniz's notion of a possible world) is that it is based on a circle. If necessity is understood as truth in all possible worlds, then possibility and actuality also are tied to possible worlds. Talk of "possible worlds" evidently already presupposes an understanding of the modalities. At best, possible worlds might be a kind of model for an uninterpreted technique of manipulating logical symbols according to transformation rules. Yet understanding the modalities in terms of a relation to the world or to worlds requires a different approach, the approach of a modal ontology, which has been developed in the history of philosophy from Aristotle via Scotus to modern and contemporary philosophy. Modal ontology is not modal logics, and I doubt that modal logics contributes anything to our understanding of the modals as long as its metaphysical presuppositions are not put under scrutiny. After all, philosophy is the critical investigation of presuppositions and not the happy acceptance of a determinate set of axioms in order to draw consequences on the basis of jejune claims to knowledge.

Contrary to what uncritical contemporary analytical metaphysics implicitly assumes—namely, that logical space has always already been there anyway, that logics should attempt to depict logical states of affairs—in what follows I want to show that logical space is only established retroactively. As we shall see, among other things, this insight completely undermines the naïve assumption that the world is a big physical object. In order to show this, I will join with two thinkers to whom physicalists and their "earth-born" kin, as Plato would say, generally pay no tribute: Schelling and Hegel. My thesis is that Schelling and Hegel develop a theory of logical space, the basic and crystal clear premise of which is: necessity can only ever be *belated necessity* (*nachträgliche Notwendigkeit*). The "hardness of the logical must" and claims about fundamental or determinative principles subtending worldly events are to be investigated by both Schelling and Hegel in terms of their "being posited." I will sketch this thought—referred to in the post-Kantian context as *Reflexionslogik*, the logic of reflection—in the first part of the present essay.

In the second part of the essay, I will point up the crucial differences between Schelling's and Hegel's conceptions of *Reflexionslogik*. In contradistinction to Schelling, Hegel assumes that a *Reflexionslogik* can fully reveal the totality of its presuppositions with its own resources, that is, that it can reach complete self-transparency. It is only by virtue of his claim to such complete transparency that Hegel can undertake his *Begriffslogik*, his logic of the Concept, in which he thematizes, as he says, "a *perfectly transparent difference*."[84] In contrast, Schelling argues that any and all theories that lay universal claim, which I call *theories of the world as world*, in principle generate a nontransparent structure. Schelling, further still, recognizes just how this insight conditions and limits his own universal theory. Schelling identifies and demarcates an essential limit to the paradigmatic logic of reflection that Hegel develops: Schelling insists that reflection, by virtue of the belatedness of all necessity, generates a certain margin of contingency (*Spielraum der Kontingenz*), which, unlike Hegel, he does not obsessively seek to overcome (*aufheben*).

1. Belated Necessity

Whenever we decide to quantify over a particular domain of objects and what exists in its scope, we necessarily posit that in this domain something happens that is different from what happens in other domains. The existential quantifier picks out something that is determined in contrast with others, both on the level of the elements it discriminates within a particular object and on the level of the domain, within which the object is distinguished as an element, because there are no domain-transcendent elements to be registered in any discourse. Therefore, to claim that something exists is to claim that there is a plurality of domains, given that domains exist and, hence, only exist in contradistinction to other domains. Were there only one domain, there would be none; the form and content of any given domain consists among other things in its difference from all others. The One that is not determined through its differentiation from others simply does not take place, as Plato already demonstrated in the *Parmenides*.

Domains of objects present us with sets of elements. However, it is crucial to distinguish *domains of objects* from *sets* in the technical sense of the term, as I have already pointed out in the Introduction. According to set theory, sets are only arrived at via a "twofold act of abstraction,"[85] as Cantor has pointed out in his founding paper of modern set theory: set theory abstracts both "from the quality" of any given elements and from "the order in which they are given."[86] Without this twofold abstraction, set theory could not open up the domain of the quantifiable. Yet, there are domains of objects, say Renaissance art or contemporary Greek politics, which cannot be made sense of in terms of this twofold abstraction. In order to understand Renaissance art, we need some insight into the order in which the elements of the domain are given and what their qualities are. Hence, domains of objects are not identical with sets in the technical sense of the term.

This also entails that any paradoxes that arise within a theory of domains of objects cannot without any further ado be solved by recourse to set-theoretical standard procedures or axioms. The theory of domains of objects, which I am laying out in this paper and throughout this collection of essays, is therefore opposed to Badiou's attempt to reduce ontology to set theory. In my view, set theory is just one domain of objects alongside others, and it remains incapable of furnishing any explanatory power when it comes to love, politics, art, or religion.

The formation of sets of elements within domains of objects is determined by definite rules about what exactly can be included in a given domain and what kinds of relations obtain between its elements, if there are any. Scientific discourses and discourses in general generate domains of objects whose regularities they methodically investigate in order both to determine what *can* (possibility) appear in a given domain and to investigate what *actually* appears within it and if the relations between what appears within them are necessary or contingent; in this way, the modalities are circumscribed by and within discourses and the domains of objects they generate and cultivate. So whatever ontological structures are presupposed by the formation of domains, they have to affect our way of thinking about objects, for there are no objects outside of a domain, because the set of all objects outside of a domain would simply be another domain defined by rules of inclusion and exclusion.

Now, if we claim that there is a particular domain, for example that of the flora and fauna of the Amazon, of the natural numbers, or of the paintings of the Renaissance, that is, when we quantify over domains, we generate ex hypothesi a higher-order domain, the task of which it is to differentiate and delineate between various domains. We therefore generate a perspective of comparison that surveys many different object domains, each of which is determined solely over against the others. That is, under this higher-order object domain we quantify over the object domains with which we started. In short, the elements of a higher-order domain are themselves domains.

If this preliminary reasoning is correct, we are permitted to ask the question of how the object domain in which all object domains are differentiated behaves, that is, how the *domain of all domains* behaves. This ultimate object domain—what Heidegger baptized as the "clearing" and what Wolfram Hogrebe calls the "domain of distinction"[87]—I here call *logical space*. Logical space encompasses inter alia everything that is possible because all object domains *überhaupt* are possible only in a logical space in which they are interrelated and can be distinguished.[88]

Domains are intelligible structures. They exist only because of rule-establishing operations. If "to exist" presupposes "to be identifiable as a determinate element in an object domain," then the DD, logical space, cannot itself be said to exist, for by logical space we mean to refer to that which cannot by definition be an element in any particular domain. To say of logical space that it exists would necessarily generate a higher-order domain, which would appear, of course, in logical space. That is, to say of logical space that it exists would be to determine it as an object within a domain and therefore to displace it from the position of the DD: we would have merely formed a higher-order DD* supposedly containing DD. Yet, DD* is identical with DD, for DD is defined as the domain within which everything takes place such that it cannot take place within itself. Logical space is for that reason simply an ontological hole, the absolute void: it is only differentiated from other domains inasmuch as it consists in not being one among others. One can speculate that Heidegger had just this in mind when he declared that in our relation to objects we ultimately "hold ourselves out into nothingness."[89] Nevertheless, whenever we speak of domains, we have to behave *as if* logical space were an object domain that truly took place on such a higher-order. Ultimately, however, the DD is that placeless place where everything takes place. We can formulate this paradox with the Russian novelist Victor Pelevin: *everything takes place nowhere.*[90]

Nevertheless, logical space is a necessary presupposition, without which the existential quantifier would have nothing to work on. Existence only takes place in domains and only so long as some thing can be differentiated from other existing things. This does not apply to logical space itself, because it is distinguished from all other domains, without, however, this difference consisting in its being merely a higher-level domain in logical space next to the flora and fauna of the Amazon or set theory. For in this way we would not have logical space itself in view, as this would no longer be the DD, but rather only its *Doppelgänger*, viz. the appearance of just another object domain.

Wittgenstein famously draws a distinction between *the world* and *logical space*. For him, the world is the totality of the *actual*, while logical space refers to the totality of the *possible*. In contrast to Wittgenstein, however, we should be clear here that neither the concept of the world nor the concept of logical space should be understood as a concept of a quantifiable totality, made up of atomic objects. For the world in the eminent singular is just as little an object of possible reference as logical space is. The world can only be determinate when we have selected *one* conceptual system of reference, *one* domain of objects. Whatever "all that is the case"[91] might be, it is neither a set nor a finite domain. It is both the case that at a certain point a spatiotemporally extended particle swarm trembles and that Markus Gabriel holds a lecture, and so forth. In the set of "all that is the case," the same would simultaneously be something other.[92]

Alain Badiou and Quentin Meillassoux have (albeit for different reasons) insightfully and rightly argued that the old European notion of an infinite totality must be replaced by and through the concept of an in principle untotalizable *transfinite.*[93] Their rationale for this move can be briefly summed up as follows: Cantor has shown that the elements of any set can be arranged into a series of subsets, the number of which exceeds the number of elements contained in the original set. Consider, for example, set *A*, consisting of three elements, x_1, x_2, and x_3. These three elements can be variously combined and arranged as sets of subsets. So we can build, for example, the sets $\{x_1, x_2\}$, $\{x_3\}$ or $\{x_1\}$, $\{x_2, x_3\}$, and so forth. The number of subsets or the power set of *A* is therefore larger than the number of elements of the original set $\{x_1, x_2, x_3\}$. This means that the so-called power set $p(A)$, that is, the set of all subsets of *A*, is necessary larger than *A*. Since this holds for all sets, there can be no universal infinite set, there can be no whole of beings or anything of the sort. The alleged whole is rather the transfinite dimension of infinite proliferation. Badiou has condensed this thought into the slogan: being as such is an inconsistent multiplicity, which is not a multiplicity consisting of determinate elements, is not given in the form of original elements. Just as in contemporary set theory, there are no ur-elements. The only quasi-element, the existence of which can be postulated, is the empty set, which is a member of every set.

Yet, things are even more complicated. If set theory cannot be the ultimate model for ontology, as I have argued in the introduction, and if instead of conceiving of being in terms of a mathematical multiplicity we have to think of it as the whole within which a multiplicity of fields of sense takes place, then we need a new transfinite in analogy to Nietzsche's new infinite, another post-Cantorian perspective, as it were.[94] There is no static eternal proliferation of elements (which are really always already sets, too) *more arithmetico*, but rather a dynamic proliferation of fields of senses due to the always other possibility of sense making. The possibilities within a given domain always exceed the domain insofar as the transgression over a domain is an inherent possibility of the domain's very constitution. Given that domains are only individuated in a context of domains, transgression is always possible, because the other domains are present as excluded. Therefore, the possible transgression of a domain is built into its constitution, even though it cannot be determined by its constitutive rules. Therefore, a possibility, which is not a possibility determined by its constitutive rules, is implicit in every domain. This possibility is its contingency. The transfinite surplus to any possible infinity (and be it Nietzsche's new infinite of interpretations or perspectives) consists in a possible transgression, which cannot be anticipated by any rules.

The world shows itself to us always only under cosmological models. Cosmological models are spheres of intelligibility under which we bring the world, and in so doing, we bring the world to order. We order the world in this manner, but we do not have any independent criterion that would allow us to assert that *any* cosmological model describes the world as it is in itself. Thus the world is a limit-concept rather than, say, a specific entity. The world is in this sense all that is the case, for its function as a limit-concept supports all domains of objects and thus all there is. The world is accessible under a variety of descriptions. That does not mean, however, that the world can somehow be a rigorously determined object in the sense of an object belonging to a first-order theory that quantifies over a domain of objects.

On our conceptual model, then, the idea of the world is different from logical space in that the former squares with a post-Cantorian theory of existence, that is, the nontotalizable, transfinite set of all distinguishable domains and all that happens therein. In contrast, logical space is the fugitive, autoretractive condition of the world, which in principle cannot be adequately thematized at all. We must thematize logical space in the mode of potency [*Potenz*], that is, from possibility: it must be recognized as possible that that which is the case is multiple and that all that is the case now could be otherwise, or could simply never have taken place at all.

Where, then, does the logical discourse that I have developed so far stand in this picture? Over the last few pages have I not incessantly quantified over logical space, which was introduced as a *singulare tantum*? Have we not against our best intentions restricted and therefore missed the "absolute," logical space, reducing it in the end to just another (Fregean) object upon which we bestow predicates, even if only the predicate of an essential predicatelessness?[95] Logical space is just like T. S. Eliot's "one-eyed merchant":

> And here is the one-eyed merchant, and this card,
> Which is blank, is something he carries on his back,
> Which I am forbidden to see.[96]

As soon as something stateable exists, a sphere of intelligibility is established: in precisely this moment (of the reciprocal constitution of the possibility of determining an object and the sphere of intelligibility, in which such determination is possible), logical space falls into the background. Logical space as such can only be glimpsed in its withdrawal, that is, only when we determine something. We must not forget, too, that upon referring to logical space as the background of our determinations, qua that which retracts upon our determining something or other, we determine it as such (logical space qua background) only by ipso facto bringing it into the fore-ground and generating yet another background. We can only refer to the background as such under excessive and improper terms, failing, too, even in the present formulation. That is to say, our means of access to logical space as such are utterly limited. And that is so because logical space does not take place under apophantic conditions, that is, under the conditions in which "something as something" takes place. As the later Schelling puts it,

> In eternity there is no "as"; something, call it A, cannot be anything with-out the exclusion of that which it is not, not A. Here, however, the subject is merely pure, that is, straightaway and utterly irreflective Being, not being posited as such. For any "being posited as such," anything "as," as such is posited in and presupposes a reflection—is a "being reflected"—is, in other words, already a Contrarium.[97]

The crucial idea that Schelling here formulates and that Hegel, too, emphasizes, is that the entire discourse we have sketched heretofore in the present essay is all performed in the medium of reflection. This means that the *pre*-supposition of logical space in the foregoing dialectic is resultant of a presup-*position*, an anterior positioning in and by reflection: that is, logical space, as that which is posited as lying before all determination, is itself posited as such (as before) by reflection. This dynamic is what Hegel refers to as "immanent *presupposing*."[98] "Reflection is the sublating of the negative of itself, it is a coincidence with itself; it therefore sublates its posi-ting, and since in its positing it sublates its positing, it is a presupposing."[99] Presuppositions, in other words, are for Hegel merely posits that behave in a certain way, namely by suspending the fact of their being posited.[100] Presuppositions are posits that are, as it were, snuck into place. They work by distorting any reflection on themselves and, in so doing, support a pre-supposition against which reflection is determined. However, through this operation reflection by no means transcends itself. For

> [i]mmediacy presents itself simply and solely as a return and is that nega-tive which is the illusory being of the beginning, the illusory being which is negated by the return. Accordingly, the return of essence is its self-repulsion. In other words, reflection-into-self is essentially the presup-posing of that from which it is the return.[101]

To return to the thought with which I began, we can now say with Hegel: no *determinate*, absolute beginning can be given that would condition reflection as such. One cannot simply set out from something, say, that there is a world that is a big physical whole composed of tiny physical objects, the arrangement of which in space and time is resultant of physical laws. Still less can we simply set out from the thought that the world is the life-world (*Lebenswelt*). The world is neither exclusively the world of *science* nor exclusively the *life-world*. In addition to these worlds, there are indeed countless other worlds that, following Goodman, one can call "world versions."[102] For example, there is the world of a Pelevin novel, the world of *La Jeteé*, the world of nineteenth-century America, that of the present residents of the Maxvorstadt in Munich, the world of the happy, the sad, and so forth. All supposedly determinate beginnings are reflections of a certain world version, are reflections that take place within certain versions of the world. All attempts, therefore, to posit a determinate beginning deny the contingency of the version of the world from which they all stem and by virtue of which they are themselves nominated as the beginning. To say it otherwise: all efforts to determine the origin of reflection and all candidates for such determinate origins are myths of origin designed by the residents of a world.

Logical space, the unconditioned, the One, Being, the Absolute, or whatever we want to call it, is thus no *determinate* absolute beginning. Yet, most theorists are not satisfied by this thought, for they want to distinguish a far more *determinate* One, "on which the sky and nature depend," as Aristotle said in the *Metaphysics*.[103] For physicalists, this is the apotheosis of quantification. In the modern world, it is well known that the natural sciences, paradigmatically Physics, stand in first place of potential successors for God, that is, a theologically determined unity. However, this effort ultimately offers only one cosmological model among others, science in toto itself consisting of a plurality of world versions. Not even at the alleged "ideal limit of inquiry" can they secure once and for all from their own resources that their cosmological model fits the world. The fact remains that there are presuppositions in play in the natural scientific world version that cannot be thematized in the established theory without thereby becoming distorted, that is, in turn generating their own presupposition. The presuppositions of theorizing can in *no* theory become fully mapped or elucidated: through this fact, all theories exhibit the form of presupposing that Schelling and Hegel investigated and exposed. Theories generate presuppositions themselves, without in any way guaranteeing the possibility of an act of self-transcendence, for such presuppositions are by no means mere determinations. Hegel, with another brilliant gesture of demystification, writes,

Reflection therefore *finds before it* an immediate, which it transcends and from which it is the return. But this return is only the presupposing of what reflection finds before it. What is thus found only *comes to be* through being *left behind*; its immediacy is a sublated immediacy.[104]

At this point, you will suspect that my reflection has maneuvered itself into a constructivist or idealist impasse. With Brandom, you might want to object that "the thought that that world is always already there anyway, regardless of the activities, if any, of knowing and acting subjects, has always stood as the most fundamental objection to any sort of idealism."[105] Yet, one must heed Brandom's delicate wording: his argument begins, after all, "*the thought* that that world is . . . " The world remains here a necessary presupposition of the theory-building process, which does not exclude but straightaway and necessarily includes the idea that the world is posited. Or, to put it with Habermas, in this objection the world appears in a straightforward manner as a "formal world-presupposition."[106] The world "in itself" (whatever that expression might mean) is not "always already there anyway" precisely because the ontological status of the "always already" only makes sense in terms of a presupposition. The modalities only come into being through thought's relation to what there is, which does not entail that all objects are mind-dependent. Existence is dependent on domains, and domains are intelligible structures. This means that objectivity is a product of thought and discourse, which does not hold for all and any objects, given that the chair I am currently sitting on is not objectivity or a domain, but a chair.

The world is first and only belatedly necessary. It is only when we reflect on the fact that there is a plurality of different reference systems that the world comes to appear: only *after* this plurality of systems appears can we even assume that it must relate to something, whatever it may be. Now, one might argue in favor of a more robust realism about the elements to be encountered in the world that a plurality of forms of arrangements of elements presuppose that the elements were already there to be arranged. However, this reasoning is far too simple. For such talk of elements already presupposes a system of reference, viz. a system of reference that quantifies over systems of reference. This higher-order reference system suffers the same conditions of possibility as the systems of reference over which it quantifies. Therefore, any talk of given elements—be they Platonic-Aristotelian forms (εἴδη), Russellian sense-data, Wittgensteinian objects, physical particles or waves, or whatever—is anything but presupposition-less. The opposite is true.[107]

The Absolute of a determinate theory is necessarily a certain, determinate Absolute and therefore not the Absolute per se, that which precedes all theories. Given that this is consistently elusive, all of our theories stay a step behind their ultimate object. In other words, there are several candidates for the Absolute, from the classical physicalistic world qua totality of all extended spatiotemporal objects (which extends beyond the life-world), the One, God, the will to power, and so forth. Ultimately, all theories generate an absolute, in that in their pronunciation of a difference between form and content, they posit the content as already there to be discovered through representation. *No element of the set "all candidates for the absolute" is absolute save in the sense that it is generated as a candidate for the absolute in the* spielraum *of contingency.* This is the essential point, and this thought is precisely what authors like Heidegger or Lacan have so vehemently articulated through radically innovative modes of presentation, in particular with the introduction of the grapheme of being *sous rature.*

Yet throughout all this we must keep in view the fact that our limited statements, stammering gestures, or once again with Wittgenstein, our "inarticulate sound,"[108] do not mean that we have penetrated the Absolute *ad maiorem Dei gloriam.* We experience, again, only a withdrawal: it does not follow from this that there is in any way something that in actual fact eludes us. With an experience of contingency we recognize a limit, which does not imply that we are therefore beyond this limit. And if contingency is to truly have the last word, we cannot even claim that this is necessary: this means that there is no theoretical operation that can guarantee even that at least contingency is necessary. For all claims, including *this one*, take place within the *spielraum* of contingency.

If we now understand necessity to mean *a hanging together* (as Sellars speaks of what goes on in logical space[109]) *of elements where nothing could be otherwise*, then all necessity is therefore relative to a system of reference. Given that all reference systems can themselves be registered as elements in a higher-order reference system, we quickly arrive at a point of insight, from which it is clear that the terms and conditions of any reference system's creation can ultimately only be determined belatedly. This entails that *all necessity is belated necessity.* The supposed "hardness of the logical must" is thus resultant of a certain sclerotic dimming or distortion: the always fragile original conditions of a theory must become practically fortified and developed and are guaranteed only through the work of power. The fundamental propositions that ground any observed necessity are not reflectively *posited* [*gesetzte*], but rather are set into circulation as *laws* [*Gesetze*].

2. With Schelling against Hegel

As the popular standard reading has it, Hegel wanted to totally eliminate contingency so as to ground a kind of spiritual monism along the lines of a simple translation of Spinoza's substance into subject. On this reading of Hegel's thought, thinking itself is figured as a teleologically developing spirit: by virtue of this, all contingency is eliminated in favor of a seemingly senseless yet assuredly teleological movement of spirit or the Idea in history.

Be that as it may, Hegel ultimately deals with the modalities in such a way as to show *the necessity of contingency*; thus he can defend himself against the reproach that his teleology of spirit is merely a sort of cheap and easy displacement of the problem of contingency. Against Hegel's thesis of the necessity of contingency, Schelling argues that necessity as such is belated. Because all necessity is ultimately repressed contingency, one can see with Schelling that Hegel's thesis of the necessity of contingency harbors a certain blind spot. It reveals itself all the more to be the opposite, that is, that all necessity is contingent, that necessity can only retroactively be established. In terms of the theory I have been developing throughout this book, the theory-building process of the arrangement of elements into a necessary order is precisely contingent on a higher order, because the theory-building process is fed by creative energies that cannot be brought under the authority of the rules of any determinate theory. The very rules, which constitute the domain of a theory, are not in the same way necessary as the relation between the elements, which are individuated by the constitutive rules. For example, it might be necessary that $7 + 5 = 12$, because the properties of 7, 5, and the relevant transformation rule called "addition" add up in such a manner that they necessitate the answer "12" when conjoined in an arithmetically relevant manner. Yet, the rules manifested in our transformation of mathematical symbols are not in the same way necessary as the relation between axioms and theorems. It could well be that "+" had a different meaning. Once its meaning is fixed in the context of arithmetic as we understand and practice it, "+" acquires the meaning + as opposed to say *quus*, to pick up Kripke's famous example.[110] Axioms and transformation rules are not necessary in the sense of the elements (theorems) generated by them in the process of accumulating knowledge. They constitute a domain, within which necessity becomes possible. For this reason, necessity is always already belated, it only comes after the fact of constitutive rules. Schelling and Hegel agree about the belatedness of necessity, with the important difference that Schelling applies belatedness to the insight into belatedness itself. According to Schelling, belatedness is, therefore, belated with respect to itself. The necessity of contingency is itself a contingent necessity.

In spite of the common thread at the ground of their respective theories, Schelling and Hegel part ways at a decisive moment: their respective accounts of the initial state of logical space. Hegel assumes that the very structure of reflection, that to which he refers by the name of "being," can be described in terms of a presupposition of reflection. "Being" is for Hegel in fact nothing other than the existence of the structure of reflection, in other words, the name for pure immanence. Therefore, everything within being just as anything determined to be different from being is immanent, in that it is in principle something knowable. There is nothing that cannot be anticipated or metabolized by our conceptual resources. "For being is posited as absolutely necessary, as self-mediation, which is absolute negation of mediation by an other, or as being which is identical only with being; an *other* that has actuality in *being*, is therefore determined simply as something *merely possible*, as empty positedness."[111]

Hegel's thesis can be translated to mean that the limit of any theory can be described using the proper language of that theory. If it were possible on this basis to develop a general theory-theory, this would amount to Hegel's thesis of totality, which states that *the immanent hanging-together of the whole cannot be exceeded because any boundary set to the whole is automatically internal to it.* For Hegel, the excluded is included as excluded, as Luhmann would have put it. Hegel refers to this idea as "absolute necessity."[112]

Absolute necessity, as Hegel says, is "that being which in its negation, in essence, is self-related and is being."[113] On my translation, this means that all theories of the world belong to the world itself, and that the stability of logical space lies in this fact. Logical space is necessarily reflexive, since it would not otherwise manifest itself in its withdrawal. That logical space is "the Absolute" in Hegel's language is clear: "Absolute necessity is thus the *reflection or form of the absolute*: the unity of being and essence, simple immediacy that is absolute negativity."[114] Logical space arises, therefore, not before our theory construction, but it is generated in our theory construction first and foremost as a paradoxical starting point, which is the central thesis of Hegel's rightly named *absolute idealism*. Logical space is, according to Hegel, a nontranscendent or immanent hanging together, and as such it is (and here is the crux) a mere aspect or moment of an absolute reflection which encompasses it. Reflection on the constitution of logical space retroactively creates its own starting point, and this starting point is thereby always already related to what follows from it.

Hegel's idea of immanence, which he describes as an absolute necessity, is also intended to make the following claim plausible. "World" is the name of an unqualified and utterly comprehensive unity, for there is absolutely nothing that does not belong to the world. This implies, however, that theories of the world must also belong to the world. The world cannot be merely an object domain in the sense of a determinate object domain of a particular first order theory. For then object domains themselves can be said to exist, so that theories are in the world alongside cats, our mental states, and Paris. Moreover, the world is itself intelligible in the sense that we can discover it as such, as a comprehensive unity, only at the peak of reflection, from which we can see directly that it is not an object among objects. In its capacity as unfolded logical space, the world bears the property of constitutive conceptual withdrawal itself, the property we attributed to logical space earlier. Nevertheless, we recognize the world constantly, not as such, but only under a certain description. All this means that no theory can be beyond the world. All theories belong to the world. Because we cannot theoretically escape the world, it is an absolute necessity. Thus spoke Hegel.

However, we can ascertain with Schelling at exactly this point a potential cut point. It presents itself immediately as the question: in which theory-language has the world *as* world been thematized? Is this talk of the world and the immanent hanging together of the whole anything more than yet another sclerotic dimming or distortion of belatedness? If all necessity is belated, which Hegel certainly concedes in his logic of reflection, then the absolute necessity as well as Hegel's entire theory-language in the *Science of Logic* is certainly not "the exposition of God as he is in his eternal essence before the creation of nature and a finite mind,"[115] as he provocatively announces at the very beginning of the book. Also suspicious is Hegel's promise of discovering "the realm of pure thought": "this realm is the truth as it is without veil and in its own absolute nature."[116] In a typical modern gesture of "lifting his hand against God,"[117] Hegel sits himself here in the place of Jesus Christ. His *Science of Logic* is precisely for this reason meant to be "way, truth, and life," because Hegel is convinced that the logic of reflection sets us on solid ground. It itself relieves us from what we have observed as the finitude of all theoretical operations and transforms its belatedness into an absolute fact for all: no way other than belated necessity.

Schelling, however, rightly always expects that the language of his own theory must remain deficient because "the truth, as it is, uncovered in and of itself," is not presentable. Each presentation of the truth, that is, each assertoric judgment, shows itself in the world under a certain description.

This obviously also holds true for judgments about judgments, which say, for instance, that all judgments are deficient. In other words, we have no means to attain to a Fregean reference free from a Fregean sense: our reference to objects is always already integral to a context, without which the individual episode to be described would remain a disconnected fragment. Such integratedness is what John McDowell describes in his eponymous essay as the necessary condition of "having the world in view."

> [T]he intentionality, the objective purport, of perceptual experience in general—whether potentially knowledge yielding or not—depends [...] on having the world in view, in a sense that goes beyond glimpses of the here and now. It would not be intelligible that the relevant episodes present themselves as glimpses of the here and now apart from their being related to a wider world view.[118]

Although we can only refer to the world by means of contingent descriptions, we are confident that there is something that we are speaking about, something to bring into language, something that strictly speaking may not even be "something" because everything that is, is such-and-so under apophantic conditions. Schelling speaks of a paradoxical primordial state of affairs that cannot be presented yet drives all presentation, the constitutive un-presentable, as "unprethinkable being."

Unprethinkable being is Schelling's name for the facticity of reason. This facticity for him is resultant of the fact that a mere dimension of distinction without anything distinct still has no relationship to a differentiation in judgments and is therefore indeed a necessary presupposition, but is only a contingently necessary presupposition. It is a necessary *pre*supposition, yet it is so only "post actum" or "a posteriori,"[119] as Schelling says, that is, only as a presup*position*. The positing is itself not necessary, it could not have taken place at all. This would not have affected the facticity of unprethinkable being. Yet, it would not have been anything determinate and, in particular, not even a necessary being. There are no modalities without positing and no positing without judgment, for positing, that is, determination, takes place only within a predicative ambience. The necessity of the presupposition is, therefore, only determinate in contradistinction to the contingency of our positing and therefore supervenient on contingency, or resultant of an accident. In other words: necessity is belated and is, for this reason, contingent.

Further, in the presupposition as such no reasons can be found, for it is from this very contingent ground that reasons as such come to be. Thus the reasons for the original decision or presupposition only come to be retrospectively, only after "I have decided between +a and −a [can it be said that] my 'being +a' is not resultant of a mere, blind whim, which would always and necessarily require thinking its contingency. Now it is not seen as a contingency because it is an intention, something willed."[120] No reasons can be unearthed in the original contingency of determinacy: it can only be eliminated by virtue of an act of what Schelling calls the "will."

Our predicative being-in-the-world is the potentialization of our presuppositions. As I have pointed out various times in this book, this logico–ontological structure of repression lies also behind the groundbreaking thesis of the late Schelling: "will is primal being [*Wollen ist Urseyn*]."[121] The transition from *x* to *F(x)* established determinacy and lies outside of determinacy. For this reason, the transition must be *willed*, an act of *decision* that leads to the very idea of a *distinction*.[122] Insofar as beings are determinate, all such determinations and therefore all beings must be willed, for otherwise the very dimension of sense would never have become established. This lets itself be stated belatedly, but cannot be conceptually anticipated. Thus, our thinking comes after an unprethinkable being and not before. This is likewise dependent on the fact that unprethinkable being as such comes to us only as that which is posited, also only as *x*, as possible subject of a judgment. That unknown *x* is then also a belated *x*—an object variable that can be determined in possible judgments.

In other words, the crucial premise in Schelling's theory of predication is: all judgments reveal a paradoxical structure of presupposition that we cannot in principle get control over through predication. Reflection ultimately draws on conceptual preferences, the registration of preferred presentations that cannot be rationally eliminated. They remain, therefore, always behind the back of reflection, just as they were originally, despite our incessant effort to represent them. This romantic-themed structure resembles the constant search for the "blue flower" (Novalis); the unknown *x* as presupposition of judgments is established hereby as the cornerstone of a counter-Hegelian *deflationary metaphysics*. For the unknown *x* is neither God nor the absolute in some twenty-four karat pure sense, but is merely the name for a constitutive withdrawal, without which we could make no judgments. This is a simple thought: that about which we judge comes before the judgment: being determines consciousness. Despite this seeming primacy of the object, we must insist with Frege: reference [*Bedeutung*] takes place only through the medium of sense [*Sinn*], from which we cannot abstract, which does not imply that meaningful [*sinnvolle*] statements mean nothing [*nichts bedeuten*]. We always relate and refer to something that can never be fully represented and therefore—as Schelling has it—the "irreducible or indivisible remainder" ["*nie aufgehende Rest*"[123]] persists as "that which with the greatest exertion cannot be resolved in understanding."[124] The dimension of presupposition that Schelling thematizes is by no means simply unknown: that said, Hegel seeks to bring this dimension to light in terms of his program of sublation in the concept [*Aufhebung in den Begriff*]. However, Hegel does so without thereby recognizing that the language and aim of his own theory is, just as Schelling's theory indicates, by no means presentation-independent. Ultimately, Hegel's *Science of Logic*, the greatest masterpiece of dialectics, is only one field of sense among others.

The crucial difference between Schelling and Hegel is that Schelling understands reflection as irrevocably finite. The structure of a posteriori or belated necessity holds therefore also for the supposed absolute necessity of reflection. That there is reflection, in other words, that thinking and theory-building processes take place, that the world thematizes itself and a logical space of possibility is opened, is according to Schelling a contingent fact. Hegel, on the contrary, endorses a *strong anthropic principle*, as it were, which states that of necessity something and thus logical space is given and that therein reflection came to be. Hegel has it that finite thinkers qua the place of reflection could not not have taken place. The necessity of reflection follows, in Hegel's eyes, from the structure of belated necessity, and entails that the actual can be completely conceptually penetrated, for all presence can be revealed as posited. In contrast, Schelling insists on the anti-idealistic intuition that there is something, the unknown x, which reflection in principle cannot so easily overcome. This he called "the unequal to itself"—a concept that today surely brings to mind Adorno's talk of the nonidentical. The unequal to itself does not show itself in already established predicative frameworks. Even the concept of the unequal to itself has a sense only in the context of a specific reference system. Therefore, all concepts fail at the unrepresentability of that which Schelling calls "unprethinkable being." And yet, this unprethinkable being provides the inexhaustible resources of our semantic expressivity. Something necessarily remains unsaid: the infinite conversation that is the life and livelihood of philosophy happens to persist in this remainder. Philosophy owes its existence to the *spielraum* of contingency in and with which it plays.

Notes

Introduction

[1] One of the most clear cut expositions of this line of thought is Locke's *Essay Concerning Human Understanding*. Locke is probably one of the first who has used the metaphor of a "horizon" of knowledge. In this way, he draws a distinction between being, as it is in itself, and what is available to us in order to investigate into "the extent of our knowledge" so as to secure the domain of knowledge. He writes, "For I thought that the first Step towards satisfying several Enquiries, the Mind of Man was very apt to run into, was, to take a Survey of our own Understandings, examine our own Powers, and to see to what Things they were adapted. Till that was done I suspected we began at the wrong end, and in vain sought for Satisfaction in a quiet and secure Possession of Truths, that most concern'd us, whilst we let loose our Thoughts into the vast Ocean of *Being* [. . .] Thus Men, extending their Enquiries beyond their Capacities, and letting their Thoughts wander in those depths, where they can find no sure Footing; 'tis no Wonder, that they raise Questions, and multiply Disputes, which never coming to any clear Resolution, are proper only to continue and increase their Doubts, and to confirm them at last in perfect Scepticism. Whereas were the Capacities of our Understandings well considered, the Extent of our Knowledge once discovered, and the Horizon found, which sets the Bounds between the enlightened and the dark Parts of Things; between what is, and what is not comprehensible by us, Men would perhaps with less scruple acquiesce in the avow'd Ignorance of the one, and imploy their Thoughts and Discourse, with more Advantage and Satisfaction in the other" (John Locke, *An Essay Concerning Human Understanding*, ed. Peter H. Nidditch, Oxford: Oxford University Press, 1975, Book I, Chapter I, §7).

[2] See, of course, Richard Rorty, *Philosophy and the Mirror of Nature*. Princeton: Princeton University Press, 1979.

[3] For this famous formula see W. V. O. Quine, *From a Logical Point of View. Nine logico-philosophical Essays* (second, revised edition), Cambridge, MA: Harvard University Press, 1963, p. 15.

[4] Heidegger elaborates on the notion of the "world" in *The Fundamental Concepts of Metaphysics: World, Finitude, Solitude*. Tr. W. McNeil and N. Walker. Bloomington: Indiana University Press, 1995. See, in particular, §68, where Heidegger "defines" the notion of the world: "World is the manifestness of beings as such as a whole." Of course, he continues to argue against "the naïve concept of the world," which understands the whole as a sum or an aggregate of things or entities, whereas the whole is for Heidegger nothing but the historically shifting domain, within which entities make sense to us.

[5] The ground-breaking work of this strand of Neo-Hegelianism is Robert Pippin, *Hegel's Idealism. The Satisfactions of Self-Consciousness*. Cambridge: Cambridge University

Press, 1989. Some recent reformulations of his basic claims can be found in John McDowell, *Having the World in View. Essays on Kant, Hegel, and Sellars.* Cambridge, Ma: Harvard University Press, 2009, in particular "Hegel's Idealism as a Radicalization of Kant", ibid., pp. 69–89; and Robert Brandom, *Reason in Philosophy. Animating Ideas.* Cambridge, MA: Harvard University Press, 2009.

[6] Bertrand Russell's appraisal comes to mind: "Philosophically, though famous in his day, he [Schelling] is not important. The import and development from Kant's philosophy was that of Hegel"; see Bertrand Russell, *History of Western Philosophy.* London: Routledge, 2004, p. 651.

[7] Slavoj Žižek, *The Indivisible Remainder. On Schelling and Related Matters.* London/New York: Verso, 1996, p. 14: "as with Hegel, the problem is not how to attain the noumenal In-itself beyond phenomena; the true problem is how and why does this In-itself split itself from itself at all, how does it acquire a distance towards itself and thus clear the space in which it can appear (to itself)?" See also Žižek's "The Abyss of Freedom" in Žižek/Schelling, *The Abyss of Freedom/Ages of the World.* Tr. J. Norman. Ann Arbor: University of Michigan Press, 1997, p. 15.

[8] Georg Wilhelm Friedrich Hegel, *Science of Logic.* Tr. A.V. Miller. Amherst, NY: Humanity Books, 1969, p. 395.

[9] In his 1804 *Wissenschaftlehre*, Fichte speaks of "a *phenomenology*, a doctrine of appearance and illusion"; see J. G. Fichte, *The Science of Knowing. J. G. Fichte's 1804 Lectures on the Wissenschaftslehre.* Tr. W. E. Wright, Albany: SUNY Press, 2005, p. 107. See further Žižek's "Fichte's Laughter" in M. Gabriel/S. Žižek, *Mythology, Madness, and Laughter. Subjectivity in German Idealism.* New York/London: Continuum Press, 2009, pp. 122–167.

[10] Immanuel Kant, *Critique of Pure Reason.* Tr. N Kemp Smith. New York: Palgrave MacMillan, 2003, cf. A247/B304: ". . . the proud name of ontology, which presumes to offer synthetic *a priori* cognitions of things in general . . . must give way to the more modest title of a transcendental analytic."

[11] See Jacobi's two crucial texts on nihilism "On Transcendental Idealism", in Brigitte Sassen (ed.), *Kant's Early Critics. The Empiricist Critique of Theoretical Philosophy.* Cambridge: Cambridge University Press, 2000; as well as his famous "Open Letter to Fichte", in Ernst Behler (ed.), *Philosophy of German Idealism.* New York: Continuum Press, 1987.

[12] Ludwig Wittgenstein, *Tractatus Logico-Philosophicus.* Tr. D. F. Pears and B. McGuinness. London: Routledge, 2001, 1. See also John McDowell, *Mind and World.* Cambridge, MA/London: Harvard University Press, 1996, p. 27: "We can formulate the point in a style Wittgenstein would have been uncomfortable with: there is no ontological gap between the sort of thing one can mean, or generally the sort of thing one can think, and the sort of thing that can be the case. When one thinks truly, what one thinks *is* what is the case. So since the world is everything that is the case (as he himself once wrote), there is no gap between thought, as such, and the world. Of course thought can be distanced from the world by being false, but there is no distance from the world implicit in the very idea of thought."

[13] McDowell, *Mind and World*, p. 33.

[14] John McDowell, *Meaning, Knowledge, and Reality.* Cambridge, MA/London: Harvard University Press, 1998, p. 392.

[15] McDowell, *Having the World in View*, p. 3. He explicitly formulates his project as the attempt to "find intentionality unproblematic."

[16] Gottlob Frege, "On Sinn and Bedeutung", in *The Frege Reader*, Ed. M. Beaney. Oxford: Blackwell Publishing, 1997, pp. 151–71, here: p. 154. See also G. Frege,

"The Thought: A Logical Inquiry", in *Mind*, New Series, Vol. 65, No. 259. (July 1956), pp. 289–311. p. 298: "Accordingly, with a proper name, it depends on how whatever it refers to is presented. This can happen in different ways and every such way corresponds with a particular sense of a sentence containing a proper name."
[17] McDowell, *Having the World in View*, p. 72.
[18] I elaborate on this distinction in Markus Gabriel, *An den Grenzen der Erkenntnistheorie. Die notwendige Endlichkeit des objektiven Wissens als Lektion des Skeptizismus*. Freiburg/München: Alber, 2008.
[19] See for instance Fichte, *1804 Wissenschaftslehre*, pp. 149, 154, 161–4, 180–90 and passim.
[20] Ibid., p. 158. See also p. 161–2, 171, 174.
[21] Ibid., p. 139.
[22] Ibid., p. 122.
[23] Friedrich Wilhelm Joseph Schelling, *The Grounding of Positive Philosophy. The Berlin Lectures*. Tr. Bruce Matthews. Albany: SUNY Press. (2007), pp. 121–8.
[24] Ibid., p. 128.
[25] For a reading along those lines see the remarkable book by Josef Simon, *Philosophy of the Sign*. Tr. G. Hefferman. Albany: SUNY Press, 2003.
[26] Kant, *Critique of Pure Reason*, A256/B312.
[27] Schelling, *Grounding of Positive Philosophy*, p. 122.
[28] See also Michael Williams, *Groundless Belief: An Essay on the Possibility of Epistemology*. Princeton: Princeton University Press, 1999, p. 48: "The upshot of this is that the sense-datum theorist is caught in a dilemma. The view that sense-data are simply discovered by introspecting one's perceptual consciousness is highly implausible. But the alternative view—that they are postulated theoretical entities—seems to conflict with the requirement that they be *given*."
[29] Anton Friedrich Koch, *Versuch über Wahrheit und Zeit*. Paderborn: Mentis, 2006.
[30] Meillassoux defines "correlationism" in the following way: "Correlationism consists in disqualifying the claim that it is possible to consider the realms of subjectivity and objectivity independently of one another." (Quentin Meillassoux, *After Finitude: An Essay on the Necessity of Contingency*. Tr. R. Brassier. New York/London: Continuum, 2008, p. 5ff.) Meillassoux believes that correlationism comes close to contemporary creationism by denying naïve realism (p. 18).
[31] Robert Brandom, *Tales of the Mighty Dead. Historical Essays in the Metaphysics of Intentionality*. Cambridge, MA/London: Harvard University Press, 2002, p. 50: "Concept *P* is *sense dependent* on concept *Q* just in case one cannot count as having grasped *P* unless one counts as having grasped *Q*. Concept *P* is *reference dependent* on concept *Q* just in case *P* cannot apply to something unless *Q* applies to something." See also p. 208.
[32] This is particularly evident in Badiou's argument for the "inexistence of the whole/all (*inexistence du tout*)"; Alain Badiou, *Logics of Worlds. Being and Event 2*. Tr. A. Toscano. New York/London: Continuum, 2009, p. 109ff.
[33] Brandom, *Tales of the Mighty Dead*, p. 193.
[34] Ibid., p. 185.
[35] Slavoj Žižek, *The Ticklish Subject. The Absent Centre of Political Ontology*. London/New York: Verso, 2008, p. 69.
[36] G. W. F. Hegel, *Phenomenology of Spirit*. Tr. A. V. Miller. Oxford: Oxford University Press, 1977, §20.
[37] As a recent example see Rolf-Peter Horstmann's essay "The *Phenomenology of Spirit* as a 'transcendentalistic' argument for a monistic ontology", in D. Moyar/ M. Quante (eds.), *Hegel's* Phenomenology of Spirit. *A Critical Guide*. Cambridge: Cambridge

University Press, 2008, pp. 43–62. Horstmann seems to identify "ontology" with a first-order theory, when he claims that Hegel's overall enterprise is designed to defend a monistic "metaphysical thesis that stands at the center of his entire effort" (p. 49). He summarizes this thesis as "the (sufficiently obscure) thesis that the entirety of reality must be seen as a single all-comprehending self-developing rational entity, which achieves knowledge of itself in a spatio-temporal process of realizing its distinctive conceptual determinations" (p. 49–50). Fortunately, there is no evidence that Hegel ever defended such a thesis about "the entirety of reality" and so forth. It is particularly odd to refer to this entirety as a "spatio-temporal process." No wonder Horstmann finds this invention of his "sufficiently obscure."

[38] See Gottlob Frege *The Foundations of Arithmetic. A logico-mathematical enquiry into the concept of number.* Tr. J. L Austin. Evanston: Northwestern University Press, 1980, §53.

[39] The most distinct representative of this tradition is, of course, Leibniz. See, for example, his 1684 "Meditations on Knowledge, Truth, and Ideas" in Georg Wilhelm Leibniz, *Philosophical Essays.* Tr. R. Ariew and D. Garber. Indianapolis: Hackett Publishing, 1989, pp. 23–8.

[40] In a similar vein, Brandom argues that "object" and "singular term" are sense-dependent concepts in Robert Brandom, *Articulating Reasons: An Introduction to Inferentialism.* Cambridge, MA.: Harvard University Press, 2000, Chapter 4. Brandom's argument there is remarkable for various reasons, but particularly relevant for the argumentation in the text because it emphasizes the necessary connection between our concept of objects and our use of singular terms. Predicative (for Brandom: inferential) structures are constitutive of objects and of the fact that we distinguish them by their properties. Of course, Brandom himself draws different consequences from this.

[41] Cf Alain Badiou, *Being and Event.* Tr. by Oliver Feltham. New York/London: Continuum, 2007, Part I. See also his explicit identification of mathematical multiplicity with "extension" and of logical multiplicity (appearance in a world) with "intension" in Badiou, *Logics of Worlds,* p. 299–303 (Introduction to book IV).

[42] See Badiou, *Logics of Worlds,* p. 208: "*Given a world and a function of appearing whose values lie in the transcendental of this world, we will call 'existence' of a being x which appears in this world the transcendental degree assigned to the self-identity of x.* Thus defined, existence is not a category of being (of mathematics), it is a category of appearing (of logic). In particular, 'to exist' has no meaning in itself. In agreement with one of Sartre's insights, who borrows it from Heidegger, but also from Kierkegaard or even Pascal, 'to exist' can only be said relatively to a world. In effect, existence is nothing but a transcendental degree. It indicates the intensity of appearance of a multiple-being in a determinate world, and this intensity is by no means prescribed by the pure multiple composition of the being in question."

[43] For a similar critique of Badiou's ontology see Žižek, *The Ticklish Subject,* pp. 191–3.

[44] Georg Cantor, *Contributions to the Founding of the Theory of Transfinite Numbers.* Tr. P. E. B. Jourdain. New York: Cosimo Books, 2007, p. 86.

[45] "In what follows, we will call *universe* the (empty) concept of a being of the Whole. We will call *world* a 'complete' situation of being (this will be gradually elucidated). Obviously, since we show that *there is no* universe, it belongs to the essence of the world that there are several worlds, since if there were only one it would be the universe" (Badiou, *Logics of Worlds,* p. 102).

[46] Badiou, *Logics of Worlds,* p. 114.

[47] Aristotle, *Metaphysics*, 992b18–20, 1003a33–4, 1026b2 (Here and throughout the text, all Aristotle citations refer to *The Complete Works of Aristotle. The Revised Oxford Translation,* (2 Volumes) Ed. Jonathan Barnes. Princeton: Princeton University Press, 1971). Badiou, however, defends the idea of the necessity of universality

for all worlds which is derived from his method of an analytic: "The analytic can also be defined as the theory of worlds, the elucidation of the most abstract laws of that which constitutes a world qua general form of appearing" (Badiou, *Logics of Worlds*, p. 299).

[48] Hegel, *Science of Logic*, p. 113.

[49] See Martin Heidegger, *The Principle of Reason*. Tr. Reginald Lilly. Indianapolis: Indiana University Press, 1991.

[50] See Martin Heidegger, *Die Kategorien- und Bedeutungslehre des Duns Scotus*. Tubingen, J. C. B. Mohr, 1916.

[51] Aristotle, *Metaphysics*, 1003a21–6.

[52] Another crucial difference between the ontological project common to all post-Kantian idealists and Badiou's ontology is their emphasis on relationality as primary. Surprisingly, despite the emphasis on the absolute, post-Kantian idealism defends a metaphysics of relationality: Being cannot be made sense of in terms of a mere *Seinslogik*, to put it with Hegel, precisely because Being in the sense of a set of "real atoms" (Badiou) can only be posited retroactively as a presupposition of determinacy. In opposition to this, Badiou defends a primacy of Being over relationality: "The extensive law of multiple being subsumes the logical form of relations. Being has the last word. It already did at the level of atomic logic, where we affirmed, under the name of 'postulate of materialism', that every atom is real" (Badiou, *Logics of Worlds*, p. 302).

[53] For a classic sophisticated refutation of the semantics underlying the projects of an intensional logic, see Hilary Putnam, "The Meaning of 'Meaning,'" in *Philosophical Papers, Vol. 2: Mind, Language and Reality*. Cambridge, Cambridge University Press, 1979.

[54] Hegel, *Science of Logic*, p. 58.

[55] "This sphere is the realm of spirit for the reason that the individual has infinite value in himself, knows himself as absolute freedom, possesses in himself the most rigid firmess and consistency, and gives up this consistency and preserves himself in what is strictly an other; love harmonizes everything, even this absolute antithesis of dependence and independence" (G. W. F. Hegel, "The Absolute Religion," translated from the second volume of Hegel's "Philosophy of Religion" by F. L. Soldan, in *The Journal of Speculative Philosophy* 16:1 (January 1882), p. 258). Cf. TWA, 17, 299: Hegel refers in particular to the fact that Jesus appears as an individual and thus the form of individuality is given an absolute, divine value. Cf. also TWA, 16, 231f.: "That which is higher in contrast to the Cultus is, then, this: subjectivity has in itself arrived at consciousness of its own infinitude; here, religion and the Cultus step wholly into the territory of freedom. The subject knows itself as infinite, and indeed as subject. This entails that the earlier unrevealed has the moment in itself to be singularity, which thus receives absolute worth [Das Höhere gegen diesen Standpunkt des Kultus ist dann dies, daß *die Subjektivität zum Bewußtsein ihrer Unendlichkeit in sich* gekommen ist; hier tritt dann die Religion und der Kultus ganz in das Gebiet der *Freiheit*. Das Subjekt weiß sich als unendlich, und zwar als Subjekt. Dazu gehört, daß jenes früher Unenthüllte an ihm selbst das Moment hat, Einzelheit zu sein, die dadurch *absoluten Wert* erhält]."

[56] Cf. Markus Gabriel, *Der Mensch im Mythos. Untersuchungen über Ontotheologie, Anthropologie und Selbstbewußtseinsgeschichte in Schellings 'Philosophie der Mythologie'*. Berlin/New York: DeGruyter, 2006; and "The Mythological Being of Reflection", in Gabriel/Žižek, *Mythology, Madness, and Laughter*. pp.15- Despite the overall primacy of ontology qua set theory over logics, Badiou is aware of some retroactive traces of appearing in being. See for example: "Nonetheless, having to

exist (or to appear) retroactively endows being with a new consistency which is distinct from its own multiple dissemination" (Badiou, *Logics of Worlds*, p. 300).

[57] See Gabriel, "The Mythological Being of Reflection," pp. 15–84.

[58] See, for example, Aristotle, *Nikomachean Ethics*, 1139a8–10. There is a vast amount of contemporary literature on contingency in German, mainly inspired by Blumenberg's work. In particular, see Gravenitz/Marquard (eds.), *Kontingenz. Poetik und Hermeneutik XVII.* München: Wilhelm Fink Verlag, 1998.

[59] See Wittgenstein, *Tractatus*, 5.634: "Everything we see could also be otherwise. Everything we can describe at all could also be otherwise. There is no order of things a priori."

[60] As Heidegger, among others, has rightly pointed out, there is another notion of truth in Aristotle, which is not defined by the possibility of error and which corresponds to the grasping (θιγεῖν) of elements (τὰ ἀσύνθετα) (*Metaphysics*, Θ10). Aristotle is well aware that there must be some form of not yet propositionally structured grasping of elements to be combined in judgment. There is, hence, a dimension of nonpropositional truth before judgment. Cf. Martin Heidegger, *Being and Time.* Tr. J. Macquarrie and E. Robinson. Malden: Blackwell Publishing, 1978, §44b, and also Heidegger, *Aristotle's Metaphysics Θ 1–3: On the Essence and Actuality of Force.* Tr. W. Brogan and P. Warnek. Bloomington: Indiana University Press, 1995.

[61] For this see Castoriadis's article "Sur la relativité de la logique," in Id., *Histoire et Création. Textes philosophiques inédits (1945–1967)*, Paris: Seuil, 2009, pp. 34–9.

[62] For an elaborate and highly original interpretation of the relation between being and understanding, see Simon, *Philosophy of the Sign*, pp. 124–40.

Chapter 1

[1] Willard V. O. Quine, "On What There Is," in *From a Logical Point of View*, pp. 1–19. Yet Quine himself evidently prefers a "physicalistic" ontology, even though he confirms that this preference is resultant of a brute decision. See his famous comparison of "physical objects" with Homer's God in "Two Dogmas of Empiricism" (Ibid., pp. 20–46, esp. p. 44): "For my part I do, qua lay physicist, believe in physical objects and not in Homer's god's; and I consider it a scientific error to believe otherwise. But in point of epistemological footing the physical objects and the gods differ only in degree and not in kind. Both sorts of entities enter our conception only as cultural posits. The myth of physical objects is epistemologically superior to most in that it has proved more efficacious than other myths as a device for working a manageable structure into the flux of experience."

[2] Kant himself uses the metaphor of a horizon in this context. Kant, *Critique of Pure Reason*, A658/B686f.: "Every concept may be regarded as a point which, as the station for an observer, has its own horizon, that is, a variety of things which can be represented, and, as it were, surveyed from that standpoint. This horizon must be capable of containing an infinite number of points, each of which has its own narrower horizon; that is, every species contains subspecies, according to the principle of specification, and the logical horizon consists exclusively of smaller horizons (subspecies), never of points which possess no extent (individuals). But for different horizons, that is, genera, each of which is determined by its own concept, there can be a common horizon, in reference to which, as from a common centre, they can all be surveyed; and from this higher genus we can proceed until we arrive at the highest of all genera, and so at the universal

and true horizon, which is determined from the standpoint of the highest concept, and which comprehends under itself all manifoldness—genera, species, and subspecies." Habermas draws on the same insight when he asserts that the world is a presupposition of discourse and not an entity. See Jürgen Habermas, *Truth and Justification*, Tr. Barbara Fultner. Cambridge, MA: The MIT Press, 2003, pp. 77, 83, 90, 99, and so forth. See also, p. 57: "A shared view of reality as a territory 'halfway between' the 'world-views' of different languages is a necessary presupposition of meaningful dialogue *überhaupt*. For the interlocutors, the concept of reality is connected with the regulative idea of a 'sum total of all that is knowable.'"

[3] Cf. Peter F. Strawson, *Skepticism and Naturalism: Some Varieties*. New York: Columbia University Press, 1985; John McDowell, *Mind, Value, and Reality*, Cambridge, MA/London: Harvard University Press, 1998, in particular, "Two Forms of Naturalism," pp. 167–97. See also the Introduction to B. Leiter (ed.), *The Future for Philosophy*, Oxford/New York: Oxford University Press, 2004, pp. 1–23. Here Leiter (p. 2) instead talks of "naturalism" and "quietism." As the highest common factor of all forms of naturalism he identifies the claim that there is nothing extra- or supernatural. Both Strawson and McDowell defend a variety of liberal naturalism in the vein of Wittgenstein.

[4] See Wilfred Sellars, "Philosophy and the Scientific Image of Man," in Id., *Science, Perception, and Reality*. Atascadero, CA: Ridgeview Publishing Company, 1991, pp. 1–40.

[5] McDowell, *Mind and World*, p. 91.

[6] Aristotle, *On the Soul*, 402a1–7.

[7] See, for example, Michael H. Williams, "Scepticism without Theory," in *The Review of Metaphysics* 61 (1988), pp. 547–88.

[8] Kant, *Critique of Pure Reason*, p. A423–5/B451–3. Kant there even defines transcendental philosophy via its skeptical method.

[9] Ibid., p. Aviii.

[10] Hegel, *Phenomenology*, §206.

[11] In G. de Giovanni and H. S. Harris (eds.), *Between Kant & Hegel: Texts in the Development of Post-Kantian Idealism*. Indianapolis: Hackett Publishing, 2000, pp. 311–63.

[12] See the discussion of Skepticism in Hegel, *Phenomenology*, §§ 197–230 and G. W. F. Hegel, *Lectures on the History of Philosophy* (Three Volumes). Tr. E. S. Haldane and F. H. Simson, Lincoln, NE: University of Nebraska Press, 1995, vol. II, pp. 328–73.

[13] Translator's note: All translations of untranslated Schelling in what follows are from the German text of Schelling's collected works. Schelling, F. W. J. *Sämmtliche Werke*. Ed. by K. F. A. Schelling, I. Abteilung Vols. 1–10, II. Abteilung Vols. 1–4. Stuttgart: Cotta, 1856-61. This edition (SW) is quoted throughout with reference to volume and page number. I have had a truly remarkable amount of help from many good philosophers in translating these passages, most importantly from Dr. Jens Rometsch (Bonn). I am deeply grateful for his help. Ultimately, however, all final translations were decided on by me: though my successful renderings are indebted to those who have helped me, all mistakes are mine alone.

[14] SW, IX, 222.

[15] In my *An den Grenzen der Erkenntnistheorie* I defend a similar set of claims.

[16] Cf. Stanley Cavell, *The Claim of Reason. Wittgenstein, Skepticism, Morality, and Tragedy*, New York: Oxford University Press, 1999, p. 45, 48, 241, and passim.

[17] Hegel, *Phenomenology*, §§197–230.

[18] Kant, *Critique of Pure Reason*, B534.

[19] Ibid., B603f.
[20] Stephen Mulhall, *Inheritance and Originality. Wittgenstein, Heidegger, Kierkegaard.* Oxford: Oxford University Press, 2001, p. 238.
[21] F. W. J. Schelling *System of Transcendental Idealism (1800).* Tr. Peter Heath. Charlottesville: University Press of Virginia, 1978. p. 27 (SW, I, 368).
[22] Kant, *Critique of Pure Reason,* B528.
[23] Ibid., B451.
[24] In order to solve the antinomies, Kant explicitly argues that the world "does not exist in itself, independently of the regressive series of my representations. . . . It exists only in the empirical regress of the series of appearances, and is not to be met with as something in itself" (Kant, *Critique of Pure Reason,* A505/B533).
[25] *Objectification* is, thus, not a deplorable mistake, but a condition for intelligibility, whereas *reification* is the proper name for a natural illusion of reason. Given that objectification is necessary for us to make sense of anything whatsoever, reification of the horizon, within which sense is made, is a natural temptation. A reified concept of the world covers up the very contingency of sense-making.
[26] Kant, *Critique of Pure Reason,* B673.
[27] SW, IX, 244.
[28] SW, IX, 209.
[29] The most prominent names are Williams, "Skepticism without Theory"; and Robert J. Fogelin, *Pyrrhonian Reflections on Knowledge and Justification.* New York: Oxford University Press, 1994.
[30] According to Strawson the radical conflict between reductive kinds of naturalism and our everyday world picture motivates a relativizing move, which solves the conflict, by relativizing the notion of reality to standpoints. He himself sets out to solve the conflict of science and life-world "by what I called the relativizing move: relativizing the concept of reality to distinct, even opposed, but not strictly incompatible, standpoints or points of view." (Strawson, *Skepticism and Naturalism,* p. 64) Strawson uses the relativizing move in order to argue for liberal naturalism, "a non-reductive variety—which recognizes the human inescapability and metaphysical acceptability of those various types of conception of reality which are challenged or put in doubt by reductive or traditionally skeptical arguments" (ibid., p. 68).
[31] SW, IX, 209, 211.
[32] SW, IX, 209.
[33] Ibid.
[34] SW, IX, 213.
[35] SW, IX, 222.
[36] SW, IX, 244.
[37] SW, IX, 244: "Wissen ist weder in dem, das immer eins bleibt, nicht aus sich hinausgeht, noch in dem, das schlechthin auseinander fällt, im Einheits-, im Zusammenhanglosen; Wissen ist Cohärenz, eins und doch vieles, stets ein anderes und doch immer eins."
[38] SW, IX, 216.
[39] Ibid.
[40] For this point, see Wolfram Hogrebe, *Prädikation und Genesis. Metaphysik als Fundamentalheuristik im Ausgang von Schellings »Die Weltalter«.* Frankfurt/Main: Suhrkamp, 1989, p. 47.
[41] Of course, this discriminatory rule cannot entail that we have to be able to distinguish an object from all other objects, which would overstrain knowledge and make it impossible a priori. Also, there is no such thing as a set of all

objects. Hence, there is no point in locating a particular object in the domain of all objects anyways. If knowledge is possible despite its finitude, its conditions for possibility have to be weaker than classical metaphysics demanded.

[42] SW, IX, 235: "Hier also der Widerspruch, daß der Mensch das, was er will, *durch* sein Wollen zunichte macht. Aus diesem Widerspruch entsteht jene innere umtreibende Bewegung, indem das Suchende das, was es sucht, gleichsam in einer beständigen Flucht vor sich her treibt."

[43] SW, IX, 217.

[44] Sextus Empiricus, *Outlines of Pyrrhonism.* Tr. R. G. Bury. Loeb Classic Library (*Sextus Empiricus in Four Volumes*, vol. I), Cambridge, MA: Harvard University Press, 1933. Hereafter cited by book and page number. Here: I, 28f.

[45] "And again, just as it is not impossible for the man who has ascended to a high place by a ladder to overturn the ladder with his foot after his ascent, so also it is not unlikely that the Sceptic after he has arrived at the demonstration of his thesis by means of the argument proving the non-existence of proof, as it were by a step-ladder, should then abolish this very argument" (Sextus Empiricus, *Against the Logicians.* Tr. R. G. Bury. Loeb Classic Library (*Sextus Empiricus in Four Volumes*, vol. II), Cambridge, MA: Harvard University Press, 1935, Book II, 481).

[46] H. Sluga "Wittgenstein and Pyrrhonism," in W. Sinnott-Armstrong (ed.) *Pyrrhonian Skepticism.* New York: Oxford University Press, 2004.

[47] Cavell, *The Claim of Reason*, p. 48.

[48] Ibid., p. 54.

[49] Ibid., p. 236.

[50] Schelling expressly opposes the model "of an absolute scientific quietism, which may appear beneficial in relation to the blind ambitions of a thinking struggling in vain, yet, at the same time it forces thought to a renunciation it cannot accept due to its very nature" (SW, XI, 277). Here he surprisingly attacks Spinoza; yet this is really an attack on Jacobi's quietism (or rather, fideism) which one sees from the fact that he takes up the idea of "scientific quietism" in his debate with Jacobi, in which this phrase first appears. (cf. SW, VIII, 111).

[51] SW, IX, 218.

[52] SW, IX, 219.

[53] Ibid.

[54] SW, IX, 209.

[55] SW, IX, 217.

[56] SW, IX, 224.

[57] SW, IX, 219. "Heraustreten" literally means "to step out," which is the translation of the latin "existere."

[58] SW, IX, 220, and elsewhere.

[59] SW, IX, 220.

[60] Here there is a doubly remarkable parallel to Jacobi. Namely, Jacobi not only claimed that he had constructed his "whole philosophy" on a "knowing non-knowing [wissendes Nichtwissen]" (Friedrich Heinrich Jacobi, "Preface and also Introduction to the Author's Collected Philosophical Works (1815)," in *The Main Philosophical Writings and the Novel Allwill*. Tr. George di Giovanni, Montreal: McGill-Queen's University Press, 1994, p. 545), but also, like Schelling, sees the unconditioned in the concept of freedom. "The concept of freedom is inextirpably rooted in the human soul as true concept of the unconditional, and compels the human soul to strive after a cognition of the unconditional that lies beyond the conditioned. Without the consciousness of this concept, nobody would know that the limitations of what is conditioned are really *limitations*" (Ibid., p. 572).

[61] SW, IX, 221.

[62] SW, IX, 224.

[63] Ibid.

[64] SW, IX, 231.

[65] For the failure of "quietism," see also Markus Gabriel, *Skeptizismus und Idealismus in der Antike.* Frankfurt/Main: Suhrkamp, 2009, §§6–7.

[66] G. W. F. Hegel, *Encyclopedia Logic: Part I of the Encyclopedia of Philosophical Sciences with the Zusätze.* Tr. T. F. Geraets, W. A. Suchting, and H. S. Harris. Indianapolis: Hackett, 1991, §85.

[67] Hegel, *Lectures on the History of Philosophy*, vol. I, p. 406. Trans. mod. TWA 18, 465f.: "Es ist Verwirrung, mit der die Philosophie überhaupt anfangen muß und die sie für sich hervorbringt; man muß an allem zweifeln, man muß alle Voraussetzungen aufgeben, um es als durch den Begriff Erzeugtes wiederzuerhalten."

[68] Ibid., vol. II, pp. 328–73.

[69] It should be noted that in Hegel's eyes Pyrrhonian skepticism is more consistent than modern skepticism, which also turns against speculative metaphysics yet leaves the convictions of common sense, not to mention physics and mathematics, totally unquestioned (Hegel, "The Relationship of Skepticism to Philosophy", in *Between Kant and Hegel*, p. 336).

[70] Hegel, "The Relationship of Skepticism to Philosophy," in *Between Kant and Hegel*, p. 339.

[71] Ibid., p. 332.

[72] Ibid., p. 336.

[73] I spell out the historical details of this in Gabriel, *Skeptizismus und Idealismus in der Antike.*

[74] Sextus, *Outline of Pyrrhonism*, I, 135.

[75] Hegel, *Encyclopedia Logic*, §45.

[76] Ibid., §32.

[77] Hegel, "The Relationship of Skepticism to Philosophy", p. 336.

[78] Hegel, *Encyclopedia Logic*, §81.

[79] Hegel, *Science of Logic*, p. 113.

[80] Ibid., p. 481ff.

[81] Ibid., p. 323ff.

[82] Hegel, *Phenomenology*, §79.

[83] Hegel, *Encyclopedia Logic*, §79.

[84] Ibid.

[85] "As has already been shown, finitude *is* only as a transcending of itself; it therefore contains infinity, the other of itself. Similarly, infinity *is* only as a transcending of the finite; it therefore essentially contains its other and is, consequently, in its own self the other of itself. The finite is not sublated by the infinite as a power existing outside it; on the contrary, its infinity consists in sublating its own self" (Hegel, *Science of Logic*, p. 145–6; cf. *Encyclopedia Logic*, §94).

[86] Brandom's identification of Hegel's "conceptual tool" of determinate negation with the "concept of material incompatibility" (Brandom, *Tales of the Mighty Dead*, p. 180) is thoroughly pre-Hegelian. As he himself asserts, for him *omnis determinatio est negatio* is a "medieval (and Spinozist) principle" (ibid., p. 179), Hegel calls "determinate negation." Yet, determinate negation might draw on a version of this principle, but it is not identical with it. Determinate negation refers to a theory-building process in reaction to a given theory. According to Hegel, the series of metaphysical definitions of the absolute is organized by

determinate negation. Fichte's conception of selfhood would be the determinate negation of Kant's transcendental synthesis of apperception, Schelling's philosophy of nature the determinate negation of Fichte's egological account of selfhood and so forth. On another level, every new position in a dialectical development is the determinate negation of its predecessor. For example, essence is the determinate negation of being. For this reason, it is sublated being, it cannot be understood without recourse to being as that which it is not. If determinate negation is reduced to the horizontal concept of "material incompatibility" one misses the vertical development Hegel envisages.

[87] Hegel, *Phenomenology*, §76.

[88] Hegel, *Lectures on the History of Philosophy*, vol. II, p. 363f.

[89] Sextus, *Outline of Pyrrhonism*, I, 197.

[90] Hegel, *Lectures on the History of Philosophy*, vol. II, p. 367.

[91] Hegel, *Phenomenology*, §§197–230.

[92] Ibid., §202.

[93] Hegel, *Phenomenology*, §205.

[94] See Sextus, *Outline of Pyrrhonism*, I, 23ff.

[95] For a good reconstruction of this point see Richard D. Hiley, *Philosophy in Question. Essays on a Pyrrhonian Theme*. Chicago: University of Chicago Press, 1988, pp. 12, 141, and passim.

[96] See, for example, Sextus, *Outline of Pyrrhonism*, l, 78.

[97] Hegel, *Phenomenology*, §205.

[98] Ibid., §206.

[99] See Hiley, *Philosophy in Question*, p. 23.

[100] Hegel, *Encyclopedia Logic*, §78.

[101] Stanley Cavell, *Philosophy the Day After Tomorrow*. Cambridge, MA/London: The Belknap Press, 2006, p. 195.

[102] Hegel, *Science of Logic*, p. 25. Trans. Mod.

[103] Wilfred Sellars, *Empiricism and the Philosophy of Mind*. Cambridge, MA: Harvard University Press, 1997, p. 76.

[104] Cf. Kant, *Critique of Pure Reason*, A101: "Nor could there be an empirical synthesis of reproduction, if a certain name were sometimes given to this, sometimes to that object, or were one and the same thing named sometimes in one way, sometimes in another, independently of any rule to which appearances are in themselves subject."

[105] For a very clear statement of this see most recently Brandom, *Reason in Philosophy*, pp. 27–51.

[106] It is often the case in philosophy that the examples given by authors are suspicious, and this is the case for Brandom as well. We read as an example of the transition from infancy to membership in a linguistic community: "For this is a change that can take place largely outside the individual —as scratching a signature onto a piece of paper can either have no legal significance or be the undertaking of a contractual obligation to pay the bank a certain sum of money every month for thirty years" (Brandom, *Tales of the Mighty Dead*, p. 31).

[107] For the old standard picture McDowell seems to be repeating see Richard Kroner, *Von Kant bis Hegel*. 2 vols., Tübingen: Mohr Siebeck, 1921–4. More recent works by many scholars have displayed the crucial function Fichte and Schelling play in the formation of German idealism.

[108] McDowell, *Having the World in View*, p. 72.

[109] G. W. F. Hegel, *Faith and Knowledge*. Tr. W. Cerf and H. S. Harris. Albany: State University of New York Press, 1977, p. 60.

[110] Ibid., p. 61.

[111] Ibid.

[112] In any event, I wholeheartedly agree with Robert Pippin that Hegel is not "an idiosyncratic Christian, romantic metaphysician," who defends a ridiculously outmoded spiritual monism (Pippin, *Hegel's Idealism*, p. 4ff.). And I believe it is necessary to add that neither Fichte, nor Schelling, nor Hegel have defended any such first-order claims about "how things really are." Yet I disagree with the Kantian disregard of ontology.

[113] Immanuel Kant, *Prolegomena to Any Future Metaphysics*. Tr. Paul Carus, Revised by James W. Ellington. Indianapolis: Hackett Publishing Company, 2001, §§22–3.

[114] McDowell, *Having the World in View*, p. 71.

[115] Kant, *Critique of Pure Reason*, A158/B197.

[116] See ibid., A19/B34–A50/B74.

[117] Ibid., B134.

[118] McDowell, *Having the World in View*, pp. 74ff.

[119] Kant of course goes even further when he explicitly states, "that the things which we intuit are not in themselves what we intuit them as being, nor their relations so constituted in themselves as they appear to us, and that if the subject, or even only the subjective constitution of the senses in general, be removed, the whole constitution and all the relations of objects in space and time, nay space and time themselves would vanish. As appearances, they cannot exist in themselves, but only in us" (Kant, *Critique of Pure Reason*, A42/B59). He thus violates even his own epistemological restrictions; this has been well known since Trendelenburg underlined this point in his "Über eine Lücke in Kants Beweis von der ausschließlichen Subjectivität des Raumes und der Zeit," in Id., *Historische Beiträge zur Philosophie*. Vol. 3, Berlin 1867, pp. 215–76.

[120] McDowell, *Having the World in View*, p. 78.

[121] "This peculiarity of our understanding, that it can produce *a priori* unity of apperception solely by means of the categories, and only by such and so many, is as little capable of further explanation as why we have just these and no other functions of judgment, or why space and time are the only forms of our possible intuition" (Kant, *Critique of Pure Reason*, B145f.).

[122] Hegel, *Faith and Knowledge*, p. 76.

[123] Ibid., p. 77.

[124] Ibid., pp. 74ff.

[125] Ibid., p. 81.

[126] Ibid., p. 72.

[127] Ibid., p. 67.

[128] Ibid., p. 72.

[129] Ibid.

[130] Hegel, *Phenomenology*, §§111–31.

[131] Brandomian inferentialism is hence more Hegelian than McDowell's variety of Kantianism, because the latter is still primarily based on an analysis of judgment. Answerability to the world presupposes responsibility. We should at no point conceive of intentionality in terms of a relation of a spontaneous subject to its epistemically transparent environment as if the latter was always already established such that we only need to explain the conditions of possibility of access to the world. Brandom comes closer to a Hegelian metaphysics of intentionality even though he misses the ontological aspect of Hegel's inferentialism. Hegel's insistence on the form of the syllogism is not just a point about the content-conferring function of inferences, but is meant as an insight into the

self-referential structure of everything that exists. Despite Brandom's Hegelian-Wittgensteinian confession, Brandomian inferentialism remains within the Cartesian confines of modern epistemology by insisting on the deontological difference between the ontological and the deontological order. For an elaboration of this critique see Gabriel, *An den Grenzen der Erkenntnistheorie*, §15.

132 Kant, *Critique of Pure Reason*, A263/B319.
133 Hegel, *Faith and Knowledge*, p. 72.
134 Ibid., p. 70.
135 See Wolfram Hogrebe, *Echo des Nichtwissens*. Berlin: Akademie Verlag, 2006, pp. 317f.
136 Dieter Sturma, *Kant über Selbstbewußtsein. Zum Zusammenhang von Erkenntniskritik und Theorie des Selbstbewußtseins*. Hildesheim/Zürich/New York: Olms, 1985, p. 53.
137 Hegel, *Faith and Knowledge*, p. 65.
138 Ibid., p. 66.
139 Ibid., p. 64.
140 Ibid., p. 65.
141 Robert Brandom, *Making It Explicit. Reasoning, Representing, and Discursive Commitment*. Cambridge, MA/London: Harvard University Press, 1998, p. 20.
142 Ludwig Wittgenstein, *Philosophical Investigations*. Tr. G. E. M. Anscombe, P. M. S. Hacker, and J. Schulte. Chichester: Blackwell Publishing, 2009, §219:

"All the steps are already taken" means: I no longer have any choice. The rule, once stamped with a particular meaning, traces the lines along which it is to be followed through the whole of space.—But if something of this sort really were the case, how would it help me?
No; my description made sense only if it was to be understood symbolically.—I should say: *This is how it strikes me*.
When I follow the rule, I do not choose.
I follow the rule *blindly*.

143 For a general reading of the philosophy of nature in German idealism along the lines of what he calls "Darstellungsphilosophie," see Thomas Sören Hoffmann, *Philosophische Physiologie. Eine Systematik des Begriffs der Natur im Spiegel der Geschichte der Philosophie*. Stuttgart-Bad Cannstatt: frommann-holzboog, 2003.
144 G. W. F. Hegel, *Elements of the Philosophy of Right*. Tr. A. Wood. Cambridge: Cambridge University Press, 1991, §146, Addition.
145 Ibid., preface, p. 23.
146 On the role of Aristotle's *De anima* in Hegel's *Philosophy of Subjective Spirit*, see Catherine Malabou, *The Future of Hegel. Plasticity, Temporality, and Dialectic*. Tr. Lisabeth During. New York: Routledge, 2005. See also Tobias Dangel, *Hegel und die Geistmetaphysik des Aristoteles* (forthcoming 2011).
147 Hegel, *Science of Logic*, p. 58.
148 Hegel, *Philosophy of Right*, §187, Remark: "Spirit attains its actuality only through internal division, by imposing this limitation and finitude upon itself, through the continuum of natural necessity and, in the very process of adapting itself to these limitations, by overcoming them and gaining its objective existence within them."
149 For a detailed reconstruction of the philosophy of subjective spirit in its context see Jens Rometsch, *Hegels Theorie des erkennenden Subjekts. Systematische Untersuchungen zur enzyklopädischen Philosophie des subjektiven Geistes*. Würzburg: Königshausen & Neumann, 2007.

[150] G. W. F. Hegel, *Philosophy of Mind. Part Three of the Encyclopaedia of the Philosophical Sciences (1830)*. Tr. William Wallace. Oxford: Oxford University Press, 1971, §383. Tr. note: The English translation by Wallace goes astray: "the special mode of mental being is '*manifestation*.'" Where I differ substantially from the Wallace, I put translation in the notes, Tom Krell.

[151] Hegel, *Philosophy of Mind*, §383: "it does not manifest or reveal *something*, but its very mode and meaning is this revelation."

[152] "Offenbaren im Begriffe": The German idiomatic expression "im Begriffe sein, etwas zu tun" means to be about to do something, to be on the point of doing something. "Revealing" is thus expression as Deleuze understands it: It creates the expressed, the sense, in the activity of expressing. Hegel, thus, makes precisely Deleuze's central point defended in his *Logic of Sense*: "sense is never a principle or an origin . . . it is produced" (Gilles Deleuze, *The Logic of Sense*. Tr. M. Lester. New York: Columbia University Press, 1990, p. 72).

[153] Hegel, *Philosophy of Mind*, §384.

[154] Ibid.

[155] Ibid., §386.

[156] In another place, Hegel interprets this as a reduction of nature. "The illusory appearance which makes spirit seem to be mediated by an Other is removed by spirit itself, since this has, so to speak, the sovereign ingratitude of ridding itself of, of mediatizing, that by which it appears to be mediated, of reducing it to something dependent solely on spirit and in this way making itself completely subsistent" (Hegel, *Philosophy of Mind*, §381Z). Cf. also the *Science of Logic*: "it is rather the nature of spirit, in a much higher sense than it is the character of the living thing in general, not to receive into itself another *original* entity, or not to let a cause continue itself into it but to break it off and to transmute it" (Hegel, *Science of Logic*, p. 562).

[157] Hegel, *Philosophy of Mind*, §392.

[158] Ibid., §§407f.

[159] On *self-feeling* in post-Kantian philosophy see Manfred Frank, *Selbstgefühl. Eine historisch-systematische Erkundung*. Frankfurt/Main: Suhrkamp, 2002.

[160] "Die Empfindung ist die Form des dumpfen Webens des Geistes in seiner bewußt- und verstandlosen Individualität, in der *alle* Bestimmtheit noch *unmittelbar* ist, nach ihrem Inhalte wie nach dem Gegensatze eines Objektiven gegen das Subjekt unentwickelt gesetzt, als seiner *besondersten*, natürlichen *Eigenheit* angehörig" (Hegel, *Philosophy of Mind*, §400, Trans. mod.).

[161] Ibid., §401.

[162] "[N]icht nur für sich immateriell, sondern die allgemeine Immaterialität der Natur, deren einfaches ideelles Leben" (Ibid., §389, trans. mod.).

[163] Aristotle, *De Anima*, 412b5–6.

[164] Aristotle, *De Anima*, 413a4–5.

[165] Hegel, *Philosophy of Mind*, §401.

[166] "[N]icht als *Weltseele*, gleichsam als ein Subjekt fixiert werden, denn sie ist nur die allgemeine *Substanz*, welche ihre wirkliche Wahrheit nur als *Einzelnheit*, Subjektivität, hat" (Ibid., §391, trans. mod.).

[167] See the quote in note 55 above.

[168] "Dieses Sich-einbinden des Besondern oder Leiblichen der Gefühlsbestimmungen in das *Sein* der Seele erscheint als eine *Wiederholung* derselben und die Erzeugung der Gewohnheit als eine *Übung*" (Hegel, *Philosophy of Mind*, §410, trans. mod.).

[169] "Subjectives Erkennen—daß es einzelne Individuen sind, welche philosophiren. Das Nacheinander des philosophischen Inhalt gehört zu dieser Erscheinung" (G. W. F. Hegel, "Notizen zum dritten Teil der Encyklopädie," in: *Gesammelte*

Werke. Published by the Nordrhein-Westfälische Akademie der Wissenschaften and the Deutsche Forschungsgemeinschaft. Vol. 13: *Enzyklopädie der philosophischen Wissenschaften im Grundrisse* (1817), Wolfgang Bonsiepen and Klaus Grotsch (ed.), under collaboration with Hans-Christian Lucas and Udo Rameil. Hamburg: Meiner, 2000, vol. 13, p. 539.

[170] "Das ganz freie, in dem reinen Elemente seiner selbst tätige *Denken* bedarf ebenfalls der Gewohnheit und Geläufigkeit, dieser Form der *Unmittelbarkeit*, wodurch es ungehindertes, durchgedrungenes Eigentum meines *einzelnen Selbsts* ist. Erst durch diese Gewohnheit existiere Ich als denkendes für mich. Selbst diese Unmittelbarkeit des denkenden Bei-sich-seins enthält Leiblichkeit" (Hegel, *Philosophy of Mind*, §410 fn.).

[171] On this point it should be pointed out that Descartes meant by "*cogitatio*" and therefore by "cogito" not only a thought in the sense of judgments or reference to objects. For "volutates," "affectus," and "judicia" are specific differentiations of the genus "cogitatio," as Descartes explains in the third Meditation (AT VII, 36f.).

[172] Hegel, *Philosophy of Mind*, §405.

[173] Ibid., §406. "Form der *Unmittelbarkeit*, in welcher die Unterschiede vom Subjektiven und Objektiven, verständiger Persönlichkeit gegen eine äußerliche Welt, und jene Verhältnisse der Endlichkeit zwischen denselben nicht vorhanden sind."

[174] "Absolutheit des räumlichen und materiellen Auseinanderseins überhaupt" (Ibid., §406, fn).

[175] Ibid., §406, fn.

[176] Ibid., §407.

[177] Ibid., §405.

[178] "Es ist dies in unmittelbarer Existenz das Verhältnis des Kindes im Mutterleibe,— ein Verhältnis, das weder bloß leiblich noch bloß geistig, sondern *psychisch* ist,—ein Verhältnis der Seele" (Ibid., §405).

[179] Ibid., §405: "anderwärts im Kreise des bewußten, besonnenen Lebens sporadische Beispiele und Spuren [vorkommen], etwa zwischen Freunden, insbesondere nervenschwachen Freundinnen (– ein Verhältnis, das sich zu den magnetischen Erscheinungen ausbilden kann), Eheleuten, Familiengliedern."

[180] Ibid., §405.

[181] As I have argued elsewhere, this is already the upshot of Plotinus's discovery of narcissism as a structural component of the psyche. See Gabriel, *Skeptizismus und Idealismus in der Antike*, §§8–11.

[182] Quoted in Michael Forster, *Hegel's Idea of a Phenomenology of Spirit*. Chicago: University of Chicago Press, 1998, p. 117.

[183] On this see Žižek, *The Ticklish Subject*, pp. 30–51.

[184] Cf. here Hogrebe's concept of a "logical pathology of spirit," which he developed through Aristotle, Hegel, and Schelling in Wolfram Hogrebe, *Archäologische Bedeutungspostulate*. Freiburg/München, 1977, §16.

[185] Cf. Hegel, *Science of Logic*, p. 625: "The judgment is the self-diremption of the Notion; *this unity* is, therefore, the ground from which the consideration of the judgment in accordance with its true *objectivity* begins. It is thus the *original division* [*Teilung*] of what is originally one; thus the word *Urteil* refers to what judgment is in and for itself."

[186] Hegel, *Philosophy of Mind*, §411.

[187] Wittgenstein, *Philosophical Investigations*, p. 152.

[188] "[D]ie Welt des verständigen Bewußtseins [. . .] ganz etwas anderes [ist] als ein Gemälde von bloßen Vorstellungen und Bildern" (Hegel, *Philosophy of Mind*, §398).

[189] Wittgenstein, *Philosophical Investigations*, §309.
[190] "Nirgend so sehr als bei der Seele und noch mehr beim Geiste ist es die
    Bestimmung der *Idealität*, die für das Verständnis am wesentlichsten fest-
    zuhalten ist, daß die Idealität *Negation* des Reellen, in dieser aber zugleich
    aufbewahrt, virtualiter enthalten ist" (Hegel, *Philosophy of Mind*, §403n.).

Chapter 2

[1] He writes in the *Freedom Essay*: "it is required that the reverse also be shown,
    that everything real (nature, the world of things) has activity, life, and freedom
    as its ground or, in Fichte's expression, that not only is I-hood all, but also the
    reverse, that all is I-hood. . . . It will always remain odd, however, that Kant, after
    having first distinguished things-in-themselves from appearances only negatively
    through their independence from time and later treating independence from
    time and freedom as correlate concepts in the metaphysical discussions of his
    Critique of Practical Reason, did not go further toward the thought of transferring
    this only possible positive concept of the in-itself to things; thereby he would
    immediately have raised himself to a higher standpoint of reflection and above
    the negativity that is the character of his theoretical philosophy" (Friedrich
    Wilhelm Josef Schelling, *Philosophical Investigations into the Essence of Human
    Freedom*. Tr. J. Love and J. Schmid, Albany: SUNY Press, 2006, p. 22).
[2] Schelling, *Freedom Essay*, p. 22.
[3] Schelling, *Freedom Essay*, p. 21.
[4] For a paradigmatic reconstruction of the relation between being and determi-
    nacy, see Konrad Utz, *Philosophie des Zufalls. Ein Entwurf.* Paderborn/München/
    Wien/Zürich: Schöningh, 2005, chapter 1.
[5] See Plato, *Parmenides*, 148a5f.
[6] Plato, *Sophist*, 237c10ff., 244d14f.
[7] On this, see Cornelius Castoriadis, *The Imaginary Institution of Society*. Tr.
    K. Blamey, Oxford: Polity Press, 1997, pp. 168f.
[8] Plato, *Sophist*, 259e5–6.
[9] Of course, there is an element of indeterminacy and withdrawal in Plato's
    notion of *chôra* in the *Timaeus*. However, Plato seems to be eager to purify his
    ontology from this remainder. For a more comprehensive treatment of this
    issue see my "*Chôra* als *différance*. Derridas dekonstruktive Lektüre von Platons
    Timaios," in Gregor Fitzi, (ed.) *Platon im Diskurs*. Heidelberg: Universitätsverlag
    Winter, 2006.
[10] SW, XI, 291, 313.
[11] Plato, *Sophist*, 254a8–9.
[12] On this see my *Der Mensch im Mythos*, pp. 104–15.
[13] See, for example, SW, XIII, 100.
[14] SW, XI, 571.
[15] SW, XI, 336.
[16] On Kierkegaard's reception of Schelling see most recently Michelle Kosch,
    Freedom and Reason in Kant, Schelling, and Kierkegaard. Oxford: Oxford University
    Press, 2006.
[17] See, for example, Aristotle, *Nichomachean Ethics*, 1139a8ff.
[18] SW, XIV, 337.
[19] SW, XIV, 341.
[20] SW, XI, 317; XIV, 346.
[21] SW, X, 282; XIII, 263–78; XIV, 342f.

[22] Speusippus, *Speusippo. Frammenti.* Ed. Margherita Isnardi Parente, Naples; Bibliopolis, 1980, fr. 72.

[23] SW, XIV, 338.

[24] Aristotle, *Metaphysics*, 1071b22–9.

[25] SW, XIII, 7, 163ff., 242; VI, 155; VII, 174, et. al.

[26] SW, XII, 53: "Denn der wahre Sinn des Ausdrucks: etwas *seyn* ist eben dieser. Wenn nämlich das Seyn *cum emphasi* gesagt wird, so ist der Ausdruck: etwas *seyn* = dem, diesem Etwas *Subjekt* seyn. Das *ist*, die Copula in jedem Satze, z.B. in dem Satze: A ist B, wenn sie nämlich überhaupt bedeutend, emphatisch, d.h. die Copula eines wirklichen Urtheils ist, so bedeutet, A ist B" so viel als: A ist dem B Subjekt, d.h. es ist nicht selbst und seiner Natur nach B (in diesem Fall wäre der Satz eine leere Tautologie), sondern: A ist das auch nicht B seyn Könnende."

[27] SW, XI, 303. Here Aristotle, Schelling, and Badiou meet. As Badiou points out, philosophy ultimately takes place at "the point where ontology and logic rub up against each other" (Badiou, *Logics of Worlds*, p. 6).

[28] SW, XI, 352, fn. 3.

[29] SW, XI, 292.

[30] SW, XI, 352, fn. 3.

[31] SW, XI, 292.

[32] SW, XI, 352, n. 3.

[33] Hogrebe, *Prädikation und Genesis*, §13.

[34] SW, XIV, 341: "Ich habe gegen dieses Seyn, das, so früh wir kommen, schon da ist, oft einwenden hören: eine solche aller Möglichkeit zuvorkommende Wirklichkeit sey nicht zu denken. Allerdings nicht durch ein dem Seyn zuvorkommendes Denken, an das wir gewöhnt sind. Das Denken setzt sich eben dieses Seyn zu seinem Ausgangspunkt, um zu dem, was ihm als das am meisten Wissenswerthe, also auch als das im Wissen am meisten Begehrenswerthe erscheint, um zu diesem als zu einem Wirklichen zu gelangen, und wirkliches Denken ist es erst im Weggehen von diesem Punkt—aber wie der *terminus a quo* einer Bewegung, in welchem selbst die Bewegung eigentlich noch nicht ist, dennoch auch mit zu der Bewegung gehört, so wird jenes Seyn im Fortgang, im Hinweggehen von ihm selbst, mit zu einem Moment des Denkens."

[35] Cf. Martin Heidegger, *On the Essence of Reasons*, Tr. Terrence Malick, Evanston: Northwestern University Press, 1969, p. 129. While Heidegger designates finite freedom as the "ground of the ground [Grund des Grundes]" in *On the Essence of Reasons* as well as in *Being and Time* (GA 2, 284f.), he modifies in the so-called "Kehre" his thinking of ground. This can be clearly seen in particular in *The Principle of Reason* in which Heidegger no longer thinks freedom, but rather being itself as the abyss (*Ab-grund*) and thereby as the "ground of the ground." Cf. Heidegger, *The Principle of Reason*, p. 12. (Reginald Lilly translates this as "reason of the reason.")

[36] SW, VII, 406ff.

[37] SW, XIV, 106: "Ewig ist, dem *keine* Potenz vorhergeht; in der Ewigkeit ist kein »als«; als etwas, z.B. als A, kann nichts gesetzt seyn ohne Ausschließung von einem nicht A. Hier aber ist das Subjekt nur noch reines, d.h. irreflektirtes, gradaus gehendes, nicht als solches gesetztes Seyn. Denn jedes *als* solches Gesetztwerden setzt eine Reflexion—ein Reflektirtwerden—also schon ein Contrarium voraus."

[38] SW, XIII, 264f., 267, 279.

[39] SW, XI, 566. A forerunner to this formulation can already be found in the *Freedom Essay*: "For only what is personal can heal what is personal, and God must become man so that man may return to God" (Schelling, *Freedom Essay*, p. 46).

[40] SW, III, 331.

[41] SW, XIII, 248–58.

[42] SW, XIII, 257.

[43] Plato, *Republic*, 509b9.

[44] Friedrich Wilhelm Josef Schelling, *Urfassung der Philosophie der Offenbarung*. Ed. by W. E. Ehrhardt, 2 vls., Hamburg: Meiner, 1992 (which I will henceforth refer to as UPO), p. 24.

[45] Ibid.

[46] Hegel, *Science of Logic*, p. 389.

[47] A metaphysics of time and freedom has recently been developed precisely along those lines by Anton Friedrich Koch in his *Versuch über Wahrheit und Zeit*. Paderborn: Mentis, 2006.

[48] SW, XIII, 206: "[d]er todte Körper hat genug an sich, und will nur *sich*. Das Thier, schon die lebendige Pflanze, der man ja einen Lichthunger zuschreibt, will etwas außer *sich*, der Mensch will etwas über *sich*. Das Thier ist durch sein Wollen außer sich gezogen, der Mensch im wahrhaft menschlichen Wollen über sich gehoben."

[49] SW, XIII, 131.

[50] SW, XII, 131: "das Reich der Wirklichkeit nicht ein abgeschlossenes, sondern ein seiner Vollendung fortwährend entgegengehendes," such that "auch der Beweis *nie* [!] abgeschlossen [ist], und darum auch diese Wissenschaft nur Philosophie."

[51] Plato, *Timaeus*, 27d6f.

[52] In 1936 Heidegger gave a lecture series on Schelling, published as volume 42 of the Heidegger *Gesamtausgabe*. The English translation is *Schelling's Treatise On the Essence of Human Freedom*. Tr. Joan Stambaugh, Athens, OH: Ohio University Press, 1985.

[53] SW, XI, 557–63.

[54] Martin Heidegger, *Contributions to Philosophy (from Enowning)*. Tr. P. Enad and K. Maly, Indianapolis: Indiana University Press, 2000, p. 120.

[55] Plato, *Republic*, 379a5ff.

[56] Aristotle, *Metaphysics*, 1026a19.

[57] Aristotle, *Metaphysics*, 1041b26.

[58] Plato, *Timaeus*, 27d6f.

[59] Heidegger, *Contributions*, pp. 46, 54: "Die Grundfrage: *wie west das Seyn?*"

[60] Heidegger, *Contributions*, pp. 45, 82f., 144, 177f., 279f., 325f., 331f., passim.

[61] Heidegger is explicit about the equation of being with an economy of sense. See *Contributions*, p. 8: "The question the 'meaning' [of being], i.e., in accordance with the elucidation in *Being and Time*, the question concerning grounding the domain of projecting-open—and then, the question of the *truth of be-ing*—is and remains *my* question, and is my *one and only* question; for this question concerns what is *most sole and unique*. [. . .] The question of the 'meaning of being' is the question of all questions. When the unfolding of this questioning is enacted, what is ownmost to what 'meaning' names here is determined, along with that in which the question dwells as mindfulness and along with what the *question* as such opens up, namely the openness for self-sheltering, i.e., truth."

[62] Heidegger, *Contributions*, p. 219. I have edited the translation here a bit. The German text says: "der Wendungspunkt in der Kehre des Ereignisses, die sich öffnende Mitte des Widerspiels von Zuruf und Zugehörigkeit, das Eigentum, verstanden wie Fürsten-tum, die herrschaftliche Mitte der Er-eignung als Zueignung des Zu-gehörigen zum Ereignis, zugleich zu ihm: Selbstwerdung" (GA 65, 311).

[63] Martin Heidegger, "Letter on Humanism", in *Pathmarks*. Ed. William McNeill. Cambridge: Cambridge University Press, 1998, p. 239.

[64] Martin Heidegger, *The Question Concerning Technology and Other Essays*. Tr. William Lovitt. New York: Harper and Rowe Publishers, 1977, p. 46.

[65] Heidegger, *Contributions*, p. 359.

[66] Heidegger, *Contributions*, p. 5.

[67] Ibid.

[68] On this distinction see ibid., p. 137.

[69] Martin Heidegger, *Introduction to Metaphysics*. Tr. Gregory Fried and Richard Polt. New Haven: Yale Nota Bene, 2000, p. 220.

[70] Badiou, *Logics of Worlds*, p. 420ff.

[71] Heidegger, *Contributions*, p. 219.

[72] Martin Heidegger, "The Age of the World Picture," in *Off the Beaten Track*. Tr. J. Young and K. Haynes, Cambridge: Cambridge University Press, 2002, p. 57.

[73] Schelling, *Grounding of Positive Philosophy*, p. 94, original wording in: SW, XIII, 7: "Weit entfernt also, daß der Mensch und sein Thun die Welt begreiflich mache, ist er selbst das Unbegreiflichste, und treibt mich unausbleiblich zu der Meinung von der Unseligkeit alles Seyns, einer Meinung, die in so vielen schmerzlichen Lauten aus alter und neuer Zeit sich kundgegeben. Gerade Er, der Mensch, treibt mich zur letzten verzweifungsvollen Frage: warum ist überhaupt etwas? warum ist nicht nichts?"

[74] Schelling has repeated this question in various phases of his thinking. See, for example, SW, VI, 155; VII, 174; XIII, 163 ff., 252.

[75] SW, XI, 352, fn. 3.

[76] In a similar vein, Castoriadis explores the concept of God in order to designate "an imaginary possessing a greater reality than the real itself" (*The Imaginary Institution of Society*, p. 128). At another passage (p. 140) he repeats this formulation referring to the "social imaginary." In other words, the ontological genesis brought about by a radical imaginary, which is not grounded in a positive ontological order, but rather grounds it, is what Castoriadis refers to as "God," which brings him close to Schelling.

[77] SW, XI, 566. Schelling there draws a distinction between the universal and personality. According to him, contemplation ultimately leads to the discovery of personality as opposed to a universal structure.

[78] See Walter Schulz, *Die Vollendung des deutschen Idealismus in der Spätphilosophie Schellings*. Stuttgart/Köln: Kohlhammer, 1944, p. 279.

[79] SW, XII, 53.

[80] Frege, *Foundations of Arithmetic*, p. 40.

[81] SW, XIII, 265; XIV, 342; UPO, 70, 82f., and so forth.

[82] SW, XIV, 337.

[83] SW, XIV, 315.

[84] SW, XIV, 337.

[85] SW, XIV, 337f.

[86] Ibid.

[87] SW, XIV, 338.

[88] SW, X, 101, 309; XIII, 230.

[89] SW, XIV, 338.

[90] Ibid.

[91] SW, XIII, 265, 267, 279.

[92] SW, XIV, 338.

[93] Ibid.

94 SW, XIV, 338.

95 SW, XI, 388.

96 Schelling's concept of unprethinkable being is heir apparent of Kant's concept of the transcendental object. See Kant, *Critique of Pure Reason*, A250ff.: "all our representations are, it is true, referred by the understanding to some object; and since appearances are nothing but representations, the understanding refers them to a *something*, as the object of sensible intuition. But this something, thus conceived, is only the transcendental object; and by that is meant something = X, of which we know, and with the present constitution of our understanding can know, nothing whatsoever, but which, as a correlate of the unity of apperception, can serve only for the unity of the manifold in sensible intuition. By means of this unity the understanding combines the manifold into the concept of an object. This transcendental object cannot be separated from the sensible data, for nothing is left through which it might be thought. Consequently it is not in itself an object of knowledge, but only the representation of appearances under the concept of an object in general—a concept which is determinable through the manifold of these appearances." Schelling goes on to ask the crucial question of how the thing itself comes to appear, that is, how unprethinkable being makes it's way into the dimension of sense. This question asks how the thing itself departs from itself and enters into thought: hereby, Schelling seeks to explain the *phenomenalization* of the Thing in thinking. Such a genetic operation goes unthought (and is perhaps even barred) in the Kantian program.

97 SW, XIV, 339.

98 SW, XIV, 338.

99 Ibid.

100 SW, XI, 464.

101 SW, XIV, 341 sq.: "[M]an muß ein solches Seyn zuweilen wohl sich vorstellen; z.B. bei Hervorbringungen, Thaten, Handlungen, deren Möglichkeit erst durch ihre Wirklichkeit begreiflich ist. Was nach einem voraus vorhandenen Begriff zu Stande kömmt, nennt niemand Original. Original ist, wovon man die Möglichkeit erst zugibt, wenn man die Wirklichkeit vor Augen sieht."

102 SW, XIV, 342.

103 SW, XIV, 350.

104 Ibid.

105 Wittgenstein, *Tractatus*, 5.634.

106 Heidegger, *Contributions*, p. 3–4.

107 SW, XI, 389.

108 SW, XIII, 257.

109 SW, XIII, 256.

110 UPO, p. 192, passim.

111 SW, XIII, 256.

112 Schelling, *Grounding of Positive Philosophy*, p. 202, original wording in: SW, XIII, 160: "Wenn Gott sein Prius im actus hat, so wird er seine Gottheit in der Potenz haben, darin daß er die *potentia universalis*, als diese das Ueberseyende, der *Herr* des Seyns ist. Aber eben darum,—um zu Gott wirklich zu gelangen, d.h. (soweit dieß möglich ist) die wirkliche Existenz der Gottheit zu beweisen, müssen wir von dem ausgehen, was ich das *bloß* Existirende genannt habe, von dem unmittelbar, einfach nothwendig Seyenden, das nothwendig ist, weil es aller Potenz, aller Möglichkeit zuvorkommt."

113 SW, XI, 564.

114 SW, XI, 185; UPO, 12.
115 UPO, 221: "Der Mensch kann diese Welt seine Welt nennen—er hat die Welt außer Gott—praeter Deum—gesetzt, indem er sich an die Stelle von Gott setzte."
116 SW, XI, 566.
117 Josef König, *Der Begriff der Intuition*. Halle: Max Niemeyer, 1926, p. 25: "Der Gang zum Sinn ist selbst sinnlos."
118 SW, XIV, 342.
119 SW, XIII, 168.
120 SW, XIII, 159.
121 SW, XIV, 343.
122 Ibid.
123 Johann Gottlieb Fichte, *Darstellung der Wissenschaftslehre. Aus den Jahren 1801/02.* Hamburg: Meiner, 1977, p. 78: "Kein absoluter Ursprung erblickt *sich*, ohne sein Nichtsein zu erblicken."
124 SW, IX, 209.
125 Niklas Luhmann, *Einführung in die Systemtheorie*. Second Edition. Heidelberg: Carl Auer, 2004, p. 62.
126 Schelling, *Grounding of Positive Philosophy*, p. 92.
127 Kant, *Critique of Pure Reason*, A505/B533.
128 See, for example, SW, XIV, 224ff.
129 SW, XIII, 206: "[D]er todte Körper hat genug an sich, und will nur *sich*. Das Thier, schon die lebendige Pflanze, der man ja einen Lichthunger zuschreibt, will etwas außer *sich*, der Mensch will etwas über *sich*. Das Thier ist durch sein Wollen außer sich gezogen, der Mensch im wahrhaft menschlichen Wollen über sich gehoben."

Chapter 3

1 Aristotle, *Metaphysics*, 1072b13–14. Elsewhere, I have tried to give the notion of "ontotheology" in Aristotle a different meaning. See "God's Transcendent Activity—Ontotheology in *Metaphysics* Λ," in: *The Review of Metaphysics* 250 (2009), pp. 385–414. There, I argue that Aristotle's God does not even think. The famous thinking of thinking is not a property of God, but rather a property of our intellect with respect to God.
2 "For Hegel, the absolute is spirit: that which is present to itself [*bei sich*] in the certainty of unconditional self-knowing. Real knowledge of beings as beings now becomes the absolute knowledge of the absolute in its absoluteness" (Heidegger, "Hegel's Concept of Experience," in *Off the Beaten Track*, p. 97). Heidegger even ascribes representationalism to Hegel (ibid., pp. 98ff.). According to Heidegger, Hegel's philosophy aims at a "theology of the absolute" (ibid., p. 152). Cf. also Heidegger's lectures on German idealism (Martin Heidegger, *Der deutsche Idealismus (Fichte, Schelling, Hegel) und die philosophische Problemlage der Gegenwart*. Frankfurt/Main: Klostermann, 1997). In Markus Gabriel, "Endlichkeit und absolutes Ich—Heideggers Fichtekritik" (forthcoming in *Fichte-Studien*). I argue against Heidegger's claim that the whole post-Kantian movement amounts to a denial of finitude on the basis of a reading of Fichte's enterprise as an analytic of finitude.
3 Martin Heidegger, *Kant and the Problem of Metaphysics*. Tr. Richard Taft. Bloomington: Indiana University Press, 1997.

[4] This corresponds to the later Schelling's interpretation of the post-Kantian development. Cf. Schelling, XI, 283. On this topic: see my *Der Mensch im Mythos*, §5; and Hogrebe, *Prädikation und Genesis*. The discussion of the transcendental ideal looms large in Hegel's defense of the ontological proof in his *Lectures on the Proof of the Existence of God*. For Hegel's interpretation of the Kantian reason qua faculty of the unconditioned, see Béatrice Longuenesse, *Hegel's Critique of Metaphysics*. New York: Cambridge University Press 2007, pp. 167–71.

[5] From a logical point of view the predicate of not having a predicate is an ordinary predicate which notoriously creates problems at the limits of expression and conception in the tradition of negative theology. A very illustrative exposition of the logical dimension of these problems can be found in: Graham Priest, *Beyond the Limits of Thought*. Cambridge: Cambridge University, Press 1995, in particular, pp. 23–5 and 61–4.

[6] Hilary Putnam, *Reason, Truth, and History*. Cambridge: Cambridge University Press, 1981, p. xi.

[7] Fichte, *1804 Wissenschaftslehre*, pp. 27ff.

[8] Georg Wilhelm Friedrich Hegel, *The Difference Between Fichte's and Schelling's System of Philosophy*. Tr. H. S. Harris and Walter Cerf. Albany: State University of New York Press, 1977, pp. 44ff.

[9] Ibid.

[10] Ibid., p. 46.

[11] Hegel, *Science of Logic*, p. 74.

[12] As Hegel himself puts it in the *Encyclopedia Logic*: "the theory of Essence is the most difficult branch of Logic. It includes the categories of metaphysic and of the sciences in general. These are the products of reflective understanding, which, while it assumes the differences to possess a footing of their own, and at the same time also expressly affirms their relativity, still combines the two statements, side by side, or one after the other, by an 'also', without bringing these thoughts into one, or unifying them into the notion" (Hegel, *Encyclopedia Logic*, §114). Slavoj Žižek and I have recently argued that the thought of Fichte, Schelling, and Hegel crucially depends on their reinterpretation of the relation between appearance and the real. See Gabriel/Žižek: *Mythology, Madness, and Laughter*.

[13] In Hegel's reading, the Kantian distinction between the thing in itself and the appearances is a modern variety of Platonism. When Hegel attacks Platonism broadly construed, he includes Kant's epistemology within the range of that concept.

[14] Hegel, *Science of Logic*, p. 529.

[15] Plato, *Republic*, 509d–513e.

[16] Hegel, *Science of Logic*, p. 529.

[17] Ibid.

[18] Ibid.

[19] It is important to insist that Hegel's recourse to the tradition of the ontological proof (and therefore to onto-theology) is not to be read as backslide into precritical metaphysics. On the contrary, it rather rests on a metacritical move. Hegel believes that Kant's critique of metaphysics was not thorough enough precisely because Kant winds up with a set of dualisms without reflecting on the fact that they are only opposed in metaphysical reflection.

[20] Cf. Wolfram Hogrebe, "Das Absolute," in *Echo des Nichtwissens*, pp. 155–69; Markus Gabriel, *Das Absolute und die Welt in Schellings Freiheitsschrift*. Bonn: Bonn University Press, 2006.

[21] On Hegel's critique of Neoplatonism see my "Hegel und Plotin,". in *Hegel und die Geschichte der Philosophie*. Ed. Heidemann, D. H./Krijnen, C. Darmstadt: Wissenschaftliche Buchgesellschaft 2007, pp. 70–83.

[22] As far as I know, Plotinus first introduced the concept of the "entirely different (τὸ πάντῃ διάφορον)" (Plotinus, *Ennead V*, Tr. A. H. Armstrong, Loeb Classical Library (*Plotinus in Seven Volumes*, vol. V), Cambridge, MA: Harvard University Press, 1984; Chapter 3, §10, line 50).

[23] Hegel, *Science of Logic*, p. 530.

[24] Ibid.

[25] "But we have to exhibit what the absolute is; but this 'exhibiting' can be neither a determining nor an external reflection from which determinations of the absolute would result; on the contrary, it is the *exposition*, and in fact the *self*-exposition, of the absolute and only a *display of what it is*" (Ibid., p. 530).

[26] Hegel, *Science of Logic*, p. 531.

[27] Ibid., p. 532.

[28] Ibid., p. 531.

[29] Ibid.

[30] Ibid.

[31] Ibid., p. 532.

[32] Ibid.

[33] Ibid.

[34] Ibid.

[35] Ibid.

[36] Ibid., p. 533.

[37] Ibid.

[38] Ibid.

[39] "As regards the attributes of which God consists, they are only infinite substances, each of which must of itself be infinitely perfect. That this must necessarily be so, we are convinced by clear and distinct reasons. It is true, however, that up to the present only two of all these infinites are known to us through their own essence; and these are thought and extension" (Benedict de Spinoza, *Short Treatise on God, Man, and his Well-Being*. Tr. A. Wolf. New York: Russell & Russell Inc., 1963, p. 52).

[40] Hegel, *Science of Logic*, p. 535.

[41] Ibid.

[42] Ibid., p. 533.

[43] Benedict de Spinoza, *Ethics*. Tr. Edwin M. Curley. London: Penguin Books, 1996, EId6exp.

[44] Yirmiyahu Yovel, "The Infinite Mode and Natural Laws in Spinoza," in Id., *God and Nature. Spinoza's Metaphysics*, Leiden/New York: Brill 1991, pp. 79–96, here, p. 91.

[45] Hegel, *Science of Logic*, p. 533.

[46] Ibid.

[47] Ibid., p. 536.

[48] Hegel develops his concept of "presupposing" (*Voraussetzen*) in the subchapter on "Positing Reflection" (ibid. pp. 400–2).

[49] Hegel, *Science of Logic*, p. 536.

[50] Cf. Georg Wilhelm Friedrich Hegel, *Lectures on the Philosophy of Religion*, Tr. Peter C. Hodgson. Berkeley: University of California Press 1988, p. 392: "God is self-consciousness; he knows himself in a consciousness that is distinct from him, which is implicitly the consciousness of God, but is also the divine consciousness

explicitly since it knows its identity with God, an identity that is mediated, however, by the negation of finitude. It is this concept that constitutes the content of
religion. We define God when we say that he distinguishes himself from himself
and is an object for himself but that in this distinction he is purely identical with
himself—that he is *spirit*." Cf. also Hegel, *Philosophy of Mind*, §564.
51 Hegel, *Science of Logic*, p. 536.
52 Ibid.
53 Ibid., p. 541.
54 Ibid., p. 829.
55 Hegel, *Philosophy of Mind*, §577. I generally agree with Nuzzo's solution of the
problem in Angelica Nuzzo, "The End of Hegel's Logic: Absolute Idea as Absolute
Method," in *Hegel's Theory of the Subject*. Ed. D. G. Carlson. Basingstoke: Palgrave
Macmillan, 2005, pp. 187–205: "the term absolute for Hegel is no longer substantive but only adjectival, as such absoluteness is predicated of each one of
the final moments of his system: *absolute knowing (absolutes Wissen), absolute idea
(absolute Idee), absolute spirit (absoluter Geist)*" (p. 188).
56 Hegel, *Science of Logic*, p. 829.
57 Hegel explicitly acknowledges this fact in *Annotations on Absolute Spirit*. See footnote 231.
58 "As for the individual, every one is a son of his time; so philosophy also is its time
apprehended in thoughts. It is just as foolish to fancy that any philosophy can
transcend its present world, as that an individual could leap out of his time or
jump over Rhodes" (Hegel, *Philosophy of Right*, pp. 21–2).
59 Hegel, *Science of Logic*, p. 824.
60 Ibid.
61 Cf. Anton Friedrich Koch's reading of the *Science of Logic* in terms of an "evolutionary theory of logical space [Evolutionstheorie des logischen Raums]"
(Anton Friedrich Koch, "Die Selbstbeziehung der Negation in Hegels Logik," in
Zeitschrift für philosophische Forschung 53 (1999), pp. 1–29, here: p. 15).
62 Hegel, *Science of Logic*, p. 824. The translation is slightly corrected from "existence" (Miller) for "Dasein" to "being there." The German text reads: "Die
Natur und der Geist sind überhaupt unterschiedene Weisen, *ihr Dasein* darzus-
tellen." I entirely agree with Nuzzo: "the absolute idea is no content but a mere
form, purely self-referential expression with nothing to express except its own
formality. This form, indeed an absolute one, is the first side of the method;
the method as formal mode (*Art und Weise*), as modality or mode of being and
knowledge at the same time. Thereby the claim that the absolute idea is method
corrects Spinoza's metaphysical claim addressed in the logic of essence that the
Absolute is mode" (Nuzzo, "The End of Hegel's Logic," p. 195).
63 Hegel, *Science of Logic*, p. 830.
64 Ibid, p. 841. For a reading of the whole enterprise of the *Science of Logic* in terms
of a theory of absolute subjectivity see Klaus Düsing, *Das Problem der Subjektivität
in Hegels Logik. Systematische und entwicklungsgeschichtliche Untersuchungen zum
Prinzip des Idealismus und zur Dialektik*. Bonn: Bouvier 1976.
65 Hegel, *Science of Logic*, p. 625, Miller's translation slightly corrected.
66 Hegel, *Science of Logic*, p. 537: "but the absolute cannot be a first, an immediate;
on the contrary, the absolute is essentially *its result*." Cf. also p. 69f.
67 For this very reason, Schelling develops an original conception of transcendence
dispensing with external reflection. For more detail see my *Das Absolute und die
Welt in Schellings Freiheitsschrift*.
68 Hegel, *Science of Logic*, p. 153.

69 The false infinite, on the contrary, is defined over against the finite. See Hegel, *Science of Logic*, pp. 139f., where Hegel claims that the contradiction between the finite and the false infinite "occurs as a direct result of the circumstance that the finite remains as a determinate being opposed to the infinite, so that there are *two* determinatenesses; *there are* two worlds, one infinite and one finite, and in the relationship the infinite is only the *limit* of the finite and is thus only a determinate infinite, an infinite which is itself finite."

70 Hegel, *Science of Logic*, p. 152.

71 An original discussion of Hegel's concept of the "true infinite" can be found in Rüdiger Bubner, "Hegels Lösung eines Rätsels," in *Das Endliche und das Unendliche in Hegels Denken*. Ed. Francesca Menegoni and Luca Illeterati. Stuttgart: Klett-Cotta 2004, pp. 17–32. See also Houlgate's excellent commentary in Stephen Houlgate, *The Opening of Hegel's Logic. From Being to Infinity*. West Lafayette, Indiana: Purdue University Press, 2006, pp. 414–20.

72 Hegel, *Philosophy of Mind*, §574.

73 Hegel, *Science of Logic*, p. 58.

74 For illuminating discussions see Thomas Sören Hoffmann, *Georg Wilhelm Friedrich Hegel. Eine Propädeutik*. Wiesbaden: Marix-Verlag, 2004, pp. 479–98, and Angelica Nuzzo, "Hegels Auffassung der Philosophie als System und die drei Schlüsse der Enzyklopädie," in *Hegels enzyklopädisches System der Philosophie*. Ed. B. Tuschling and U. Volgel. Stuttgart: Frommann Holzboog, 2004, pp. 459–80.

75 Hegel, *Philosophy of Mind*, §577.

76 Cf. Longuenesse, *Hegel's Critique of Metaphysics*, pp. 110–59.

77 Cf. Thomas Sören Hoffmann, *Die absolute Form. Modalität, Individualität und das Prinzip der Philosophie nach Kant und Hegel*. Berlin/New York: De Gruyter, 1991, who further develops the basic ideas of Josef Simon, *Das Problem der Sprache bei Hegel*. Stuttgart: Kohlhammer-Verlag, 1966.

78 David Lewis, *On the Plurality of Worlds*. Oxford: Oxford University Press, 1986, p. 1.

79 Ibid.

80 Tr. Note: *handgreiflich*. It is worth noting that "handgreiflich" means both "haptic" or "grabbable" and "to be violent towards someone with one's hands." When someone gets in a fistfight, they become "handgreiflich."

81 Ibid., p. 2: "there are so many other worlds, in fact, that absolutely every way that a world could possibly be is a way that some world is."

82 Ibid., p. 3.

83 Ibid., p. 5.

84 Hegel, *Science of Logic*, p. 571.

85 Cantor, *Contributions to the Founding of the Theory of Transfinite Numbers*, p. 86.

86 Ibid.

87 See Hogrebe, *Echo des Nichtwissens*, p. 317f. Hogrebe here describes the "space in which the distinctions we meet in the world are cleaved" as "the space of all possible differences, which we can call: the dimension of distinction [*Distinktionsdimension*]. Any claim about fundamental distinctions takes this dimension from the outset as given and complete. It cannot be distinguished from other spaces and simply cannot be positively identified: nevertheless, we need it because otherwise we could not create a universe through our distinctions. It is the semantically completely diaphanous background or protoplasm of all semantic contrasts, the transcendental condition of their possibility."

88 At this point I leave open the question of whether the set of all logical impossibilities also belongs to logical space.

89 Heidegger, *Kant and the Problem of Metaphysics*, p. 51.
90 Victor Pelevin, *Buddha's Little Finger*. Tr. Andrew Bromfield, New York: Penguin Books, 2001, pp. 139–41.
91 Wittgenstein, *Tractatus*, 1.
92 One could argue here (as I will further along) that identity is tied to the retroactive gathering of the plurality of means of access to the world.
93 See Badiou, *Being and Event*, and Meillassoux, *After Finitude*.
94 Friedrich Nietzsche, *The Gay Science*. Tr. Walter Kaufmann. New York: Vintage Books, 1974, §374: "But I should think that today we are at least far from the ridiculous immodesty that would be involved in decreeing from our corner that perspectives are permitted only from this corner. Rather has the world become 'infinite' for us all over again, inasmuch as we cannot reject the possibility that *it may include infinite interpretations?*"
95 On the predicate of predicatelessness see Schelling, SW, VII, 406–7.
96 Thomas S. Eliot, *The Waste Land*. Ed. M. North, New York/London: W. W. Norton, 2001, p. 7, vs. 52–4.
97 SW, XIV, 106.
98 Hegel, *Science of Logic*, p. 733.
99 Ibid., p. 401.
100 Quine's notion of "posits" (in particular see §6 of *Word and Object*. Cambridge MA: MIT Press, 1960) comes clse to this truth of the *Reflexionslogik*. See p. 22: "Everything to which we concede existence is a posit from the standpoint of a description of the theory-building process, and simultaneously real from the standpoint of the theory that is being built."
101 Hegel, *Science of Logic*, p. 401.
102 See, naturally, Nelson Goodman, *Ways of Worldmaking*. Indianapolis: Hackett, 1978.
103 Aristotle, *Metaphysics*, 1073b13–14.
104 Hegel, *Science of Logic*, p. 402.
105 Brandom, *Tales of the Mighty Dead*, p. 208.
106 See Habermas, *Truth and Justification*, pp. 77, 83, 90, 99, and so forth. See also, p. 57: "A shared view of reality as a territory 'halfway between' the 'world-views' of different languages is a necessary presupposition of meaningful dialogue überhaupt. For the interlocutors, the concept of reality is connected with the regulative idea of a 'sum total of all that is knowable.'"
107 See Anton Friedrich Koch's convincing rejection of the possibility of "primordial states of affairs (*Ursachverhalte*)" in *Versuch über Wahrheit und Zeit*, §13.
108 Wittgenstein, *Philosophical Investigations*, §261.
109 Tr. Note: Throughout the present essay I translate "Zusammenhang," which is typically translated as context, connection, interconnection or something to that effect, as "hanging together," so as to highlight a certain reference to Sellars. I take it that what Gabriel has in mind in the present essay when he writes "*Zusammenhang*" is the same thing that Sellars wants to expose through his synoptic concept of logical space, viz. the way "things in the broadest sense of the term *hang together* in the broadest possible sense of the term" (Sellars, *Science, Perception, and Reality*, p. 1, my italics, Tom Krell.)
110 Saul A. Kripke, *Wittgenstein on Rules and Private Language*. Cambridge, MA: Harvard University Press, 1982.
111 Hegel, *Science of Logic*, p. 553.
112 Ibid., pp. 550–4.
113 Ibid., p. 552.

[114] Ibid.

[115] Hegel, *Science of Logic*, p. 50.

[116] Ibid.

[117] In the *Natorp-Bericht* Heidegger determines this act as the expression of the essential atheism of philosophy as such. See Martin Heidegger, "Anzeige der hermeneutischen Situation (1922)," in *Heidegger Gesamtausgabe*. Bd. 62. Ed. by G. Neumann. Frankfurt am Main: Klostermann, 2005, p. 363, fn. 54.

[118] McDowell, *Having the World in View*, p. 7.

[119] SW, XIV, 338.

[120] Ibid.

[121] SW, XI, 388.

[122] With Carl Schmitt we can assert, therefore, that any "order is based on a decision"; see Carl Schmitt, *Political Theology. Four Chapters on the Concept of Sovereignty.* Tr. G. Schwab. Chicago: University of Chicago Press, 2006, p. 10.

[123] Tr. Note: I translate "nie aufgehende Rest" here as "irreducible or indivisible remainder," to square with both translations at play on the contemporary scene. This translation is sufficient in at least one respect, viz. that it captures the mathematical ring of "nie aufgehende Rest": this phrase brings to mind the thought of doing a complex math problem and arriving at an unexpected result—in English we would say something does not "add up" or "work out." However, it strikes me that "nie aufgehende Rest" also has points to night and to darkness, for in German one says "die Sonne geht auf."

[124] Schelling, *Freedom Essay*, p. 29. Schelling here borrows heavily from Friedrich Schlegel's essay "On Unintelligibility."

Bibliography

Aristotle. *The Complete Works of Aristotle. The Revised Oxford Translation.* 2 vols. Ed. Jonathan Barnes. Princeton: Princeton University Press, 1971.

Badiou, A. *Being and Event.* Tr. Oliver Feltham. New York/London: Continuum, 2007.

— *Logics of Worlds. Being and Event 2.* Tr. A. Toscano. New York/London: Continuum, 2009.

Brandom, R. *Making It Explicit. Reasoning, Representing, and Discursive Commitment.* Cambridge, MA/London: Harvard University Press, 1998.

— *Articulating Reasons. An Introduction to Inferentialism.* Cambridge, MA: Harvard University Press, 2000.

— *Tales of the Mighty Dead. Historical Essays in the Metaphysics of Intentionality.* Cambridge, MA/London: Harvard University Press, 2002.

— *Reason in Philosophy. Animating Ideas.* Cambridge, MA: Harvard University Press, 2009.

Bubner, R. "Hegels Lösung eines Rätsels," in *Das Endliche und das Unendliche in Hegels Denken.* Ed. Francesca Menegoni/Luca Illeterati Stuttgart: Klett-Cotta, 2004, pp. 17–32.

Cantor, G. *Contributions to the Founding of the Theory of Transfinite Numbers.* Tr. P. E. B. Jourdain. New York: Cosimo Books, 2007.

Castoriadis, C. *The Imaginary Institution of Society.* Tr. Kathleen Blamey. Oxford: Polity Press, 1997.

— "Sur la relativité de la logique," in *Histoire et Création. Textes philosophiques inédits (1945–1967),* Paris: Seuil, 2009, pp. 34–9.

Cavell, S. *The Claim of Reason. Wittgenstein, Skepticism, Morality, and Tragedy.* New York: Oxford University Press, 1999.

— *Philosophy the Day After Tomorrow.* Cambridge, MA/London: The Belknap Press, 2006.

Dangel, D. *Hegel und die Geistmetaphysik des Aristoteles.* (forthcoming 2011).

Deleuze, G. *The Logic of Sense.* Tr. M. Lester. New York: Columbia University Press, 1990.

Düsing, K. *Das Problem der Subjektivität in Hegels Logik. Systematische und entwicklungs-geschichtliche Untersuchungen zum Prinzip des Idealismus und zur Dialektik.* Bonn: Bouvier, 1976.

Eliot, T. S. *The Waste Land.* Ed. Michael North. New York/London: W. W. Norton, 2001.

Fichte, J. G. *Darstellung der Wissenschaftslehre. Aus den Jahren 1801/02.* Hamburg: Meiner, 1977.

— *The Science of Knowing. J. G. Fichte's 1804 Lectures on the Wissenschaftslehre.* Tr. W. E. Wright. Albany: SUNY Press, 2005.

Fogelin, R. J. *Pyrrhonian Reflections on Knowledge and Justification.* New York: Oxford University Press, 1994.

Forster, M. *Hegel's Idea of a Phenomenology of Spirit.* Chicago: University of Chicago Press, 1998.

Frank, M. *Selbstgefühl. Eine historisch-systematische Erkundung.* Frankfurt/Main: Suhrkamp, 2002.

Frege, G. "The Thought: A Logical Inquiry," in *Mind*, New Series, 65:259 (July 1956), pp. 289–311.

— *The Foundations of Arithmetic. A Logico-mathematical Enquiry Into the Concept of Number.* Tr. J. L Austin. Evanston: Northwestern University Press, 1980.

— "On Sinn and Bedeutung," in *The Frege Reader.* Ed. M. Beaney. Oxford: Blackwell Publishing, 1997, pp. 151–71.

Gabriel, M. *Das Absolute und die Welt in Schellings Freiheitsschrift.* Bonn: Bonn University Press 2006.

— *Der Mensch im Mythos. Untersuchungen über Ontotheologie, Anthropologie und Selbstbewußtseinsgeschichte in Schellings "Philosophie der Mythologie".* Berlin/New York: DeGruyter, 2006.

— "*Chôra* als *différance.* Derridas dekonstruktive Lektüre von Platons *Timaios*," in *Platon im Diskurs.* Ed. Gregor Fitzi. Heidelberg: Winter 2006.

— "Hegel und Plotin", in *Hegel und die Geschichte der Philosophie.* Ed. Dietmar H. Heidemann/Christian Krijnen. Darmstadt: Wissenschaftliche Buchgesellschaft, 2007, pp. 70–83.

— *An den Grenzen der Erkenntnistheorie. Die notwendige Endlichkeit des objektiven Wissens als Lektion des Skeptizismus.* Freiburg/München: Alber, 2008.

— "God's Transcendent Activity— Ontotheology in *Metaphysics* Λ," *The Review of Metaphysics* 250 (2009), pp. 385–414.

— *Skeptizismus und Idealismus in der Antike.* Frankfurt/Main: Suhrkamp, 2009.

— "Endlichkeit und absolutes Ich— Heideggers Fichtekritik." (forthcoming in *Fichte-Studien*).

Gabriel, M., and Žižek, S. *Mythology, Madness, and Laughter. Subjectivity in German Idealism.* New York/London: Continuum Press, 2009.

de Giovanni, G., and Harris H. S., (eds.) *Between Kant & Hegel: Texts in the Development of Post-Kantian Idealism.* Indianapolis: Hackett Publishing, 2000.

Goodman, N. *Ways of Worldmaking.* Indianapolis: Hackett, 1978.

Habermas, J. *Truth and Justification.* Tr. Barbara Fultner. Cambridge, MA: The MIT Press, 2003.

Hegel, G. W. F. "The Absolute Religion." Tr. from the second volume of Hegel's "Philosophy of Religion" by F. L. Soldan. *The Journal of Speculative Philosophy* 16:1 (January 1882).

— *Science of Logic.* Tr. A. V. Miller. Amherst, NY: Humanity Books, 1969.

— *Philosophy of Mind: Part Three of the Encyclopaedia of the Philosophical Sciences (1830).* Tr. William Wallace. Oxford: Oxford University Press, 1971.

— *Phenomenology of Spirit.* Tr. A. V. Miller. Oxford: Oxford University Press, 1977.

— *The Difference Between Fichte's and Schelling's System of Philosophy.* Tr. H. S. Harris and W. Cerf. Albany: State University of New York Press, 1977.

— *Faith and Knowledge.* Tr. W. Cerf and H. S. Harris. Albany: State University of New York Press, 1977.

— *Lectures on the Philosophy of Religion.* Tr. P. C. Hodgson. Berkeley: University of California Press, 1988.

— *Elements of the Philosophy of Right.* Tr. A. Wood. Cambridge: Cambridge University Press, 1991.

— *Encyclopedia Logic. Part I of the Encyclopedia of Philosophical Sciences with the Zusätze.* Tr. T. F. Geraets, W. A. Suchting, and H. S. Harris. Indianapolis: Hackett, 1991.

— *Lectures on the History of Philosophy* (Three Volumes). Tr. E. S. Haldane and F. H. Simson. Lincoln, NE: University of Nebraska Press, 1995.

— "Notizen zum dritten Teil der Encyklopädie," in *Gesammelte Werke.* Edited in Cooperation with the Deutsche Forschungsgemeinschaft by the Nordrhein-Westfälische Akademie der Wissenschaften. Vol. 13: *Enzyklopädie der philosophischen Wissenschaften im Grundrisse* (1817), prepared by Hans-Christian Lucas and Udo Rameil, edited by Wolfgang Bonsiepen and Klaus Grotsch. Hamburg: Meiner, 2000.

— *Lectures on the Proofs of the Existence of God.* Tr. Peter C. Hodgson. Oxford: Oxford University Press, 2007.

Heidegger, M. *Die Kategorien-und Bedeutungslehre des Duns Scotus.* Tübingen: J. C. B. Mohr, 1916.

— *On the Essence of Reasons.* Tr. T. Malick. Evanston: Northwestern University Press, 1969.

— *The Question Concerning Technology and Other Essays.* Tr. W. Lovitt. New York: Harper and Rowe Publishers, 1977.

— *Being and Time.* Tr. J. Macquarrie and E. Robinson. Malden: Blackwell Publishing, 1978.

— *Schelling's Treatise On the Essence of Human Freedom.* Tr. J. Stambaugh, Athens, OH: Ohio University Press, 1985.

— *The Principle of Reason.* Tr. R. Lilly. Indianapolis: Indiana University Press, 1991.

— *Aristotle's Metaphysics Θ 1–3: On the Essence and Actuality of Force.* Tr. W. Brogan and P. Warnek. Bloomington: Indiana University Press, 1995.

— *The Fundamental Concepts of Metaphysics: World, Finitude, Solitude.* Tr. W. McNeil and N. Walker. Bloomington: Indiana University Press, 1995.

— *Der deutsche Idealismus (Fichte, Schelling, Hegel) und die philosophische Problemlage der Gegenwart.* Frankfurt/Main: Klostermann, 1997.

— *Kant and the Problem of Metaphysics.* Tr. R. Taft. Bloomington: Indiana University Press, 1997.

— "Letter on Humanism," in *Pathmarks.* Ed. William McNeill. Cambridge: Cambridge University Press, 1998.

— *Contributions to Philosophy (from Enowning).* Tr. P. Enad and K. Maly. Bloomington: Indiana University Press, 2000.

— *Introduction to Metaphysics.* Tr. G. Fried and R. Polt. New Haven: Yale Nota Bene, 2000.

— "Hegel's Concept of Experience," in *Off the Beaten Track.* Tr. J. Young and K. Haynes. Cambridge: Cambridge University Press, 2002.

— "The Age of the World Picture," in *Off the Beaten Track.* Tr. J. Young and K. Haynes, Cambridge: Cambridge University Press, 2002.

— "Anzeige der hermeneutischen Situation (1922)," in *Heidegger Gesamtausgabe.* Vol. 62, pp. 343–4. Ed. G. Neumann. Frankfurt/Main: Klostermann, 2005.

Hiley, R. D. *Philosophy in Question. Essays on a Pyrrhonian Theme.* Chicago: University of Chicago Press, 1988.

Hoffmann, T. S. *Die absolute Form. Modalität, Individualität und das Prinzip der Philosophie nach Kant und Hegel.* Berlin/New York: De Gruyter, 1991.

— *Georg Wilhelm Friedrich Hegel. Eine Propädeutik.* Wiesbaden: Marix-Verlag, 2004.

— *Philosophische Physiologie. Eine Systematik des Begriffs der Natur im Spiegel der Geschichte der Philosophie.* Stuttgart-Bad Cannstatt: frommann-holzboog, 2003.

Hogrebe, W. *Archäologische Bedeutungspostulate.* Freiburg/München: Alber, 1977.

— *Prädikation und Genesis: Metaphysik als Fundamentalheuristik im Ausgang von Schellings «Die Weltalter».* Frankfurt/Main: Suhrkamp, 1989.

— "Das Absolute," in his *Echo des Nichtwissens.* Berlin: Akademie-Verlag, 2006, pp. 155–69.

Horstmann, R.-P. "The *Phenomenology of Spirit* as a 'transcendentalistic' argument for a monistic ontology," in *Hegel's* Phenomenology of Spirit. *A Critical Guide.* Ed. Dean Moyar and Michael Quante. Cambridge: Cambridge University Press, 2008, pp. 43–62.

Houlgate, S. *The Opening of Hegel's Logic. From Being to Infinity.* Indiana: Purdue University Press, 2006.

Jacobi, C. G. J. "Open Letter to Fichte," in *Philosophy of German Idealism.* Ed. E. Behler. New York: Continuum Press, 1987.

— "Preface and also Introduction to the Author's Collected Philosophical Works (1815)", in *The Main Philosophical Writings and the Novel Allwill.* Tr. G. di Giovanni. Montreal: McGill-Queen's University Press, 1994.

— "On Transcendental Idealism," in *Kant's Early Critics. The Empiricist Critique of Theoretical Philosophy.* Ed. Brigitte Sassen. Cambridge: Cambridge University Press, 2000.

Kant, I. *Prolegomena to Any Future Metaphysics.* Tr. P. Carus, Revised by J. W. Ellington. Indianapolis: Hackett Publishing Company, 2001.

— *Critique of Pure Reason.* Tr. N. Kemp Smith. New York: Palgrave MacMillan, 2003.

Koch, A. F. "Die Selbstbeziehung der Negation in Hegels Logik," in *Zeitschrift für philosophische Forschung* 53 (1999), pp. 1–29.

— *Versuch über Wahrheit und Zeit.* Paderborn: Mentis, 2006.

König, J. *Der Begriff der Intuition.* Halle: Max Niemeyer, 1926.

Kosch, M. *Freedom and Reason in Kant, Schelling, and Kierkegaard.* Oxford: Oxford University Press, 2006.

Kripke, S. A. *Wittgenstein on Rules and Private Language.* Cambridge, MA: Harvard University Press, 1982.

Kroner, R. *Von Kant bis Hegel.* 2 vols, Tübingen: Mohr Siebeck, 1921–4.

Leibniz, G. W. *Philosophical Essays.* Tr. R. Ariew and D. Garber. Indianapolis: Hackett Publishing, 1989.

Leiter, B. (ed). *The Future for Philosophy.* Oxford/New York: Oxford University Press, 2004.

Lewis, D. *On the Plurality of Worlds.* Oxford: Oxford University Press, 1986.

Locke, J. *An Essay Concerning Human Understanding.* Ed. Peter H. Nidditch. Oxford: Oxford University Press, 1975.

Longuenesse, B. *Hegel's Critique of Metaphysics.* New York: Cambridge University Press, 2007.

Luhmann, N. *Einführung in die Systemtheorie.* Second Edition. Heidelberg: Carl Auer, 2004.

Malabou, C. *The Future of Hegel. Plasticity, Temporality, and Dialectic.* Tr. L. During. New York: Routledge, 2005.

McDowell, J. *Mind and World.* Cambridge, MA/London: Harvard University Press, 1996.

— *Meaning, Knowledge, and Reality.* Cambridge, MA/London: Harvard University Press, 1998.

— *Mind, Value, and Reality.* Cambridge, MA/London: Harvard University Press, 1998.

— *Having the World in View. Essays on Kant, Hegel, and Sellars.* Cambridge, MA: Harvard University Press, 2009.

Meillassoux, Q. *After Finitude. An Essay on the Necessity of Contingency.* Tr. R. Brassier. New York/London: Continuum, 2008.

Muhall, S. *Inheritance and Originality. Wittgenstein, Heidegger, Kierkegaard.* Oxford: Oxford University Press, 2001.

Nietzsche, F. *The Gay Science.* Tr. W. Kaufmann. New York: Vintage Books, 1974.

Nuzzo, A. "Hegels Auffassung der Philosophie als System und die drei Schlüsse der Enzyklopädie," in *Hegels enzyklopädisches System der Philosophie.* Ed. Burkhar. Tuschling and Ulrich. Vogel. Stuttgart: Frommann Holzboog, 2004.

— "The End of Hegel's Logic: Absolute Idea as Absolute Method," in *Hegel's Theory of the Subject.* Ed. David G. Carlson. Basingstoke: Palgrave Macmillan, 2005.

Pelevin, V. *Buddha's Little Finger.* Tr. Andrew Bromfield. New York: Penguin Books, 2001.

Pippin, R. *Hegel's Idealism. The Satisfactions of Self-Consciousness.* Cambridge: Cambridge University Press, 1989.

Plotinus. *Ennead V.* Tr. A. H. Armstrong. Loeb Classical Library (*Plotinus in Seven Volumes,* vol. V), Cambridge, MA: Harvard University Press, 1984.

Priest, G. *Beyond the Limits of Thought.* Cambridge: Cambridge University Press, 1995.

Putnam, H. "The Meaning of 'Meaning'," in *Philosophical Papers, Vol. 2: Mind, Language and Reality.* Cambridge: Cambridge University Press, 1979.

— *Reason, Truth, and History.* Cambridge: Cambridge University Press, 1981.

Quine, W. V. O. *Word and Object.* Cambridge, MA: MIT Press, 1960.

— *From a Logical Point of View. Nine logico-philosophical Essays.* Second, Revised Edition. Cambridge, MA: Harvard University Press, 1963.

Rometsch, J. *Hegels Theorie des erkennenden Subjekts. Systematische Untersuchungen zur enzyklopädischen Philosophie des subjektiven Geistes.* Würzburg: Königshausen & Neumann, 2007.

Rorty, R. *Philosophy and the Mirror of Nature.* Princeton: Princeton University Press, 1979.

Russell, B. *History of Western Philosophy.* London: Routledge, 2004.

Schelling, F. W. J. *Sämmtliche Werke.* Ed. K. F. A. Schelling. I. Abteilung Vols. 1–10, II. Abteilung Vols. 1–4. Stuttgart: Cotta, 1856–61.

— *System of Transcendental Idealism (1800)*. Tr. P. Heath. Charlottesville: University Press of Virginia, 1978.

— *Urfassung der Philosophie der Offenbarung*. Ed. Walter E. Ehrhardt. 2 vols, Hamburg: Meiner, 1992 (cited as: UPO).

— *Philosophical Investigations into the Essence of Human Freedom*. Tr. J. Love and J. Schmid. Albany, NY: SUNY Press, 2006.

— *The Grounding of Positive Philosophy. The Berlin Lectures*. Tr. B. Matthews. Albany, NY: SUNY Press, 2007.

Schmitt, C. *Political Theology. Four Chapters on the Concept of Sovereignty*. Tr. G. Schwab. Chicago: University of Chicago Press, 2006.

Schulz, W. *Die Vollendung des deutschen Idealismus in der Spätphilosophie Schellings*. Stuttgart/Köln: Kohlhammer, 1954.

Sellars, W. "Philosophy and the Scientific Image of Man," in *Science, Perception, and Reality*. Atascadero, CA: Ridgeview Publishing Company, 1991, pp. 1–40.

— *Empiricism and the Philosophy of Mind*. Cambridge, MA: Harvard University Press, 1997.

Sextus Empiricus. *Outlines of Pyrrhonism*. Tr. R. G. Bury. Loeb Classic Library (*Sextus Empiricus in Four Volumes*, vol. I). Cambridge, MA: Harvard University Press, 1933.

— *Against the Logicians*. Tr. R. G. Bury. Loeb Classic Library (*Sextus Empiricus in Four Volumes*, vol. II). Cambridge, MA: Harvard University Press, 1935.

Simon, J. *Das Problem der Sprache bei Hegel*. Stuttgart: Kohlhammer-Verlag, 1966.

— *Philosophy of the Sign*. Tr. G. Hefferman. Albany, NY: SUNY Press, 2003.

Sluga, H. "Wittgenstein and Pyrrhonism," in *Pyrrhonian Skepticism*. Ed. Walter. Sinnott-Armstrong. New York: Oxford University Press, 2004.

Speusippus. *Speusippo. Frammenti*. Ed. Margherita Isnardi Parente. Naples: Bibliopolis, 1980.

de Spinoza, B. *Short Treatise on God, Man, and his Well-Being*. Tr. A. Wolf. New York: Russell & Russell Inc., 1963.

— *Ethics*. Tr. E. M. Curley. London: Penguin Books, 1996.

Strawson, P. F. *Skepticism and Naturalism. Some Varieties*. New York: Columbia University Press, 1985.

Sturma, D. *Kant über Selbstbewußtsein. Zum Zusammenhang von Erkenntniskritik und Theorie des Selbstbewußtseins*. Hildesheim/Zürich/New York: Olms, 1985.

Trendelenburg, F. A. "Über eine Lücke in Kants Beweis von der ausschließlichen Subjectivität des Raumes und der Zeit," in *Historische Beiträge zur Philosophie*. Vol. 3, Berlin: G. Bethge Verlag, 1867, pp. 215–76.

Utz, K. *Philosophie des Zufalls. Ein Entwurf*. Paderborn/München/Wien/Zürich: Schöningh, 2005.

Williams, M. "Scepticism without Theory," in *The Review of Metaphysics* 61 (1988), pp. 547–88.

— *Groundless Belief: An Essay on the Possibility of Epistemology*. Princeton: Princeton University Press, 1999.

Wittgenstein, L. *Tractatus Logico-Philosophicus*. Tr. D. F. Pears and B. McGuinness. London: Routledge, 2001.

Wittgenstein, L. *Philosophical Investigations*. Tr. G. E. M. Anscombe, P. M. S. Hacker, and J. Schulte. Chichester: Blackwell Publishing, 2009.

Yovel, Y. "The Infinite Mode and Natural Laws in Spinoza," in Id., H, *God and Nature. Spinoza's Metaphysics.* Leiden/New York: Brill, 1991, pp. 79–96.

Žižek, S. *The Indivisible Remainder. On Schelling and Related Matters.* London/New York: Verso, 1996.

— *The Ticklish Subject. The Absent Centre of Political Ontology.* London/New York: Verso, 2008.

Žižek, S. and Schelling F. W. J. *The Abyss of Freedom/Ages of the World.* Tr. J. Norman. Ann Arbor: University of Michigan Press, 1997.

Index

CPSIA information can be obtained at www.ICGtesting.com
Printed in the USA
LVOW01s1957130115

422676LV00004B/56/P